PRAISE FOR *CUDA FOR ENGINEER*

"First there was FORTRAN, circa 1960, which enabled us to program mainframes. Then there was BASIC, circa 1980, which enabled us to program the first microcomputers. And now there is CUDA, which enables us to program super-microcomputers.

"*CUDA for Engineers* allows researchers in engineering and mathematics to perform calculations hundreds of times faster than was previously possible on microcomputers. This permits new kinds of calculations to be performed and reveals this book to be a game changer."

—*Richard H. Rand, professor of mechanical and aerospace engineering, and of mathematics, Cornell University*

"*CUDA for Engineers* has been put together in a very thoughtful and practical way. The reader is quickly immersed in the world of parallel programming with CUDA and results are seen right away. This book is a great introduction and helps readers from many different scientific and engineering disciplines become exposed to the benefits of GPU programming. This book is an enjoyable read and has great support through top-notch example programs and exercises."

—*Dr. Mark Staveley, senior program manager, Azure High Performance Computing*

"*CUDA for Engineers* lives up to its name by stepping the reader through concepts, strategies, terminology, and examples, which work together to form an educational framework so that experts and non-experts alike can approach high-performance computing with foresight and understanding."

—*Joseph M. Iaquinto, Ph.D., research specialist, VA Puget Sound*

"This book reflects a practical approach that is in perfect agreement with the way I teach numerical methods for engineers. It would make a fine supplement for engineering students or practitioners to add CUDA to their numerical toolbox, and thus embark on the study of high-performance scientific computing. It's perfect for newcomers to CUDA who already have a foundation in programming. I recommend following the authors' advice and working immediately with the hands-on exercises, step by step. After this immersion, you will approach proficiency by simply adding some personal projects in GPU computing and delving into the NVIDIA CUDA Guide and developer community."

—*Lorena A. Barba, associate professor of mechanical and aerospace engineering, The George Washington University*

CUDA for Engineers

CUDA for Engineers

An Introduction to High-Performance Parallel Computing

Duane Storti

Mete Yurtoglu

✦✦Addison-Wesley

New York • Boston • Indianapolis • San Francisco
Toronto • Montreal • London • Munich • Paris • Madrid
Capetown • Sydney • Tokyo • Singapore • Mexico City

For information about buying this title in bulk quantities, or for special sales opportunities (which may include electronic versions; custom cover designs; and content particular to your business, training goals, marketing focus, or branding interests), please contact our corporate sales department at corpsales@pearsoned.com or (800) 382-3419.

For government sales inquiries, please contact governmentsales@pearsoned.com.

For questions about sales outside the U.S., please contact international@pearsoned.com.

Visit us on the Web: informit.com/aw

Library of Congress Cataloging-in-Publication Data
Names: Storti, Duane, author. | Yurtoglu, Mete.
Title: CUDA for engineers : an introduction to high-performance parallel
    computing / Duane Storti, Mete Yurtoglu.
Description: New York : Addison-Wesley, 2015. | Includes bibliographical
    references and index.
Identifiers: LCCN 2015034266 | ISBN 9780134177410 (pbk. : alk. paper)
Subjects: LCSH: Parallel computers. | CUDA (Computer architecture)
Classification: LCC QA76.58 .S76 2015 | DDC 004/.35—dc23
LC record available at http://lccn.loc.gov/2015034266

ISBN-13: 978-0-13-417741-0
ISBN-10: 0-13-417741-X
Text printed in the United States on recycled paper at RR Donnelley in Crawfordsville, Indiana.
First printing, November 2015

Editor-in-Chief
Mark L. Taub

Executive Editor
Laura Lewin

Development Editor
Songlin Qiu

Managing Editor
John Fuller

Project Editor
Elizabeth Ryan

Copy Editor
Teresa Barensfeld

Indexer
Jack Lewis

Proofreader
Anna Popick

Technical Reviewers
Tom Bradley
Richard Rand
Mark Staveley

Editorial Assistant
Olivia Basegio

Cover Designer
Chuti Prasertsith

Compositor
The CIP Group

To the family, friends, and teachers
who inspire us to keep learning cool things
and to share what we have learned.

Contents

Acknowledgments

The authors wish to express their thanks to a variety of people without whom this book would never have come into existence.

Thank you to all the family members who received a bit less attention while we were consumed by the writing of this book. Thank you to Laura Lewin and everyone at Pearson who contributed to the editing, production, and marketing efforts. Thank you to Nicholas Wilt (formerly at NVIDIA and currently at Amazon), who first put us in contact with Laura and really got the ball rolling. Thanks also to our technical reviewers Thomas Bradley of NVIDIA, Mark Staveley of Microsoft, and Richard Rand of Cornell University, all of whom provided helpful comments, corrections, and insights.

Thank you to the many colleagues here at the University of Washington–Seattle Department of Mechanical Engineering who contributed via discussions ranging from big-picture perspective down to the finest technical details. That list includes but is not limited to Mark Ganter, Di Zhang, and Ben Weiss (who helped create several of the figures and also provided us with some lifesaving software to support logical tags and automated code formatting). We would also like to thank Mechanical Engineering Department Chair Per Reinhall for his approval for us to offer the class that helped to inspire the creation of much of the book's content. Additional thanks go to our colleagues David Haynor of University of Washington Department of Radiology and William Ledoux of the Seattle VA Hospital, whose research initiatives continue to motivate meaningful journeys into CUDA territory.

We wish to say a special thank you to the good folks at NVIDIA, including CEO Jen-Hsun Huang who not only had, but also acted on, a vision of what could be accomplished by enhancing access to GPU-based parallel computing; Chandra Cheij, Academic Programs Manager; Kimberly Powell, Director of Higher Education and Healthcare Industries; Jon Saposhnik and Bob Crovella, helpful and inspirational CUDA gurus; and last, but definitely not least, Jay White, Director of Strategic Marketing, who sustains the Seattle-area GPU-computing meet-up group and serves as our local go-to guy.

We would also like to thank all the students who had the sense of adventure to participate in the initial CUDA-based class offerings at the University of Washington, especially former ME graduate student Grant Marchelli (now Grant Marchelli, Ph.D., CTO of Envitrum Inc.), who played a key role in everything from setting up the lab to providing code samples and delivering guest lectures. A special thank you goes to Gerald Barnett, who was so generous with his time and expertise when it came time to edit the first draft.

Finally, a big thanks to you, the reader. The value of having something important to share depends on having people to share it with; we appreciate your interest, and we sincerely hope this book provides you with useful and productive experiences.

About the Authors

Duane Storti received a Ph.D. in theoretical and applied mechanics from Cornell University in 1984. Since then, he has served as a professor of mechanical engineering at the University of Washington–Seattle. Duane has 35 years of experience in teaching and research in the areas of engineering mathematics, dynamics and vibrations, computer-aided design, 3D printing, and applied GPU computing. When not on campus, he can often be found in the gym, coaching youth volleyball.

Mete Yurtoglu received a B.S. in physics and a B.S. in mechanical engineering in 2008, and an M.S. in 2011 from Bogazici University in Istanbul, Turkey. He is currently a graduate student at the University of Washington–Seattle pursuing an M.S. in applied mathematics and a Ph.D. in mechanical engineering. His research interests focus on GPU-based methods for computer vision and machine learning. Mete enjoys family time, playing soccer, and working out.

Introduction

GPUs are massively parallel

Welcome to *CUDA for Engineers*. The goal of this book is to give you direct, hands-on engagement with personal high-performance computing. If you follow along on our foray into the CUDA world, you will gain the benefit of massive parallelism and be able to perform computations on a basic gaming computer that until very recently required a supercomputer. The material presented in this book will help you make sense of more sophisticated CUDA literature and pursue your own CUDA projects.

Let's get started by explaining CUDA and our strategy for getting up to speed as efficiently as possible.

What Is CUDA?

CUDA is a hardware/software platform for parallel computing created and supported by NVIDIA Corporation to promote access to high-performance parallel computing. The hardware aspect of CUDA involves graphics cards equipped with one or more CUDA-enabled **graphics processing units (GPUs)**. The NVIDIA CUDA Toolkit software provides a development environment based on the C/C++ family of programming languages [1].

The GPU-based approach to massively parallel computing used by CUDA is also the core technology used in many of the world's fastest and most energy-efficient supercomputers. The key criterion has evolved from **FLOPS (floating point operations per second)** to FLOPS/watt (i.e., the ratio of computing productivity to energy consumption), and GPU-based parallelism competes well in terms of FLOPS/watt. In fact, between June 2012 and December 2013, the list of the top ten most energy-efficient supercomputers in the world changed from being 100% based on IBM's Blue Gene system (containing PowerPC CPUs) to

100% based on NVIDIA's GPU systems [2]. In this rapid shift to GPU-based computing, the ratio of computation to power consumption more than doubled and continues to increase.

What Does "Need-to-Know" Mean for Learning CUDA?

GPU-based parallel computing is truly a game-changing technology. You need to know about GPU-based parallel computing to keep up with developments in fields related to applied computation, engineering design and analysis, simulation, machine learning, vision and imaging systems, or any number of other computing-intensive fields. GPU-based parallel computing reduces the time for some computing tasks by orders of magnitude, so big computations (like training a machine learning system on a large data set) that took weeks can now happen in hours, and moderate-sized computations (like producing a 3D contour plot) that took minutes can happen interactively in real time. And these gains can be achieved at very reasonable costs in terms of both developer effort and the hardware required. You need to know about CUDA because CUDA is currently the best-supported and most accessible platform for tapping into the power of GPU-based parallel computing.

We will also do our best to provide you with everything you need to know (and as little as possible of what you do not need to know!) to get you to your first direct experiences with CUDA. This book is not intended to be an encyclopedic guide to CUDA; good books of that sort are already available. We will provide links to such reference resources, and we hope you will explore them as you develop a sophisticated working knowledge of CUDA. The challenge with such guides, however, is that they assume that the reader already knows enough about parallel computing and CUDA to make sense of their lingo and context.

Our goal here is to present the essentials of CUDA in a clear, concise manner without assuming specialized background or getting lost in a jungle of details. We aim for the most direct path to meaningful hands-on experiences. You will not need to read 100 pages of background material before actively engaging with CUDA. We provide short appendices if you need to set up a basic CUDA-enabled system or catch up on the essentials of C programming. Your first hands-on engagement with CUDA that involves running some standard sample programs comes in Chapter 1, "First Steps," and by the end of Chapter 3, "From Loops to

Grids," you should be running small CUDA programs you have created yourself. The ensuing chapters present numerous complete examples that you can build, run, and modify, as well as suggested projects to provide additional hands-on CUDA experience. Get ready for a fast and exciting ride, focused on what you really need to know to get up to speed with CUDA.

What Is Meant by "for Engineers"?

Our focus is a technically literate engineering audience. If you are a practicing engineer or a university student with a year's worth of engineering courses, this book is for you. The examples presented, intended to be readily recognizable and to directly connect engineers to CUDA-powered computing, include the following:

- Visualizing functions in two dimensions (2D) and three dimensions (3D)

- Solving differential equations while changing the initial or boundary conditions

- Viewing/processing images or image stacks

- Computing inner products and centroids

- Solving systems of linear algebraic equations

- Monte Carlo computations

We assume that you have some, but not necessarily extensive, computing experience. An introductory computing course using C or C++ provides an ideal foundation. If your previous experience involves some other programming language, Appendix C, "Need-to-Know C Programming," is designed to get you quickly up to speed. When you can create applications with functions that involve arrays and `for` loops, you have the essential background to appreciate the contrast between serial computing typical of CPU-based systems and parallel computing implemented on the GPU with CUDA.

As for mathematics, some previous exposure to differential equations, finite difference approximations, and linear algebra will be helpful for some of the examples, but here too we provide the essentials. Brief descriptions of relevant math and engineering concepts are provided at the start of examples that involve specialized background so you can appreciate even the examples that lie outside your specialty area.

Equally important as the necessary background is what you do *not* need to jump into CUDA with us. You do *not* need to be a computer scientist or an experienced, professional programmer. You do *not* need to have a background in any particular technical field. You do *not* need to have access to high-end or exotic computing systems.

What Do You Need to Get Started with CUDA?

You need to have access to a computer—not even a particularly fancy computer— with a CUDA-enabled GPU: something on the order of a decent gaming system. You also need some special software that is freely available and readily accessible. If you are fortunate enough to be associated with an organization that provides you with access to CUDA-enabled computing resources, then you are ahead of the game. However, we definitely want to include those of you who will be using your personal computer as your CUDA platform. Appendix A, "Hardware Setup," and Appendix B, "Software Setup," will walk you through the details of setting up your own system. We aim to support users across a range of operating systems, so specifics are included to enable you to build and run applications under Windows and UNIX-like systems including Linux and OS X.

How Is This Book Structured?

In addition to this introduction, there are nine chapters and four appendices. The chapters lay out the need-to-know path for most readers, while the appendices deal with background issues or topics off the critical path. Our presentation encourages you to be actively engaged with CUDA. To get the most out of the book, plan on creating, testing, and modifying the applications (which we will refer to as **apps**) as you work through the chapters.

- Chapter 1, "First Steps," provides an active start into the CUDA world that checks out your CUDA system. You will run existing sample CUDA apps to ensure that you have a CUDA-enabled system and run a couple simple C codes to make sure that you are ready to create, compile, and execute programs. These first C codes evaluate a function that calculates the distance from a reference point for a set of input values: first one input value at a time and then for an array of input values. These apps serve as the initial candidates for parallelization with CUDA.

- If you run into issues with any of these basic CUDA requirements, take a detour into the appendices. Appendix A, "Hardware Setup," covers how to check if you have a CUDA-enabled GPU and how to obtain and install one if you don't. Appendix B, "Software Setup," shows you how to install CUDA software, and Appendix C, "Need-to-Know C Programming," covers the essential aspects of C programming.

- After reading the necessary appendices and completing Chapter 1, "First Steps," you are ready for Chapter 2, "CUDA Essentials," which presents the basic CUDA model for parallelism and essential extensions of C for CUDA programming.

The rest of the book is organized around a sequence of example apps that introduce and implement fundamental CUDA concepts.

- Chapter 3, "From Loops to Grids," shows how to parallelize the distance function evaluation codes introduced in Chapter 1, "First Steps." This process presents the bare essentials of parallel computing with CUDA and introduces the typical pattern of transferring data between CPU and GPU. We also briefly introduce unified memory, which may allow you to streamline your development process. By the end of Chapter 3, "From Loops to Grids," you will be ready for hands-on experience using our example programs to create your own CUDA apps. This chapter also includes the first reference to Appendix D, "CUDA Practicalities: Timing, Profiling, Error Handling, and Debugging," which discusses CUDA development tools.

- Chapter 4, "2D Grids and Interactive Graphics," extends the distance function evaluation example to higher dimensions. Once we have created a 2D array of data (which can be treated as an image), we'll take advantage of the opportunity to provide just enough about OpenGL interoperability to enable graphical display with real-time keyboard/mouse interactivity. We'll also introduce the basics of simulation using differential equations, and we will launch the simulation code simultaneously for numerous initial conditions to implement a parallel stability analysis.

- In Chapter 5, "Stencils and Shared Memory," we start to deal with the reality that the computations in different threads are not always independent. The simplest case, and also one of the most common, involves threads that interact with their neighbors in a computational grid, leading to what is called a stencil pattern. We present the basics in an intuitive image filtering context and then introduce an alternate stencil to solve for a steady-state temperature distribution. The discussion takes us through the concepts of tiling and shared memory that are useful in a wide variety of applications.

- Chapter 6, "Reduction and Atomic Functions," deals with the challenging scenario of thread interaction in which all the threads interact during the computation. We start with the simple example of computing the dot product of two vectors to identify the challenges (and some solutions), and then proceed to a more interesting application involving centroids.

- Chapter 7, "Interacting with 3D Data," ventures into parallel computing with 3D grids, which builds directly on earlier looks at 1D and 2D grids. We then explore slicing, volume rendering, and raycasting as methods that employ 2D grids to achieve interactive visualization of data from the 3D grid.

- Chapter 8, "Using CUDA Libraries," provides an introduction to CUDA libraries so you will have some idea of what kinds of preexisting codes are available and when and how you might want to use them. We use CUDA libraries to present both new apps and re-implementations of select apps from previous chapters.

- When you get to the end of this book, there will still be plenty of things to learn and materials left to explore. Chapter 9, "Exploring the CUDA Ecosystem," directs you to additional CUDA resources, including books, blogs, websites, videos, and examples, that will continue to enhance your CUDA experience.

To put it all together, Figure 0.1 shows a flowchart of ways to work through the book.

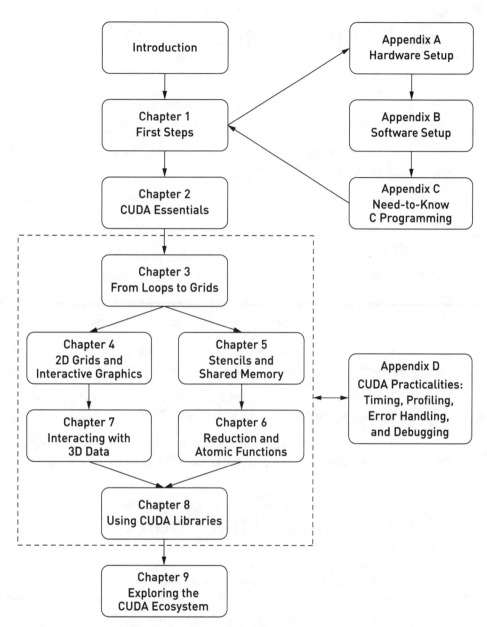

Figure 0.1 Chapter dependencies

Conventions Used in This Book

This book uses the following conventions:

- To distinguish from normal English, programming code, filenames, and menu selections are typeset in a special monospace font.

- Titled sidebars provide information that is contextually connected but independent from the flow of the text.

- We often refer to UNIX-like systems including Linux and OS X simply as **Linux**.

- We refer to complete working example programs as applications or, for short, **apps**.

- We use an arrow (⇒) to show nested menu selections.

- Following common usage, "one-dimensional," "two-dimensional," and "three-dimensional" are abbreviated as 1D, 2D, and 3D, respectively.

- Some figures have been altered to enhance grayscale contrast. Full-color versions are available at www.cudaforengineers.com.

- Each chapter ends with a list of suggested projects to provide the reader with opportunities for additional hands-on CUDA experiences.

- A number enclosed in square brackets formatted as plain text indicates a reference located at the end of the current chapter or appendix.

Code Used in This Book

Codes for apps presented in this book are available online through the www.cudaforengineers.com website. While the book contains some snippets and "skeleton" codes, code that appears labeled as a **Listing** that includes line numbers is intended to be real working code. We have made a serious attempt to make sure that the codes have been tested and run successfully on multiple systems including Windows 7, Windows 8.1, Linux (Ubuntu 14.04 LTS), and OS X 10.10 (with one clearly identified exception that occurs at the very end of Chapter 3, "From Loops to Grids.")

The codes presented in this book have been created with a high priority on being concise, readable, explainable, and understandable. As a result, the codes typically do not include the error-checking and performance-evaluation functionality that would be present in commercial codes. These topics are covered in Appendix D, "CUDA Practicalities: Timing, Profiling, Error Handling, and Debugging," so you can add those functionalities as desired.

CUDA apps can be developed using either C or C++ programming style. We primarily use a C programming style to minimize the programming background required of the reader.

User's Guide

Our mission in writing *CUDA for Engineers* is to get a broad technical audience actively involved in GPU-based parallel computing using CUDA. Thinking metaphorically, we are inviting you to take a trip into the land of GPU-based parallel computing, and *CUDA for Engineers* is the guidebook for that trip. The travel guidebook analogy is appropriate in numerous ways, including the following:

- If you only read the guidebook and never actually make the trip, the book has not really accomplished its intended mission. Please take the trip!

- Most guidebooks deal with things you need to do before starting the trip. Instead of inoculations and passports, the hardware setup and software setup required for the trip are covered in Appendices A and B, respectively.

- Travel to foreign lands often involves dealing with a new language and perhaps a specific dialect. For this trip, the language is C, and the dialect is CUDA. If you are comfortable with C (or C++), you are in good shape. If C is still foreign to you, the basics needed to start the trip are covered in Appendix C.

- Guidebooks generally provide a list of must-see places and must-do activities. Our must-see places are in Chapters 1 and 2, where you will experience the power of CUDA sample codes and gain initial exposure to the special CUDA dialect. The must-do activity is in Chapter 3, where you'll see how to convert serial C codes into parallel CUDA codes.

- For those desiring the more extensive CUDA tour, just proceed through the chapters in sequence.

- Abbreviated and targeted trips are possible, and the departure point is Chapter 3, where we create our first parallel applications. If you have a sense of urgency to get to a particular destination, jump right into Chapter 3. If it makes sense to you, just push forward from there. If not, back up to Chapters 1 and 2 (and/or the appendices) to fill in the gaps as you encounter them. From there you can proceed in various directions:

  - If your goal involves interactive graphics, scientific visualization, gaming, and the like, proceed to Chapters 4 and 7.

  - If your goal is scientific computing, partial differential equations, or image processing, proceed to Chapters 5 and 6.

  - If your primary goal is to utilize existing CUDA-powered libraries, jump directly to Chapter 8.

- Long tour or short, it is nice to see new things, but actually *doing* new things enhances the long-term impact of the experience. So don't just read. When codes are presented, create, compile, and execute them. Modify them, and test out your modifications. Do some of the projects at the end of each chapter, or start up a project of your own.

- On some tours you go solo, and sometimes you travel with a group and a guide. We have worked hard to produce a book that provides good support for a solo trip. However, if you end up using the book in a classroom setting, by all means take advantage of opportunities to interact with instructors and classmates. Asking and answering questions is a great way to learn, and a second pair of eyes is perhaps the best debugging tool.

- On any trip, things may go awry or additional directions or scheduling information may be needed. Material for addressing such issues is located in Appendix D and Chapter 9, which provides pointers to additional resources to help you start "exploring the CUDA ecosystem."

Historical Context

This book is the result of several years of adventures into CUDA territory that started with research projects involving volumetric medical imaging, registration of 2D and 3D imaging (i.e., fluoroscopy and CT scans), and novel approaches to computer-aided design and additive manufacturing. As the utility and importance of CUDA became apparent, it also became clear that sharing the appreciation of CUDA was the right thing to do. The result was a special topics course on applications of CUDA offered to students from a wide range of departments with no prerequisites other than an introductory computing class. The writing of this book follows the third offering of the course, which has evolved to include system setup, exploration of CUDA Samples, a very fast introduction to C programming, CUDA's model for parallelism—along with the few things beyond basic C needed to implement it—and a survey of useful CUDA features including atomic functions, shared memory, and interactive graphics. All of that happens in the first half of a 10-week quarter, and the remaining time is dedicated to projects and presentations. Each student in the class gives a short presentation of their project topic in week 5 and then a final presentation in week 10 of what they have accomplished. Class meetings in between are a combination of consulting hours and presentations (by instructor or guest speakers) on experiences creating and using CUDA-powered applications. In terms of the contents of the book, the course translates roughly as follows:

- System setup and initial CUDA Sample run: Appendices A and B, Chapter 1.

- Brief introduction to C: Appendix C.

- CUDA, its model for parallelism, and language essentials: Chapters 2 and 3.

- Interactive graphics: Chapter 4.

- Shared memory: First part of Chapter 5.

- Atomic functions: First part of Chapter 6.

- Project: Turn the students loose to explore the remainder of Chapters 5–9 for project inspiration, encourage active writing of code, and provide as much help as possible getting over hurdles that arise.

While the organization of the book has some relation to the course, the content is largely the result of a mostly unguided foray into the CUDA world, which turns out to be a big place where it is not hard to get lost. We have filtered through a lot of material including books, sample codes, research papers, and seminar presentations, with the goal of getting down to the gist of what engineers from outside the field would really need to know to get a handle on what can be done with a powerful parallel computing tool like CUDA and understand how they can actually make use of that tool themselves. It is our sincere hope that the result is a book that can fulfill the dual purposes of enabling individual learning and supporting classroom experiences, and we sincerely hope that this book helps to make your voyage into the world of CUDA more efficient, more enjoyable, more rewarding, and less overwhelming.

References

[1] NVIDIA Corporation, "CUDA Toolkit," NVIDIA CUDA Zone, 2015, https://developer .nvidia.com/cuda-toolkit.

[2] CompuGreen, LLC, "The Green 500 List—June 2014," The Green 500, June 2014, Accessed July 1, 2015, http://www.green500.org/lists/green201406.

Chapter 1

First Steps

The goal of this chapter is to get you to plunge right into the world of parallel computing with CUDA. We'll start by running a sample app provided with the CUDA Toolkit. The sample app provides both serial and parallel implementations so you can compare performance measures to get an initial feel for how CUDA can enhance your computing capabilities. Note that the procedures for building and executing apps depend on your operating system, and we'll provide enough detail to get the sample running under Windows and Linux/OS X. At the end of the chapter, we present two simple C apps that will provide initial candidates for parallelization with CUDA.

This chapter contains several crucial checkpoints that direct you to the appendices if there is an issue or capability that needs attention. Please believe us when we tell you that a trip to the appendices is likely to save you more time than you will lose by forging ahead without verifying that the checkpoint criterion is satisfied.

That said, we now encounter the first **checkpoint**: You need to be working on a CUDA-enabled system that has a CUDA-enabled graphics card and CUDA development software. If there is any question about the status of your system, go to Appendix A, "Hardware Setup," to verify your hardware status and Appendix B, "Software Setup," to verify your software status.

Running CUDA Samples

Let's start by running a sample app, the nbody CUDA Sample, to get a meaningful initial CUDA experience. The app computes, and provides graphic visualization of, the motions of a large number of gravitationally interacting masses.

CUDA SAMPLES UNDER WINDOWS

If you are on a fully CUDA-enabled Windows system, you have a CUDA-enabled GPU and software including an appropriate driver for the GPU, the CUDA Toolkit, and Microsoft Visual Studio with NVIDIA's Nsight plug-in. The code and discussions in this book are based on CUDA 7.5, Nsight Visual Studio Edition 4.7, and Visual Studio Community 2013 with 64-bit compilation (specified by setting the Solution Platforms selection to x64 not Win32).

Here we also assume that you know how to locate and run the CUDA Samples. This is another **checkpoint**: If you do not know how to find or run a CUDA Sample, go directly to Appendix B, "Software Setup," and return after you have learned to run CUDA Samples.

Go to the CUDA Samples folder shown in Figure 1.1, where you will see subfolders for the various categories of CUDA Samples and the highlighted bin folder.

Figure 1.1 The CUDA Samples folder

Navigate to the `bin/win64/Release` subfolder where the executable files are stored, as shown in Figure 1.2. **Checkpoint**: If you do not see these executable files in the `Release` folder, go to Appendix B, "Software Setup," for directions on building the CUDA Sample codes into executables.

In the `Release` folder, find the executable for the `nbody` sample, which is highlighted in Figure 1.2, and double-click to start an interesting and relevant application. Two windows should open: a graphics window, shown in Figure 1.3, and a console window with a command-line interface (the last line of which should verify your GPU model number and compute capability), shown in Figure 1.4. (You may need to move the graphics window so you can see the contents of the console window.) The `nbody` application simulates the gravitational interaction between thousands of particles and displays a graphical version of the resulting motion. The title bar of the graphics window also contains some details including the number of bodies in the simulation, the number of binary interactions computed per second, the total GFLOPS, and the precision.

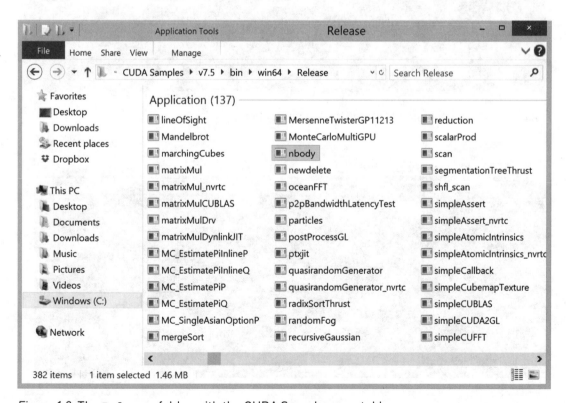

Figure 1.2 The `Release` folder with the CUDA Sample executables

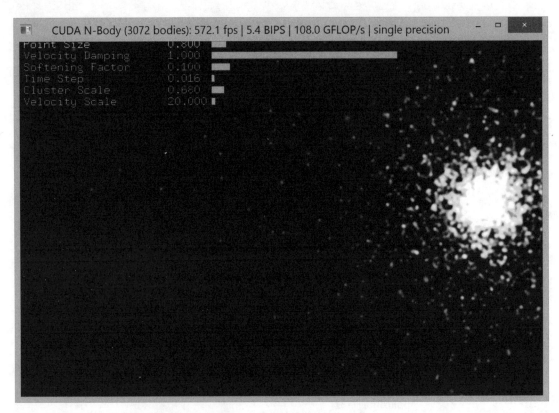

Figure 1.3 Graphical output from the nbody simulation

C:\ProgramData\NVIDIA Corporation\CUDA Samples\v7.5\bin\win64\Release\nbody.exe

```
Run "nbody -benchmark [-numbodies=<numBodies>]" to measure perfomance.
        -fullscreen       (run n-body simulation in fullscreen mode)
        -fp64             (use double precision floating point values for simulation)
        -hostmem          (stores simulation data in host memory)
        -benchmark        (run benchmark to measure performance)
        -numbodies=<N>    (number of bodies (>= 1) to run in simulation)
        -device=<d>       (where d=0,1,2.... for the CUDA device to use)
        -numdevices=<i>   (where i=(number of CUDA devices > 0) to use for simulation)
        -compare          (compares simulation results running once on the default GPU and once on the CPU)
        -cpu              (run n-body simulation on the CPU)
        -tipsy=<file.bin> (load a tipsy model file for simulation)

NOTE: The CUDA Samples are not meant for performance measurements. Results may vary when GPU Boost is enabled.

> Windowed mode
> Simulation data stored in video memory
> Single precision floating point simulation
> 1 Devices used for simulation
> Compute 5.0 CUDA device: [GeForce 840M]
```

Figure 1.4 nbody console window providing optional command-line arguments

It is also useful to be able to run CUDA Samples from a command prompt, which you can do as follows. First, let's note another **checkpoint**: If you run into any questions carrying out the suggestions in the following paragraph, go to Appendix B, "Software Setup," to locate the answers.

Start Visual Studio and open a `Visual Studio Command Prompt` (available in the `TOOLS` menu). Using the File Explorer, copy the address of the `Release` folder (where the CUDA Samples executables reside). Change to the `Release` folder by typing `cd` at the command prompt and pasting in the folder address, then execute the command `nbody` to run the simulation.

CUDA SAMPLES UNDER LINUX

Let's start with a **checkpoint**: If you run into any questions carrying out the suggestions in the following paragraph, go to Appendix B, "Software Setup," to locate the answers.

Open a command line and `cd` to your `NVIDIA_CUDA-7.5_Samples/5_Simulations/nbody` directory. Build the `nbody` executable using `make` (if you have not already done so), then type `./nbody` to run the simulation. Using a similar procedure, you can build and run whichever CUDA Samples are of interest.

ESTIMATING "ACCELERATION"

In the lingo of the GPU-based parallel community, getting a computation to run *N* times as fast is called "*N*x acceleration." (This imprecise use of "acceleration" may be painful to those of us who have studied dynamics, but we'll just have to get over it since the lingo is not likely to change.)

This is a good time to generate some initial acceleration estimates, and the nbody app actually provides a means of doing so. The nbody console window provides a list of optional arguments that can be employed when nbody is run from the command prompt. We are going to use three of those options, and you may want to experiment with some of the others:

- The –benchmark option makes the simulation run in a mode that suppresses the graphics output and produces quantitative performance estimates.

- The –cpu option makes the simulation execute on the CPU instead of the GPU.

- The –fp64 option makes the simulation run using double-precision 64-bit arithmetic instead of single-precision 32-bit arithmetic.

The nbody console window also displays the disclaimer "The CUDA Samples are not meant for performance measurement," so let's do some nbody benchmark tests to get some rough acceleration estimates but maintain a bit of healthy skepticism and not read too much into the results.

Start by running nbody -benchmark (./nbody -benchmark in Linux/OS X) and noting results, including the number of GFLOPS reported after execution on the GPU. Next, run nbody with the flags -benchmark -cpu and note the corresponding numbers for execution on the CPU. Repeat both tests with the additional -fp64 option.

On our notebook computer with a GeForce 840M, the GPU produced a single-precision GFLOPS estimate that exceeded the CPU estimate by a factor of about 120x. Using double precision, the GPU produces an acceleration of about 6x. Here we reach another **checkpoint**: You should actually run these computations and get a concrete idea of the acceleration achieved on your system before you continue reading.

Note that the disclaimer is well-founded in that the CPU implementation may not be fully optimized while the GPU implementation has been heavily optimized. (In fact, the docs subfolder of the nbody sample includes a full GPU Gems paper on optimizing the GPU implementation.) Despite the disclaimer, we can learn a couple things from these initial tests: (1) GPU-based parallelism can provide significant gains in computational throughput, and (2) the performance multiplier achieved by a GeForce card is significantly higher for single-precision than for double-precision computations.

The speed-ups you achieve may well reflect the CUDA rule of thumb that you can gain an initial increase in performance when you first parallelize your computation on the GPU; you can often gain a second performance increase by choosing the right memory model (we'll discuss the available choices) and/or buying a higher-end GPU (especially if double precision is important to you, and you can afford a Tesla card); and the third big increase in performance typically requires advanced tuning involving hardware-specific details. Our discussions will focus on the first two speed-ups, and we'll refer you to other sources for information about the third.

That wraps up our look at the nbody sample, but let's run one more sample before we move on. Run the volumeRender sample from the 2_Graphics directory (as shown in Figure 1.1) to interact with a 3D data set by moving the mouse to change your view of the data in real time. We'll be creating our own version of a 3D visualization app in Chapter 7, "Interacting with 3D Data."

Feel free to continue exploring the CUDA Samples, but you are now ready to move on to the next section.

Running Our Own Serial Apps

The time has come to move beyond the CUDA Samples and build/run apps of our own. In this section we present the code for two apps, dist_v1 and dist_v2, that do the same task. Each app computes an array of distances from a reference point to each of N points uniformly spaced along a line segment. This task is chosen to be about as simple as possible while still having meaning for engineers, and you will have little trouble imagining how to generalize these apps to perform the more general task of evaluating other functions for specified input values.

Note that while dist_v1 and dist_v2 perform the same task, they are organized to accomplish that task in different ways:

- The dist_v1 app has a single for loop that scales the loop index to create an input location and then computes/stores the distance from the reference location. Here we create a distance() function that computes the distance from the reference location for a single point, and call the function N times.

- The dist_v2 app starts by creating the array of input points, then passing a pointer to that array to the distanceArray() function that we define to compute/store to the entire array of distance values as the result of a single call.

The apps dist_v1 and dist_v2 will serve as our initial candidates for parallelization in Chapter 3, "From Loops to Grids." The code listings are presented here, and detailed explanations with instructions for creating, building, and executing each app are presented in Appendix C, "Need-to-Know C Programming." This brings us to another **checkpoint**: You need to be able to build and run both dist_v1 and dist_v2; if you run into any trouble doing so, go to Appendix C, "Need-to-Know C Programming," to find the information to resolve the trouble.

dist_v1

The code for the dist_v1 app consists of one file, main.cpp, which is shown in Listing 1.1. The corresponding Linux Makefile is shown in Listing 1.2.

Listing 1.1 `dist_v1/main.cpp`

```
 1 #include <math.h> // Include standard math library containing sqrt
 2 #define N 64 // Specify a constant value for array length
 3
 4 // A scaling function to convert integers 0,1,...,N-1
 5 // to evenly spaced floats ranging from 0 to 1
 6 float scale(int i, int n)
 7 {
 8   return ((float)i)/(n - 1);
 9 }
10
11 // Compute the distance between 2 points on a line
12 float distance(float x1, float x2)
13 {
14   return sqrt((x2 - x1)*(x2 - x1));
15 }
16
17 int main()
18 {
19   // Create an array of N floats (initialized to 0.0)
20   // We will overwrite these values to store our results.
21   float out[N] = {0.0f};
22
23   // Choose a reference value from which distances are measured
24   float ref = 0.5f;
25
26   /* for loop to scale the index to obtain coordinate value,
27    *  compute the distance from the reference point,
28    *  and store the result in the corresponding entry of out */
29   for (int i = 0; i < N; ++i)
30   {
31     float x = scale(i, N);
32     out[i] = distance(x, ref);
33   }
34
35   return 0;
36 }
```

Listing 1.2 `dist_v1/Makefile`

```
NVCC = /usr/local/cuda/bin/nvcc
NVCC_FLAGS = -g -G -Xcompiler -Wall
main.exe: main.cpp
    $(NVCC) $(NVCC_FLAGS) $< -o $@
```

dist_v2

The code for `dist_v2` consists of three files: `main.cpp` (shown in Listing 1.3), `aux_functions.cpp` (shown in Listing 1.4), and the header file `aux_functions.h` (shown in Listing 1.5). The Linux Makefile is shown in Listing 1.6.

Listing 1.3 `dist_v2/main.cpp`

```
 1 #include "aux_functions.h"
 2 #include <stdlib.h> // supports dynamic memory management
 3
 4 #define N 20000000 // A large array size
 5
 6 int main()
 7 {
 8   float *in = (float*)calloc(N, sizeof(float));
 9   float *out = (float*)calloc(N, sizeof(float));
10   const float ref = 0.5f;
11
12   for (int i = 0; i < N; ++i)
13   {
14     in[i] = scale(i, N);
15   }
16
17   distanceArray(out, in, ref, N);
18
19   // Release the heap memory after we are done using it
20   free(in);
21   free(out);
22   return 0;
23 }
```

Listing 1.4 `dist_v2/aux_functions.cpp`

```
 1 #include "aux_functions.h"
 2 #include <math.h>
 3
 4 float scale(int i, int n)
 5 {
 6   return ((float)i) / (n - 1);
 7 }
 8
 9 float distance(float x1, float x2)
10 {
11   return sqrt((x2 - x1)*(x2 - x1));
12 }
13
14 void distanceArray(float *out, float *in, float ref, int n)
15 {
16   for (int i = 0; i < n; ++i)
17   {
18     out[i] = distance(in[i], ref);
19   }
20 }
```

Listing 1.5 `dist_v2/aux_functions.h`

```
 1 #ifndef AUX_FUNCTIONS_H
 2 #define AUX_FUNCTIONS_H
 3
```

```
 4 // Function to scale input on interval [0,1]
 5 float scale(int i, int n);
 6 // Compute the distance between 2 points on a line
 7 float distance(float x1, float x2);
 8 // Compute scaled distance for an array of input values
 9 void distanceArray(float *out, float *in, float ref, int n);
10
11 #endif
```

Listing 1.6 `dist_v2/Makefile`

```
 1 NVCC = /usr/local/cuda/bin/nvcc
 2 NVCC_FLAGS = -g -G -Xcompiler -Wall
 3
 4 all: main.exe
 5
 6 main.exe: main.o aux_functions.o
 7    $(NVCC) $^ -o $@
 8
 9 main.o: main.cpp aux_functions.h
10    $(NVCC) $(NVCC_FLAGS) -c $< -o $@
11
12 aux_functions .o: aux_functions.cpp aux_functions.h
13    $(NVCC) $(NVCC_FLAGS) -c $< -o $@
```

Here we reach the chapter's final **checkpoint**: Before proceeding, you need to have run `dist_v1` and `dist_v2` and, using a debugger, verified that the distance values computed start at 0.5 (the distance from a scaled value of 0 to the reference point at 0.5), decrease toward zero near the middle of the array, and increase back to 0.5 (corresponding to the distance from 0.5 to a scaled value of 1.0). If you encounter any trouble, read the necessary portions of Appendix C, "Need-to-Know C Programming," before going on.

Summary

In this chapter, we ran some CUDA Samples to get an immediate experience with GPU-based parallel computing. We also presented two serial apps that will serve as initial candidates for parallelization: `dist_v1` provides about the simplest example for parallelization, and `dist_v2` illustrates a useful structure and more typical data flow.

You should now be ready to move on to Chapter 2, "CUDA Essentials," for a discussion of CUDA's model of parallel computing, after which, in Chapter 3, "From Loops to Grids," we'll get down to the actual business of parallelization with CUDA.

Suggested Projects

Projects 1–5 are about running some of the other CUDA Samples.

1. Run `deviceQuery` from `1_Utilities` to find out information about the CUDA GPUs on your system (if you did not already do so in Appendix A, "Hardware Setup").

2. Run `Mandelbrot` from `2_Graphics`. Simulation options will appear in the command window. You can quit the simulation with the `Esc` key.

3. Run `volumeFilter` from `2_Graphics`. Simulation options will appear in the command window.

4. Run `smokeParticles` from `5_Simulations`. Right-click on the simulation to see interaction options.

5. Run `fluidsGL` from `5_Simulations`. Left-click and drag on the simulation to play with fluid particles (`r` resets the simulation).

6. We defined `distance()` to return `sqrt((x2 - x1)*(x2 - x1))`. An alternative way to compute the square root of a square is to use absolute value. Create an alternative implementation of `distance()` based on absolute value. See http://en.cppreference.com/w/c/numeric/math for information on common mathematical functions.

Chapter 2

CUDA Essentials

Our discussion in Chapter 1, "First Steps," left off with the function `distanceArray()`, which computes distance values from a reference point to an array of input locations. The computation is completely serial; the values are computed in a sequence as the index i in a `for` loop increments over the range of input array elements. However, the computation of any one of the distance values is independent of the other computations. In a serial implementation, we do not take advantage of the independence and instead wait until one entry in the array is computed before moving on to the next. There is no particular downside to the serial approach if you are using a simple system that can only do one computation at a time. However, with **general purpose GPU (GPGPU) computing** we have access to hundreds or thousands of hardware units that can compute simultaneously. To take advantage of the many processors at our disposal, we change from a serial model, in which computing tasks happen one at a time while the others wait their turn, to a parallel model, in which a large number of computations execute simultaneously. This chapter describes CUDA's model for parallelism, the basic language extensions, and the **application programming interface (API)** for creating CUDA apps [1,2].

CUDA's Model for Parallelism

The change from serial to parallel CUDA computing involves a change in both hardware and software. The hardware change involves chips that include multiple computing units and mechanisms for scheduling computations and data transfers. The software change involves an API and extensions to the programming language.

Host and Device

To refine our terminology a bit, **host** refers to the CPU and its memory, and **device** refers to the GPU and its memory.

The most essential property of a GPU that enables parallelization is that the **device** contains not one or several computing units (like a modern multicore CPU) but hundreds or thousands of computing units. If you can organize your computation into a large number of independent subtasks, the numerous computing units give you the capability to perform many of those tasks in parallel; that is, to execute tasks simultaneously instead of sequentially. Realizing such parallelization involves some major organizational questions: How does a particular computing unit know which subtask to perform? How do a large number of computing units get access to the instructions and data they need without causing a major communications traffic jam?

CUDA employs the **single instruction multiple thread (SIMT)** model of parallelization. CUDA GPUs contain numerous fundamental computing units called **cores**, and each core includes an arithmetic logic unit (ALU) and a floating-point unit (FPU). Cores are collected into groups called **streaming multiprocessors (SMs)**.

We parallelize a computing task by breaking it up into numerous subtasks called **threads** that are organized into **blocks**. Blocks are divided into **warps** whose size matches the number of cores in an SM. Each warp gets assigned to a particular SM for execution. The SM's control unit directs each of its cores to execute the same instructions simultaneously for each thread in the assigned warp, hence the term "single instruction multiple thread."

Executing the same instructions is not just an exercise in redundancy, because each thread performs distinct computations using unique index values that are provided by CUDA [3]. The SIMT approach is **scalable** because computational throughput can be increased by providing more SMs to share the computing load. Figure 2.1 illustrates the contrast between the architecture of a CPU and a GPU. The CPU has a few computing cores occupying a small portion of the chip and a large area dedicated to control and cache to help those few cores run fast. It is a general rule (and a recurring CUDA theme) that the time required to access data increases with the distance between the computing core and the memory location where the data is stored. The time that a core spends waiting

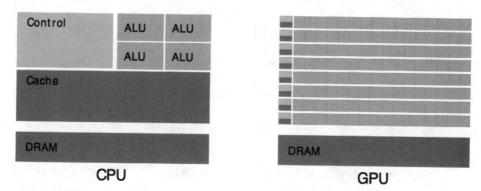

Figure 2.1 Illustration of architecture difference between CPU and GPU. (Figure from the CUDA Programming Guide, used with permission of NVIDIA Corporation.)

for data is called **latency**, and a CPU is designed to minimize latency by dedicating lots of space to storing data where it can be accessed quickly.

The allocation of space on the GPU is very different. Most of the chip area is dedicated to lots of computing cores organized into SMs with a shared control unit. Instead of minimizing latency (which would require a significant amount of cache per core), the GPU aims to hide latency. When execution of a warp requires data that is not available, the SM switches to executing another warp whose data is available. The focus is on overall computing throughput rather than on the speed of an individual core.

Now we are ready to consider the software aspect of CUDA's SIMT implementation. The essential software construct is a special kind of function called a **kernel** that spawns a large collection of computational threads organized into groups that can be assigned to SMs. In CUDA jargon, we **launch a kernel** to create a computational **grid** composed of **blocks** of **threads** (or **threadblocks**). In order to replace sequential computations, we need a way to tell each thread which part of the computation to do; that is, which entry of the input to process and/or which entry of the output to compute/store. CUDA addresses this need by providing each thread with built-in index variables. These CUDA index variables replace the loop index in serial code. The process of launching a kernel, creating a computational grid, and indexing the blocks and threads is presented in the next section.

Need-to-Know CUDA API and C Language Extensions

The basic tasks needed for CUDA parallelism include the following:

- Launching a kernel with specified grid dimensions (numbers of blocks and threads)

- Specifying that functions should be compiled to run on the device (GPU), the host (CPU), or both

- Accessing and utilizing block and thread index values for a computational thread

- Allocating memory and transferring data

Let's start with specifying a kernel launch. As discussed above, a kernel is a kind of function and a kernel launch looks very much like a regular function call; that is, it starts with a name such as aKernel and ends with parentheses containing a comma-separated argument list. Now for the language extension: To indicate the parallel nature and to specify the dimensions of the computational grid, the grid dimensions and block dimensions (inside **triple angle brackets** or **triple chevrons**) are inserted between the name and the parentheses holding the arguments:

```
aKernel<<<Dg, Db>>>(args)
```

Note that Dg, the number of blocks in the grid, and Db, the number of threads in a block, together constitute the **execution configuration** and specify the dimensions of the kernel launch.

This establishes the syntax for launching a kernel, but there is still the issue of how to declare a function that is called from the host but executed on the device. CUDA makes this distinction by prepending one of the following **function type qualifiers**:

- __global__ is the qualifier for kernels (which can be called from the host and executed on the device).

- __host__ functions are called from the host and execute on the host. (This is the default qualifier and is often omitted.)

- __device__ functions are called from the device and execute on the device. (A function that is called from a kernel needs the __device__ qualifier.)

- Prepending __host__ __device__ causes the system to compile separate host and device versions of the function.

Dynamic Parallelism

As of CUDA 5.0, it is possible to launch kernels from other kernels on CUDA devices of compute capability 3.5 or above [1,4,5,6]. Calling __global__ functions from the device is referred to as **dynamic parallelism**, which is beyond the intended scope of this book.

Kernels have several notable capabilities and limitations:

- Kernels cannot return a value, so the return type is always void, and kernel declarations start as follows:

  ```
  __global__ void aKernel(typedArgs)
  ```

- Kernels provide dimension and index variables for each block and thread.

  Dimension variables:

  - gridDim specifies the number of blocks in the grid.

  - blockDim specifies the number of threads in each block.

  Index variables:

  - blockIdx gives the index of the block in the grid.

  - threadIdx gives the index of the thread within the block.

- Kernels execute on the GPU and do not, in general, have access to data stored on the host side that would be accessed by the CPU.

Developments in Memory Access

Recent developments aim to unify access to the memory available to the CPU and one or more GPUs. We will cover what needs to be done to manage memory transfer between host and device. The alternative of unified memory access is introduced near the end of Chapter 3, "From Loops to Grids."

The CUDA Runtime API provides the following functions for transferring input data to the device and transferring results back to the host:

- `cudaMalloc()` allocates device memory.

- `cudaMemcpy()` transfers data to or from a device.

- `cudaFree()` frees device memory that is no longer in use.

Kernels enable multiple computations to occur in parallel, but they also give up control of the order of execution. CUDA provides functions to synchronize and coordinate execution when necessary:

- `__syncThreads()` synchronizes threads within a block.

- `cudaDeviceSynchronize()` effectively synchronizes all threads in a grid.

- Atomic operations, such as `atomicAdd()`, prevent conflicts associated with multiple threads concurrently accessing a variable.

In addition to the functions and qualifiers described above, CUDA also provides support for some additional useful data types:

- `size_t`: dedicated type for variables that indicate amounts of memory.

- `cudaError_t`: dedicated type for variables used in error handling.

- Vector types: CUDA extends the standard C data types to vectors of length up to 4. Individual components are accessed with the suffixes `.x`, `.y`, `.z`, and `.w`.

Essential Use of Vector Types

CUDA uses the vector type `uint3` for the index variables, `blockIdx` and `threadIdx`. A `uint3` variable is a vector with three unsigned integer components.

CUDA uses the vector type `dim3` for the dimension variables, `gridDim` and `blockDim`. The `dim3` type is equivalent to `uint3` with unspecified entries set to 1. We will use `dim3` variables for specifying execution configurations.

Summary

You now have access to the tools needed to start creating apps that take advantage of the parallel computing power of the GPU using CUDA, and that is just what we will start doing in Chapter 3, "From Loops to Grids."

Suggested Projects

1. Go to the CUDA Zone and enroll as a registered CUDA developer (if you have not already done so).

2. View the video at www.nvidia.com/object/nvision08_gpu_v_cpu.html to see an entertaining demonstration of the contrast between serial and parallel execution.

3. Read the "Introduction" to the *CUDA Programming Guide* at http://docs .nvidia.com/cuda/pdf/CUDA_C_Programming_Guide.pdf.

4. Watch the video, "GPU Computing: Past, Present, and Future," by David Luebke, from the 2011 GPU Tech Conference to get an interesting perspective on the origins and directions of GPU computing. (Do not worry about the occasional unfamiliar term. Think of this talk as an opportunity to gain exposure to CUDA jargon.) The video can be found at http://on-demand-gtc.gputechconf.com/ content/includes/gtc/video/stream-david-luebke-june2011.html.

References

[1]   NVIDIA Corporation, "CUDA C Programming Guide," NVIDIA Developer Zone, CUDA Toolkit Documentation, 2015, http://docs.nvidia.com/cuda/cuda-c-programming-guide/index.html#abstract.

[2]   Jason Sanders and Edward Kandrot, *CUDA by Example* (Boston, MA: Addison-Wesley, 2011).

[3]   Rob Farber, "The CUDA Execution Model," Chap. 4 in *CUDA Application Design and Development* (Waltham, MA: Morgan Kaufmann, 2011), 85–108.

[4] NVIDIA Corporation, *Dynamic Parallelism in CUDA*, 2012, http://developer
     .download.nvidia.com/assets/cuda/files/CUDADownloads/TechBrief_Dynamic_
     Parallelism_in_CUDA.pdf.

[5] Stephen Jones, *Introduction to Dynamic Parallelism* (2012), http://on-demand
     .gputechconf.com/gtc/2012/presentations/S0338-GTC2012-CUDA-
     Programming-Model.pdf.

[6] Andrew Adinetz, "Adaptive Parallel Computation with CUDA Dynamic Parallel-
     ism," *Parallel Forall* (blog), May 2014, http://devblogs.nvidia.com/parallelforall/
     introduction-cuda-dynamic-parallelism/.

Chapter 3

From Loops to Grids

We are now ready to apply the basics presented in Chapter 2, "CUDA Essentials," to parallelize the C codes presented in Chapter 1, "First Steps," and Appendix C, "Need-to-Know C Programming." Recall that we created two versions of the distance app. In dist_v1 we used a for loop to compute an array of distance values. In dist_v2 we created an array of input values and then called the function distanceArray() to compute the entire array of distance values (again in serial using a for loop). In this chapter, we use CUDA to parallelize the distance apps by replacing serial passes through a loop with a computational grid of threads that can execute together.

We will be creating, building, and executing new apps, but the focus is on parallelization with CUDA. If you run into problems with non-CUDA-specific issues such as building and executing C apps, please refer to Appendix C, "Need-to-Know C Programming."

Parallelizing dist_v1

For this initial foray into parallelization, we'll go through the steps of getting from the code for dist_v1 to the parallel version dist_v1_cuda before presenting the complete code, which appears in Listing 3.1. Here are the basic steps that you should follow along with:

1. Create a dist_v1_cuda project containing a kernel.cu file:

   a. In Linux, create a dist_v1_cuda directory and create the file kernel.cu within that directory.

    b. In Visual Studio, create a new CUDA 7.5 Runtime Project named `dist_v1_cuda`, which will include a `kernel.cu` file. Delete the sample code from `kernel.cu`.

2. Copy and paste the contents of `dist_v1/main.cpp` into `kernel.cu`. Modify the code in `kernel.cu` as follows:

    a. Delete `#include <math.h>` because CUDA-internal files already include `math.h`, and insert `#include <stdio.h>` to enable printing output to the console.

    b. Below the current `#define` statement, add another, `#define TPB 32`, to indicate the number of threads per block that will be used in our kernel launch.

    c. Copy the entire for loop and paste a copy just above `main()`. We'll return to edit this into a kernel definition.

    d. Replace the for loop in `main()` with the kernel call `distanceKernel<<<N/TPB, TPB>>>(d_out, ref, N);` which consists of three elements:

      i. The function name `distanceKernel`.

      ii. Triple chevrons enclosing the execution configuration parameters. In this case, we specify `N/TPB` blocks (2) each with `TPB` threads (32).

      iii. The list of arguments including a pointer to the output array `d_out`, the reference location `ref`, and the array length `N`.

    e. Convert the copy of the for loop above `main()` into a kernel definition as follows:

      i. Replace the first line of the loop (everything before the braces) with the kernel declaration consisting of the following:

        1. The qualifier `__global__`

        2. The return type `void`

        3. The function name `distanceKernel`

        4. Parentheses enclosing a comma-separated list of typed arguments `(float *d_out, float ref, int len)`

ii. Insert as the first line inside the braces the following formula for computing an index i (to replace the loop index of the same name, which has now been removed) using the built-in index and dimension variables that CUDA provides with every kernel launch:

```
const int i = blockIdx.x*blockDim.x + threadIdx.x;
```

iii. Change the name of the array on the left-hand side of the assignment from out[i] to d_out[i]

iv. Insert as the last line inside the braces the following printf() statement:

```
printf("i = %2d: dist from %f to %f is %f.\n", i, ref, x,
d_out[i]);
```

f. Prepend the qualifier __device__ to the definitions of scale() and distance().

g. Manage storage as follows:

i. At the start of main(), remove the statement defining out (which will not be used here) with the following code to create a device array d_out that can store N floats:

```
float *d_out;
cudaMalloc(&d_out, N*sizeof(float));
```

ii. Just above the return statement at the end of main(), free the memory allocated for d_out with the following:

```
cudaFree(d_out);
```

To make sure all the pieces come together properly, the code for dist_v1_cuda/kernel.cu is shown in Listing 3.1.

Listing 3.1 dist_v1_cuda/kernel.cu

```
1 #include <stdio.h>
2 #define N 64
3 #define TPB 32
4
5 __device__ float scale(int i, int n)
6 {
7   return ((float)i)/(n - 1);
8 }
9
10 __device__ float distance(float x1, float x2)
11 {
```

```
12    return sqrt((x2 - x1)*(x2 - x1));
13 }
14
15 __global__ void distanceKernel(float *d_out, float ref, int len)
16 {
17    const int i = blockIdx.x*blockDim.x + threadIdx.x;
18    const float x = scale(i, len);
19    d_out[i] = distance(x, ref);
20    printf("i = %2d: dist from %f to %f is %f.\n", i, ref, x, d_out[i]);
21 }
22
23 int main()
24 {
25    const float ref = 0.5f;
26
27    // Declare a pointer for an array of floats
28    float *d_out = 0;
29
30    // Allocate device memory to store the output array
31    cudaMalloc(&d_out, N*sizeof(float));
32
33    // Launch kernel to compute and store distance values
34    distanceKernel<<<N/TPB, TPB>>>(d_out, ref, N);
35
36    cudaFree(d_out); // Free the memory
37    return 0;
38 }
```

A few comments are in order before building and executing the parallelized app. We hope that your efforts in following along have gotten you to the point where you can now look at the complete listing and have a reasonable idea of the motivation for and purpose of all the components of the code.

We also want to remind you of some special aspects of kernel functions since they provide our primary tool for parallelization in CUDA. The big thing to remember is that the kernel (distanceKernel in this case) executes on the device, so it cannot return a value to the host; hence the mandatory return type void. The kernel generally has access to device memory, not to host memory, so we allocate device memory for the output array using cudaMalloc() (rather than host memory using malloc()) and use the name d_out where the prefix d_ serves as a convenient (but definitely not mandatory) reminder that d_out is a device array. Finally, note that the kernel definition is written as if we only have to write code for a single thread. Everything that happened previously with loops is now taken care of by the fact that each thread can determine i, its overall index in the computational grid, from the index and dimension variables provided automatically to each thread by CUDA.

Choosing the Execution Configuration

Note that choosing the specific execution configuration that will produce the best performance on a given system involves both art and science. For now, let's not get hung up in the details and just point out that choosing the number of threads in a block to be some multiple of 32 is reasonable since that matches up with the number of CUDA cores in an SM. There are also limits on the sizes supported for both blocks and grids. A handy table including those limits can be found in the CUDA C Programming Guide [1]. One particularly relevant limit is that a single block cannot contain more than 1,024 threads. Since grids may have total thread counts well over 1,024, you should expect your kernel launches to include lots of blocks, and plan on doing some execution configuration experiments to see what works best for your app running on your hardware. For such larger problems, reasonable values to test for the number of threads per block include 128, 256, and 512.

EXECUTING dist_v1_cuda

With the code complete, it is time to build and execute the app. Since the code now includes a kernel launch (which is not part of C/C++), we need to invoke the NVIDIA C Compiler, nvcc. In Windows, Visual Studio recognizes the .cu extension and automatically invokes the nvcc compiler, so go ahead and press F7 to build the app. Under Linux, build the app with the Makefile shown in Listing 3.2 that specifies compilation using nvcc.

Listing 3.2 dist_v1_cuda/Makefile

```
NVCC = /usr/local/cuda/bin/nvcc
NVCC_FLAGS = -g -G -Xcompiler -Wall

main.exe: kernel.cu
    $(NVCC) $(NVCC_FLAGS) $^ -o $@
```

Note that in Listing 3.1 we included the standard input/output library on line 1 and inserted a printf() statement on line 20 to print results to the screen, so now you can execute the app and view the output printed to the terminal. Verify that the values agree with those computed using the serial apps dist_v1 and dist_v2.

Notes on printf()

Be advised that using printf() from a kernel is not supported for GPUs with compute capability less than 2.0. If you are not familiar with printf() (or inserting strings into the output stream, `cout`, for the C++ inclined), please see your favorite C/C++ language reference. We are doing this for expediency, but be advised that `printf()` should not be considered as a general purpose debugging tool.

More on Debugging

The usual C/C++ debugging tools provided by Visual Studio or `gdb` are not capable of displaying the values in device memory, but there are CUDA-specific debugging tools available for this purpose. A discussion of CUDA debugging tools, including methods for inspecting values stored in device memory, is provided in Appendix D, "CUDA Practicalities: Timing, Profiling, Error Handling, and Debugging."

The first thing you may notice is that the printed output is not necessarily presented with the index ordered from 0 to 63. This is a fundamental difference between serial and parallel apps: In a serial app, we get to specify the order in which computations are performed in a loop. In the CUDA approach to parallelism, we give up some control of the order of computations to gain the computational acceleration associated with the massive parallelism provided by hundreds or thousands of processors doing multiple evaluations at the same time.

The second thing to check (and the issue of paramount importance) is that the distance values correspond with the ones you computed with the serial distance apps, `dist_v1` and `dist_v2`. All the parallelization in the world is not helpful if it produces incorrect outputs!

Parallelizing `dist_v2`

The first parallelized distance app, `dist_v1_cuda`, is atypical in that it does not involve a significant amount of input data. Now we are ready to parallelize the second distance app, `dist_v2`, a more typical case that involves processing an array of input values. The plan for processing an array of data on the GPU is straightforward:

1. Create an array in device memory (on the GPU) whose type and size matches that of the input array stored in host memory (on the CPU side).

2. Create an array in device memory to store the output data. (There will be occasions where you choose to store the output by overwriting the input array, but let's consider separate input and output arrays for now.)

3. Copy the input array from host memory to the corresponding array in device memory.

4. Launch a kernel to perform the computation and store the output values in the output device array.

5. Copy the output array from device memory to the corresponding array in host memory.

6. Free the memory allocated to hold the device arrays.

The steps listed above fit in nicely with the organization we established for dist_v2, which included a main.cpp file (primarily to contain the code for main()), a separate file (named aux_functions.cpp) to hold code defining auxiliary functions, and a header file (named aux_functions.h) for inclusion of prototypes for functions like distanceArray() that are "visible" and can be called from other files (including main.cpp).

Since Step 4 involves a CUDA kernel call, we will replace aux_functions.cpp (and its corresponding header file) with kernel.cu (and its corresponding header file, which is called kernel.h). The full codes are shown in Listings 3.3, 3.4, and 3.5, along with the Makefile in Listing 3.6.

Listing 3.3 dist_v2_cuda/main.cpp

```
 1 #include "kernel.h"
 2 #include <stdlib.h>
 3 #define N 64
 4
 5 float scale(int i, int n)
 6 {
 7   return ((float)i)/(n - 1);
 8 }
 9
10 int main()
11 {
12   const float ref = 0.5f;
13
14   float *in  = (float*)calloc(N, sizeof(float));
15   float *out = (float*)calloc(N, sizeof(float));
16
17   // Compute scaled input values
18   for (int i = 0; i < N; ++i)
19   {
20     in[i] = scale(i, N);
21   }
22
23   // Compute distances for the entire array
24   distanceArray(out, in, ref, N);
25
```

```
26    free(in);
27    free(out);
28    return 0;
29 }
```

The code for dist_v2_cuda/main.cpp is almost the same as dist_v2/main.cpp except that the scale() function is moved to main.cpp and kernel.h is included instead of aux_functions.h. All the significant changes occur in the new definition of distanceArray() contained in kernel.cu.

Listing 3.4 dist_v2_cuda/kernel.cu

```
 1 #include "kernel.h"
 2 #include <stdio.h>
 3 #define TPB 32
 4
 5 __device__
 6 float distance(float x1, float x2)
 7 {
 8    return sqrt((x2 - x1)*(x2 - x1));
 9 }
10
11 __global__
12 void distanceKernel(float *d_out, float *d_in, float ref)
13 {
14    const int i = blockIdx.x*blockDim.x + threadIdx.x;
15    const float x = d_in[i];
16    d_out[i] = distance(x, ref);
17    printf("i = %2d: dist from %f to %f is %f.\n", i, ref, x, d_out[i]);
18 }
19
20 void distanceArray(float *out, float *in, float ref, int len)
21 {
22    // Declare pointers to device arrays
23    float *d_in = 0;
24    float *d_out = 0;
25
26    // Allocate memory for device arrays
27    cudaMalloc(&d_in, len*sizeof(float));
28    cudaMalloc(&d_out, len*sizeof(float));
29
30    // Copy input data from host to device
31    cudaMemcpy(d_in, in, len*sizeof(float), cudaMemcpyHostToDevice);
32
33    // Launch kernel to compute and store distance values
34    distanceKernel<<<len/TPB, TPB>>>(d_out, d_in, ref);
35
36    // Copy results from device to host
37    cudaMemcpy(out, d_out, len*sizeof(float), cudaMemcpyDeviceToHost);
38
39    // Free the memory allocated for device arrays
40    cudaFree(d_in);
41    cudaFree(d_out);
42 }
```

There are a few aspects of `dist_v2_cuda/kernel.cu` worth noting:

1. The `distanceKernel()` function is slightly different from the version in `dist_v1_cuda/kernel.cu`. Here, the arguments include a pointer, `d_in`, to an array of input values that have already been scaled.

2. The new definition of `distanceArray()` performs all five of the steps in the plan outlined above. Input and output device arrays are declared and allocated on lines 23–28; input data is copied from the host array to the device array on line 31; the GPU-parallelized execution results from the kernel call on line 34; the output distance values are copied from device to host on line 37; and the memory allocated for the device arrays is freed on lines 40–41.

3. The function, `distanceArray()` calls the kernel function, `distanceKernel()`. Such functions are referred to as **wrapper** or **launcher** functions.

Execution Configuration Involves Integer Arithmetic

The kernel execution configuration is specified so that each block has `TPB` threads, and there are `N/TPB` blocks (since `N` is the value of `len` passed by the function call). We have used #define to set `TPB` = 32 and `N` = 64, so this works out to 2 blocks of 32 threads, just as we had before, but remember that the dimension variables are vectors of type `int` and use integer arithmetic. If you set `N=65`, you would still get 65/32 = 2 blocks of 32 threads, and the last entry in the array would not get computed because there is no thread with the corresponding index in the computational grid. The simple trick to ensure the grid covers the array length is to change the specified number of blocks from `N/TPB` to `(N+TPB-1)/TPB` to ensure that the block number is rounded up. This also means that the grid index can exceed the maximum legal array index, and a control statement is then needed in the kernel to prevent execution with indices that would exceed array dimensions and produce segmentation violation errors. We'll stick with the simple version here, but we'll put the more reliable specification to work in future apps.

Recall that the grid and block dimensions within the triple chevrons actually have type `dim3`. In this 1D context, the integer values are interpreted as the `.x` components of a `dim3` whose unspecified `.y` and `.z` components have the default value 1. The execution configuration `<<<len/TPB, TPB>>>` is shorthand for `<<<dim3(len/TPB, 1, 1), dim3(TPB, 1, 1)>>>`. We'll introduce meaningful values for the `.y` and `.z` components when we get to higher dimensional grids.

Listing 3.5 `dist_v2_cuda/kernel.h`

```
1 #ifndef KERNEL_H
2 #define KERNEL_H
3
4 // Kernel wrapper for computing array of distance values
5 void distanceArray(float *out, float *in, float ref, int len);
6
7 #endif
```

Listing 3.6 `dist_v2_cuda/Makefile`

```
 1 NVCC = /usr/local/cuda/bin/nvcc
 2 NVCC_FLAGS = -g -G -Xcompiler -Wall
 3
 4 all: main.exe
 5
 6 main.exe: main.o kernel.o
 7    $(NVCC) $^ -o $@
 8
 9 main.o: main.cpp kernel.h
10    $(NVCC) $(NVCC_FLAGS) -c $< -o $@
11
12 kernel.o: kernel.cu kernel.h
13    $(NVCC) $(NVCC_FLAGS) -c $< -o $@
```

With all the code in hand, you can now build and execute `dist_v2_cuda`. Verify that the distance values are correctly computed, and take a moment to notice that essentially all of the CUDA code is sequestered in `kernel.cu`. Compare the `distanceArray()` prototypes in `dist_v2/aux_functions.h` and `dist_v2_cuda/kernel.h`. Note that the prototypes are identical, but the function definition has changed. In software development terms, we have changed the implementation while maintaining the interface. This approach provides a model for creating CUDA-powered versions of existing applications.

Standard Workflow

Looking at what typically appears, let's identify the parts of the workflow that represent CUDA's costs and benefits. The costs should be rather obvious: creating mirror arrays and transferring data between host and device are additional tasks that are not needed when doing serial computation on the CPU. In return for the costs of these "overhead" memory operations, we get access to the benefits associated with the ability to execute operations concurrently on the hundreds or thousands of processing cores on the GPU. These considerations lead directly to a simple game plan for using CUDA productively:

• Copy your input data to the device *once* and leave it there.

• Launch a kernel that does a significant amount of work (so the benefits of massive parallelism are significant compared to the cost of memory transfers).

• Copy the results back to the host *only once*.

Nothing about this is set in stone, but it does provide a useful rule of thumb, and at this point, you have all the tools you need to execute this typical workflow. However, before we move on to higher dimensional problems, let's go off on a quick tangent to look at an alternative approach that can enable you to simplify your development process.

Simplified Workflow

While the standard workflow detailed above constitutes the "dominant paradigm," some see it as involving too much bookkeeping so the good folks at NVIDIA put their heads together and provided a streamlined alternative called **unified memory**. This approach breaks down the barrier between host memory and device memory so that you can have one array that is (or at least appears to be) accessible from both host and device.

UNIFIED MEMORY AND MANAGED ARRAYS

The good news is that unified memory relieves you from having to create separate copies of an array (on the host and the device) and from explicitly calling for data transfers between CPU and GPU. Instead, you can create a single **managed array** that can be accessed from both host and device. In reality, the data in the array needs to be transferred between host and device, but the CUDA system schedules and executes those transfers so you don't have to. Note that managed memory arrays involve a tradeoff between development efficiency and execution efficiency. Letting the system manage the data transfers may simplify and accelerate the process of developing your app, but there is no guarantee that the system will "automagically" manage the data transfers as well as you can. There may come a stage in your development process where you find that the bottleneck in your code involves data transfers, and you may decide at that point it is worth taking explicit control of allocating storage and transferring data. More on that topic later when we get more into the details of performance issues, but for now let's look at the basics of unified memory and implement a managed memory version of the distance app.

Important notes regarding unified memory:

- Unified memory has particular system requirements, including a GPU with compute capability not less than 3.0 and a 64-bit version of either Linux or Windows [1]. (Unified memory is not currently available on OS X.)

- The other large potential benefit is significant for those of you who prefer object-oriented C++ code; unified memory addressing is much better suited to dealing with transfer of structured data and helps to avoid "deep copy" issues [2].

- Concerns about performance costs of managed arrays may be alleviated when GPUs shift from software emulation of unified memory to implementation in hardware.

DISTANCE APP WITH `cudaMallocManaged()`

When we parallelized `dist_v2` to create `dist_v2_cuda`, we followed the dominant paradigm by creating redundant arrays and by explicitly transferring data back and forth between host and device across the PCIe bus using `cudaMemcpy()`.

Here we look at the details of the streamlined implementation made possible with the introduction of unified memory so that a single array is accessible from both host and device. The essential addition to the CUDA extensions of C is the function `cudaMallocManaged()`, which we will use to allocate memory for managed arrays (after declaration of an appropriate pointer, just as with `cudaMalloc()`).

Once again, we will keep the discussion short and get right into the code for a version of the distance app that takes advantage of unified memory as shown in Listing 3.7. There are a number of changes worth noting:

- The code for `distanceArray()` is greatly simplified since there is no need to allocate arrays or explicitly call for a data transfer; all the function has to do is launch the compute kernel (and call `cudaDeviceSynchronize()` to make sure that execution is complete before returning).

- Only a single version is created of each of the relevant arrays. In main(), pointers are declared to in and out. Unified memory is allocated for the arrays using cudaMallocManaged() and then freed with cudaFree() after the computation is completed.

- For purposes of concise presentation, we chose to put all the code in a single file. This time we create a .cu file rather than the .cpp file used in Chapter 1, "First Steps," when the code included only C code with no CUDA language extensions.

- Note the qualifier (or lack thereof) for each function:

  - scale() is called within the for loop executed on the CPU to generate the input data. The appropriate qualifier is __host__, but we can leave it out because it is the default qualifier.

  - distance(), which is called from within the kernel and will execute on the GPU, gets qualified with __device__.

  - distanceKernel(), which like all kernels can be called from the host and executed on the device, gets the qualifier __global__ and the return type void.

Listing 3.7 `dist_v2_cuda_unified/kernel.cu`

```
1  #include <stdio.h>
2  #define N 64
3  #define TPB 32
4
5  float scale(int i, int n)
6  {
7    return ((float)i)/(n - 1);
8  }
9
10 __device__
11 float distance(float x1, float x2)
12 {
13   return sqrt((x2 - x1)*(x2 - x1));
14 }
15
16 __global__
17 void distanceKernel(float *d_out, float *d_in, float ref)
18 {
19   const int i = blockIdx.x*blockDim.x + threadIdx.x;
20   const float x = d_in[i];
21   d_out[i] = distance(x, ref);
22   printf("i = %2d: dist from %f to %f is %f.\n", i, ref, x, d_out[i]);
23 }
24
25 int main()
26 {
```

```
27   const float ref = 0.5f;
28   // Declare pointers for input and output arrays
29   float *in = 0;
30   float *out = 0;
31
32   // Allocate managed memory for input and output arrays
33   cudaMallocManaged(&in, N*sizeof(float));
34   cudaMallocManaged(&out, N*sizeof(float));
35
36   // Compute scaled input values
37   for (int i = 0; i < N; ++i)
38   {
39     in[i] = scale(i, N);
40   }
41
42   // Launch kernel to compute and store distance values
43   distanceKernel <<<N/TPB, TPB>>>(out, in, ref);
44   cudaDeviceSynchronize();
45
46   // Free the allocated memory
47   cudaFree(in);
48   cudaFree(out);
49
50   return 0;
51 }
```

Once again, we have come to the point where we need to build and execute the app, then inspect the results to see if the computation produced correct results. (The Linux Makefile shown in Listing 3.2 can be used to build this project.) We included a `printf()` statement on line 22 to print the results to the console, but you can also inspect the results using your debugging tools.

In Linux, you can view the values in the managed array using `cuda-gdb` the same way you view the values of any variables (with `print out[0]@64`).

Using Visual Studio under Windows, you may see out in the `Locals` pane, but only a single value is available there. However, you can view the other values as follows:

1. Set a breakpoint at line 47, just before freeing the memory.

2. Start debugging (F5).

3. Select DEBUG ⇒ QuickWatch (Shift+F9).

4. When the QuickWatch window opens, enter out, 64.

5. Click the triangle next to the name to open the list of entries in out.

For a closer look at CUDA-specific debugging tools, see Appendix D, "CUDA Practicalities: Timing, Profiling, Error Handling, and Debugging."

Summary

In this chapter, we used CUDA to create `dist_v1_cuda` and `dist_v2_cuda`, the parallel versions of `dist_v1` and `dist_v2`.

`dist_v2_cuda` provided a nice example of typical workflow in a CUDA app. Here is a concise recap of what happened (and what generically happens in CUDA apps):

- Create input and output host arrays that provide the input data and a place to which results will be copied.

- Declare pointers and allocate memory for analogous input and output arrays on the device.

- Copy the input data from the host array to the corresponding array on the device.

- Launch a kernel on the device to do the computing and write the results to the output device array.

- Copy the results from the output device array to the corresponding array on the host.

- Free the memory allocated for the arrays.

Congratulations are in order because you have crossed the threshold into the world of massively parallel computing. Now you can (and should!) start modifying the example apps and the CUDA Samples to create your own CUDA-powered apps. Note that we have maintained our "need-to-know" approach to get across the CUDA threshold as quickly and clearly as possible. We implemented the standard CUDA workflow (with separate copies of arrays on host and device and explicit calls for data transfers) and touched briefly on the simplified development approach that becomes possible with unified memory.

While we have achieved our initial goal of becoming CUDA-capable as quickly as possible, it is worth noting that we have leapt ahead without worrying about important things (error handling, CUDA debugging, timing, and profiling) that you will need (or at least really want) to know about when you take on larger

CUDA projects. Those subjects are discussed in Appendix D, which you should now have the background to read. At this point, we recommend that you proceed on to the next chapter and read about the practicalities in Appendix D whenever you reach a point where you need to know about the specifics of error handling, debugging, timing, and profiling.

Suggested Projects

1. Experiment with changing the number of elements in the distance array. What, if any, problems arise if you define N to be 128? 1024? 63? 65?

2. Compute a distance array with 4,096 elements, and experiment with changing TPB. What is the largest block size (and smallest number of blocks) you can run on your system? Note that the answer to this question depends on the compute capability of your GPU. Refer to the CUDA C Programming Guide [1] to see if your result agrees with limit listed there for "maximum number of threads per block."

References

[1]   NVIDIA Corporation, "CUDA C Programming Guide," NVIDIA Developer Zone, CUDA Toolkit Documentation, 2015, http://docs.nvidia.com/cuda/cuda-c-programming-guide/index.html#abstract.

[2]   Mark Harris, "Unified Memory in CUDA 6," *Parallel Forall* (blog), November 2013. http://devblogs.nvidia.com/parallelforall/unified-memory-in-cuda-6/.

Chapter 4

2D Grids and Interactive Graphics

In this chapter, we see that the CUDA model of parallelism extends readily to two dimensions (2D). We go through the basics of launching a 2D computational grid and create a skeleton kernel you can use to compute a 2D grid of values for functions of interest to you. We then specialize the kernel to create `dist_2d`, an app that computes the distance from a reference point in the plane to each member of a uniform 2D grid of points. By identifying the grid of points with pixels in an image, we compute data for an image whose shading is based on distance values.

Once we are generating image data, it is only natural to take advantage of CUDA's **graphics interoperability** (or **graphics interop** for short) capability, which supports cooperation with standard graphics **application programming interfaces (APIs)** including **Direct3D** [1] and **OpenGL** [2]. We'll use OpenGL, and maintaining our need-to-know approach, we'll very quickly provide just the necessities of OpenGL to get your results on the screen at interactive speeds.

By the end of this chapter you will have run a `flashlight` app that interactively displays an image with shading based on distance from a reference point that you can move using mouse or keyboard input and a `stability` app that interactively displays the results of several hundred thousand numerical simulations of the dynamics of an oscillator. This experience should get you to the point where you are ready to start creating your own CUDA-powered interactive apps.

Launching 2D Computational Grids

Here we expand on our earlier examples that involved a 1D array (points distributed regularly along a line segment) and move on to consider applications involving points regularly distributed on a portion of a 2D plane. While we will encounter other applications (e.g., simulating heat conduction) that fit this scenario, the most common (and likely most intuitive) example involves digital image processing. To take advantage of the intuitive connection, we will use image-processing terminology in presenting the concepts—all of which will transfer directly to other applications.

A digital raster image consists of a collection of picture elements or **pixels** arranged in a uniform 2D rectangular grid with each pixel having a quantized intensity value. To be concrete, let's associate the width and height directions with the x and y coordinates, respectively, and say that our image is W pixels wide by H pixels high. If the quantized value stored in each pixel is simply a number, the data for an image matches exactly with the data for a matrix of size W x H.

As we move on from 1D to 2D problems in CUDA, we hope you will be pleasantly surprised by how few adjustments need to be made. In 1D, we specified integer values for block and grid sizes and computed an index i based on `blockDim.x`, `blockIdx.x`, and `threadIdx.x` according to the formula

```
int i = blockIdx.x*blockDim.x + threadIdx.x;
```

Here we reinterpret the expression on the right-hand side of the assignment as the specification of a new index c that keeps track of what column each pixel belongs to. (As we traverse a row of pixels from left to right, c increases from its minimum value 0 to its maximum value W-1.) We also introduce a second index r to keep track of row numbers (ranging from 0 to H-1). The row index is computed just as the column index is, but using the `.y` components (instead of the `.x` components), so the column and row indices are computed as follows:

```
int c = blockIdx.x*blockDim.x + threadIdx.x;
int r = blockIdx.y*blockDim.y + threadIdx.y;
```

To keep data storage and transfer simple, we will continue to store and transfer data in a "flat" 1D array, so we will have one more integer variable to index into the 1D array. We will continue to call that variable i, noting that i played this role in the 1D case, but in other places (including the CUDA Samples) you will see variables named `idx`, `flatIdx`, and `offset` indexing the 1D array. We place values in the 1D array in row major order—that is, by storing the data from row 0, followed by the data from row 1, and so on—so the index i in the 1D array is now computed as follows:

```
int i = r*w + c;
```

To describe the 2D computational grid that intuitively matches up with an image (or matrix or other regular 2D discretization), we specify block and grid sizes using dim3 variables with two nontrivial components. Recall that an integer within the triple chevrons of a kernel call is treated as the .x component of a dim3 variable with a default value of 1 for the unspecified .y and .z components. In the current 2D context, we specify nontrivial .x and .y components. The .z component of the dim3, which here has the default value 1, will come into play when we get to 3D grids in Chapter 7, "Interacting with 3D Data."

Without further ado, let's lay out the necessary syntax and get directly to parallel computation of pixel values with a 2D grid.

SYNTAX FOR 2D KERNEL LAUNCH

The 2D kernel launch differs from the 1D launch only in terms of the execution configuration. Computing data for an image involves W columns and H rows, and we can organize the computation into 2D blocks with TX threads in the x-direction and TY threads in the y-direction. (You can choose to organize your 2D grid into 1D blocks, but you will run into limits on both maximum block dimension and total number of threads in a block. See the CUDA C Programming Guide [3] for details.)

We specify the 2D block size with a single statement:

```
dim3 blockSize(TX, TY); // Equivalent to dim3 blockSize(TX, TY, 1);
```

and then we compute the number of blocks (bx and by) needed in each direction exactly as in the 1D case.

```
int bx = (W + blockSize.x - 1)/blockSize.x ;
int by = (H + blockSize.y - 1)/blockSize.y ;
```

The syntax for specifying the grid size (in blocks) is

```
dim3 gridSize = dim3(bx, by);
```

With those few details in hand, we are ready to launch:

```
kernelName<<<gridSize, blockSize>>>(args)
```

DEFINING 2D KERNELS

The prototype or declaration of a kernel to be launched on a 2D grid will look exactly as before: it starts with the qualifier __global__ followed by return type void and a legal name, such as kernel2D, and ends with a comma-separated list of typed arguments (which better include a pointer to a device array d_out where the computed image data will be stored, along with the width and height of the image and any other required inputs). The kernel2D function begins by computing the row, column, and flat indices and testing that the row and column indices have values corresponding to a pixel within the image. All that is left is computing the value for the pixel.

Putting the pieces together, the structure of a typical 2D kernel is given in Listing 4.1.

Listing 4.1 "Skeleton" listing for a kernel to be launched on a 2D grid. Replace INSERT_CODE_
HERE with your code for computing the output value.

```
 1 __global__
 2 void kernel2D(float *d_out, int w, int h, … )
 3 {
 4    // Compute column and row indices.
 5    const int c = blockIdx.x * blockDim.x + threadIdx.x;
 6    const int r = blockIdx.y * blockDim.y + threadIdx.y;
 7    const int i = r * w + c; // 1D flat index
 8
 9    // Check if within image bounds.
10    if ((c >= w) || (r >= h))
11      return;
12
13    d_out[i] = INSERT_CODE_HERE; // Compute/store pixel in device array.
14 }
```

A Note on Capitalization of Variable Names

We need to refer to parameter values such as the width and height of an image inside of function definitions where they are considered as input variables, but the input value in the function call will typically be a constant value specified using #define. We will follow the prevailing convention by using uppercase for the constant value and the same name in lowercase for the input variable. For example, the function kernel2D() in Listing 4.1 has the prototype

void kernel2D(uchar4 *d_out, int w, int h, …)

and the function call

```
#define W 500
#define H 500
kernel2D<<<gridSize, blockSize>>>(d_out, W, H, ... )
```

indicates that the input values for width and height are constants, here with value 500.

One detail worth dealing with at this point is a common data type for images. The quantized value stored for each pixel is of type uchar4, which is a vector type storing four unsigned character values (each of which occupies 1 byte of storage). For practical purposes, you can think of the four components of the uchar4 (designated as usual by suffixes .x, .y, .z, and .w) as specifying integer values ranging from 0 to 255 for the red, green, blue, and alpha (opacity) display channels. This format for describing pixel values in an image is often abbreviated as **RGBA**.

Putting the pieces together, the structure of a typical 2D kernel for computing an image is given in Listing 4.2.

Listing 4.2 *"Skeleton"* listing for computing data for an image. RED_FORMULA, GREEN_FORMULA, and BLUE_FORMULA should be replaced with your code for computing desired values between 0 and 255 for each color channel.

```
1 __global__
2 void kernel2D(uchar4 *d_output, int w, int h, ... )
3 {
4   // Compute column and row indices.
5   int c = blockIdx.x*blockDim.x + threadIdx.x;
6   int r = blockIdx.y*blockDim.y + threadIdx.y;
7   int i = r * w + c; // 1D flat index
8
9   // Check if within image bounds.
10  if ((r >= h) || (c >= w)) {
11      return;
12  }
13
14  d_output[i].x = RED_FORMULA;     //Compute red
15  d_output[i].y = GREEN_ FORMULA; //Compute green
16  d_output[i].z = BLUE_ FORMULA;   //Compute blue
17  d_output[i].w = 255; // Fully opaque
18 }
```

dist_2d

Let's tie the general discussion of 2D grids together with our earlier examples involving distance apps by coding up an app that produces a 2D array of distances from a reference point, and then we'll adapt the app to produce an array of data for an RGBA image. Listing 4.3 provides all the code for computing distances on a 2D grid.

Listing 4.3 Computing distances on a 2D grid

```
 1  #define W 500
 2  #define H 500
 3  #define TX 32 // number of threads per block along x-axis
 4  #define TY 32 // number of threads per block along y-axis
 5
 6  __global__
 7  void distanceKernel(float *d_out, int w, int h, float2 pos)
 8  {
 9    const int c = blockIdx.x*blockDim.x + threadIdx.x;
10    const int r = blockIdx.y*blockDim.y + threadIdx.y;
11    const int i = r*w + c;
12    if ((c >= w) || (r >= h)) return;
13
14    // Compute the distance and set d_out[i]
15    d_out[i] = sqrtf((c - pos.x)*(c - pos.x) +
16                     (r - pos.y)*(r - pos.y));
17  }
18
19  int main()
20  {
21    float *out = (float*)calloc(W*H, sizeof(float));
22    float *d_out; // pointer for device array
23    cudaMalloc(&d_out, W*H*sizeof(float));
24
25    const float2 pos = {0.0f, 0.0f}; // set reference position
26    const dim3 blockSize(TX, TY);
27    const int bx = (W + TX - 1)/TX;
28    const int by = (W + TY - 1)/TY;
29    const dim3 gridSize = dim3(bx, by);
30
31    distanceKernel<<<gridSize, blockSize>>>(d_out, W, H, pos);
32
33    // Copy results to host.
34    cudaMemcpy(out, d_out, W*H*sizeof(float), cudaMemcpyDeviceToHost);
35
36    cudaFree(d_out);
37    free(out);
38    return 0;
39  }
```

The kernel, lines 6–17, is exactly as in Listing 4.1 but with a result computed using the Pythagorean formula to compute the distance between the location {c, r} and a reference location pos. (Note that we have defined pos to have type float2 so it can store both coordinates of the reference location {pos.x, pos.y}.) The rest of the listing, lines 19–39, gives the details of main() starting with declaration of an output array of appropriate size initialized to zero. Lines

22–23 declare a pointer to the device array d_out and allocate the memory with cudaMalloc(). Line 25 sets the reference position, and lines 26–29 set the kernel launch parameters: a 2D grid of bx × by blocks each having TX × TY threads. Line 31 launches the kernel to compute the distance values, which are copied back to out on the host side on line 34. Lines 36–37 free the allocated device and host memory, then main() returns zero to indicate completion.

Next we make a few minor changes to produce an app that computes an array of RGBA values corresponding to a distance image. The full code is provided in Listing 4.4.

Listing 4.4 Parallel computation of image data based on distance from a reference point in 2D

```
1  #define W   500
2  #define H   500
3  #define TX 32 // number of threads per block along x-axis
4  #define TY 32 // number of threads per block along y-axis
5
6  __device__
7  unsigned char clip(int n) { return n > 255 ? 255 : (n < 0 ? 0 : n); }
8
9  __global__
10 void distanceKernel(uchar4 *d_out, int w, int h, int2 pos)
11 {
12   const int c = blockIdx.x*blockDim.x + threadIdx.x;
13   const int r = blockIdx.y*blockDim.y + threadIdx.y;
14   const int i = r*w + c;
15   if ((c >= w) || (r >= h)) return;
16
17   // Compute the distance (in pixel spacings)
18   const int d = sqrtf((c - pos.x) * (c - pos.x) +
19                       (r - pos.y) * (r - pos.y));
20   // Convert distance to intensity value on interval [0, 255]
21   const unsigned char intensity = clip(255 - d);
22
23   d_out[i].x = intensity; // red channel
24   d_out[i].y = intensity; // green channel
25   d_out[i].z = 0; // blue channel
26   d_out[i].z = 255; // fully opaque
27 }
28
29 int main()
30 {
31   uchar4 *out = (uchar4*)calloc(W*H, sizeof(uchar4));
32   uchar4 *d_out; // pointer for device array
33   cudaMalloc(&d_out, W*H*sizeof(uchar4));
34
35   const int2 pos = {0, 0}; // set reference position
36   const dim3 blockSize(TX, TY);
37   const int bx = (W + TX - 1)/TX;
38   const int by = (W + TY - 1)/TY;
```

[handwritten margin notes: "splitter-like code" and "Also a good way of displaying RDM data"]

```
39    const dim3 gridSize = dim3(bx, by);
40
41    distanceKernel<<<gridSize, blockSize>>>(d_out, W, H, pos);
42
43    // Copy results to host.
44    cudaMemcpy(out, d_out, W*H*sizeof(uchar4), cudaMemcpyDeviceToHost);
45
46    cudaFree(d_out);
47    free(out);
48    return 0;
49 }
```

Here the distance is computed in pixel spacings, so the reference position, pos, now has type int2, and the distance d has type int. The distance value is then converted to intensity of type unsigned char, whose value is restricted to the allowed range of 0 to 255 using the function clip(). The output arrays, out and d_out, have the corresponding vector type uchar4. The assignments d_out[i].x = intensity and d_out[i].y = intensity store the intensity value in the red and green channels to produce a yellow distance image. (We set the blue component to zero and the alpha to 255, corresponding to full opacity, but you should experiment with other color specifications.)

Live Display via Graphics Interop

Now that we can construct apps that produce image data, it makes sense to start displaying those images and exploring what CUDA's massive parallelism enables us to do in real time.

Real-time graphic interactivity will involve CUDA's provision for interoperability with a standard graphics package. We will be using OpenGL, which could be (and is) the subject of numerous books all by itself [2,4,5], so we will take our usual need-to-know approach. We introduce just enough OpenGL to display a single textured rectangle and provide a few examples of code to support interactions via keyboard and mouse with the help of the **OpenGL Utility Toolkit (GLUT)**. The idea is that the rectangle provides a window into the world of your app, and you can use CUDA to compute the pixel shading values corresponding to whatever scene you want the user to see. CUDA/OpenGL interop provides interactive controls and displays the changing scene as a texture on the displayed rectangle in real time (or, more accurately, at a rate comparable to the ~60Hz refresh rate typical of modern visual display systems).

Figure 4.1 Interactive spot of light in the finished application

Here we present the code for a sample app that opens a graphics window and interactively displays an image based on distance to a reference point that can be changed interactively using keyboard or mouse input. We call the app `flashlight` because it produces a directable circle of light whose intensity diminishes away from the center of the "spot." Figure 4.1 shows the screenshot of the app in its finished state.

This entire app requires a total of less than 200 lines of code, which we have organized into three files:

- `main.cpp` contains the essentials of the CUDA/OpenGL set up and interop. It is about 100 lines of code (half of the total), and while we will provide a brief explanation of its contents, you should be able to create your own apps by using `flashlight` as a template by making only minor changes to `main.cpp`.

- `kernel.cu` contains the essential CUDA code, including the `clip()` function described above, the definition of the `kernelLauncher()` function, and the definition of the actual kernel function (here `distanceKernel()`), which must write its output to a `uchar4` array.

- `interactions.h` defines the **callback** functions `keyboard()`, `mouseMove()`, and `mouseDrag()` to specify how the system should respond to inputs.

While we will go through the entire code, the important point is that you can use the `flashlight` app as a template to readily create your own apps in just a few steps:

1. Create a new app based on `flashlight` by making a copy of the code directory under Linux or by creating a new project using `flashlight` as a template in Visual Studio under Windows.

2. Edit the kernel function to produce whatever data you want to display.

3. In `interactions.h`, edit the callback functions to specify how your app should respond to keyboard and mouse inputs, and edit `printInstructions()` to customize the instructions for user interactions.

4. Optionally, edit the `#define TITLE_STRING` statement in `interactions.h` to customize the app name in the title bar of the graphics window.

Listings 4.5, 4.6, 4.7, and 4.8 show all the code necessary to display a distance image on your screen using CUDA/OpenGL interop, and we will walk you through the necessities while trying not to get hung up on too many details.

Listing 4.5 `flashlight/main.cpp`

```
 1 #include "kernel.h"
 2 #include <stdio.h>
 3 #include <stdlib.h>
 4 #ifdef _WIN32
 5 #define WINDOWS_LEAN_AND_MEAN
 6 #define NOMINMAX
 7 #include <windows.h>
 8 #endif
 9 #ifdef __APPLE__
10 #include <GLUT/glut.h>
11 #else
12 #include <GL/glew.h>
13 #include <GL/freeglut.h>
14 #endif
15 #include <cuda_runtime.h>
16 #include <cuda_gl_interop.h>
17 #include "interactions.h"
18
19 // texture and pixel objects
20 GLuint pbo = 0;     // OpenGL pixel buffer object
21 GLuint tex = 0;     // OpenGL texture object
22 struct cudaGraphicsResource *cuda_pbo_resource;
23
24 void render() {
25    uchar4 *d_out = 0;
26    cudaGraphicsMapResources(1, &cuda_pbo_resource, 0);
27    cudaGraphicsResourceGetMappedPointer((void **)&d_out, NULL,
28                                         cuda_pbo_resource);
```

```
29    kernelLauncher(d_out, W, H, loc);
30    cudaGraphicsUnmapResources(1, &cuda_pbo_resource, 0);
31 }
32
33 void drawTexture() {
34    glTexImage2D(GL_TEXTURE_2D, 0, GL_RGBA, W, H, 0, GL_RGBA,
35                 GL_UNSIGNED_BYTE, NULL);
36    glEnable(GL_TEXTURE_2D);
37    glBegin(GL_QUADS);
38    glTexCoord2f(0.0f, 0.0f); glVertex2f(0, 0);
39    glTexCoord2f(0.0f, 1.0f); glVertex2f(0, H);
40    glTexCoord2f(1.0f, 1.0f); glVertex2f(W, H);
41    glTexCoord2f(1.0f, 0.0f); glVertex2f(W, 0);
42    glEnd();
43    glDisable(GL_TEXTURE_2D);
44 }
45
46 void display() {
47    render();
48    drawTexture();
49    glutSwapBuffers();
50 }
51
52 void initGLUT(int *argc, char **argv) {
53    glutInit(argc, argv);
54    glutInitDisplayMode(GLUT_RGBA | GLUT_DOUBLE);
55    glutInitWindowSize(W, H);
56    glutCreateWindow(TITLE_STRING);
57 #ifndef __APPLE__
58    glewInit();
59 #endif
60 }
61
62 void initPixelBuffer() {
63    glGenBuffers(1, &pbo);
64    glBindBuffer(GL_PIXEL_UNPACK_BUFFER, pbo);
65    glBufferData(GL_PIXEL_UNPACK_BUFFER, 4*W*H*sizeof(GLubyte), 0,
66                 GL_STREAM_DRAW);
67    glGenTextures(1, &tex);
68    glBindTexture(GL_TEXTURE_2D, tex);
69    glTexParameteri(GL_TEXTURE_2D, GL_TEXTURE_MIN_FILTER, GL_NEAREST);
70    cudaGraphicsGLRegisterBuffer(&cuda_pbo_resource, pbo,
71                                 cudaGraphicsMapFlagsWriteDiscard);
72 }
73
74 void exitfunc() {
75    if (pbo) {
76       cudaGraphicsUnregisterResource(cuda_pbo_resource);
77       glDeleteBuffers(1, &pbo);
78       glDeleteTextures(1, &tex);
79    }
80 }
81
82 int main(int argc, char** argv) {
83    printInstructions();
```

```
84     initGLUT(&argc, argv);
85     gluOrtho2D(0, W, H, 0);
86     glutKeyboardFunc(keyboard);
87     glutSpecialFunc(handleSpecialKeypress);
88     glutPassiveMotionFunc(mouseMove);
89     glutMotionFunc(mouseDrag);
90     glutDisplayFunc(display);
91     initPixelBuffer();
92     glutMainLoop();
93     atexit(exitfunc);
94     return 0;
95 }
```

This is the brief, high-level overview of what is happening in main.cpp. Lines 1–17 load the header files appropriate for your operating system to access the necessary supporting code. The rest of the explanation should start from the bottom. Lines 82–95 define main(), which does the following things:

- Line 83 prints a few user interface instructions to the command window.

- initGLUT initializes the GLUT library and sets up the specifications for the graphics window, including the display mode (RGBA), the buffering (double), size (W x H), and title.

- gluOrtho2D(0, W, H, 0) establishes the viewing transform (simple orthographic projection).

- Lines 86–89 indicate that keyboard and mouse interactions will be specified by the functions keyboard, handleSpecialKeypress, mouseMove, and mouseDrag (the details of which will be specified in interactions.h).

- glutDisplayFunc(display) says that what is to be shown in the window is determined by the function display(), which is all of three lines long. On lines 47–49, it calls render() to compute new pixel values, drawTexture() to draw the OpenGL texture, and then swaps the display buffers.

  - drawTexture() sets up a 2D OpenGL texture image, creates a single quadrangle graphics primitive with texture coordinates (0.0f, 0.0f), (0.0f, 1.0f), (1.0f, 1.0f), and (1.0f, 0.0f); that is, the corners of the unit square, corresponding with the pixel coordinates (0, 0), (0, H), (W, H), and (W, 0).

  - Double buffering is a common technique for enhancing the efficiency of graphics programs. One buffer provides memory that can be read to "feed" the display, while at the same time, the other buffer provides memory into which the contents of the next frame can be written. Between frames in a graphics sequence, the buffers swap their read/write roles.

- `initPixelBuffer()`, not surprisingly, initializes the pixel buffer on lines 62–72. The key for our purposes is the last line which "registers" the OpenGL buffer with CUDA. This operation has some overhead, but it enables low-overhead "mapping" that turns over control of the buffer memory to CUDA to write output and "unmapping" that returns control of the buffer memory to OpenGL for display. Figure 4.2 shows a summary of the interop between CUDA and OpenGL.

- `glutMainLoop()`, on line 92, is where the real action happens. It repeatedly checks for input and calls for computation of updated images via `display` that calls `render`, which does the following:

  - Maps the pixel buffer to CUDA and gets a CUDA pointer to the buffer memory so it can serve as the output device array

  - Calls the wrapper function `kernelLauncher` that launches the kernel to compute the pixel values for the updated image

  - Unmaps the buffer so OpenGL can display the contents

- When you exit the app, `atexit(exitfunc)` performs the final clean up by undoing the resource registration and deleting the OpenGL pixel buffer and texture before zero is returned to indicate completion of `main()`.

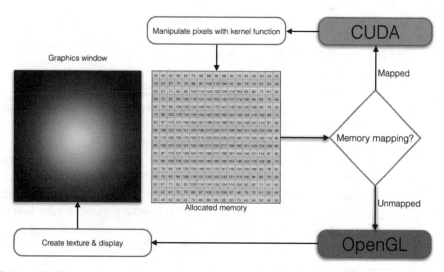

Figure 4.2 Illustration of alternating access to device memory that is mapped to CUDA to store computational results and unmapped (i.e., returned to OpenGL control) for display of those results

Of all the code in `main.cpp`, the only thing you need to change when you create your own CUDA/OpenGL interop apps is the `render()` function, where you will need to update the argument list for `kernelLauncher()`.

Listing 4.6 `flashlight/kernel.cu`

```
1 #include "kernel.h"
2 #define TX 32
3 #define TY 32
4
5 __device__
6 unsigned char clip(int n) { return n > 255 ? 255 : (n < 0 ? 0 : n); }
7
8 __global__
9 void distanceKernel(uchar4 *d_out, int w, int h, int2 pos) {
10    const int c = blockIdx.x*blockDim.x + threadIdx.x;
11    const int r = blockIdx.y*blockDim.y + threadIdx.y;
12    if ((c >= w) || (r >= h)) return; // Check if within image bounds
13    const int i = c + r*w; // 1D indexing
14    const int dist = sqrtf((c - pos.x)*(c - pos.x) +
15                           (r - pos.y)*(r - pos.y));
16    const unsigned char intensity = clip(255 - dist);
17    d_out[i].x = intensity;
18    d_out[i].y = intensity;
19    d_out[i].z = 0;
20    d_out[i].w = 255;
21 }
22
23 void kernelLauncher(uchar4 *d_out, int w, int h, int2 pos) {
24    const dim3 blockSize(TX, TY);
25    const dim3 gridSize = dim3((w + TX - 1)/TX, (h + TY - 1)/TY);
26    distanceKernel<<<gridSize, blockSize>>>(d_out, w, h, pos);
27 }
```

The code from `kernel.cu` in Listing 4.6 should look familiar and require little explanation at this point. The primary change is a wrapper function `kernelLauncher()` that computes the grid dimensions and launches the kernel. Note that you will not find any mention of a host output array. Computation and display are both handled from the device, and there is no need to transfer data to the host. (Such a transfer of large quantities of image data across the PCIe bus could be time-consuming and greatly inhibit real-time interaction capabilities.) You will also not find a `cudaMalloc()` to create space for a device array. The `render()` function in `main.cpp` declares a pointer `d_out` that gets its value from `cudaGraphicsResourceGetMappedPointer()` and provides the CUDA pointer to the memory allocated for the pixel buffer.

The header file associated with the kernel is shown in Listing 4.7. In addition to the include guard and kernel function prototype, `kernel.h` also contains forward declarations for `uchar4` and `int2` so that the compiler knows of their existence before the CUDA code (which is aware of their definitions) is built or executed.

Listing 4.7 `flashlight/kernel.h`

```
1 #ifndef KERNEL_H
2 #define KERNEL_H
3
4 struct uchar4;
5 struct int2;
6
7 void kernelLauncher(uchar4 *d_out, int w, int h, int2 pos);
8
9 #endif
```

Listing 4.8 `flashlight/interactions.h` that specifies callback functions controlling interactive behavior of the `flashlight` app

```
 1 #ifndef INTERACTIONS_H
 2 #define INTERACTIONS_H
 3 #define W 600
 4 #define H 600
 5 #define DELTA 5 // pixel increment for arrow keys
 6 #define TITLE_STRING "flashlight: distance image display app"
 7 int2 loc = {W/2, H/2};
 8 bool dragMode = false; // mouse tracking mode
 9
10 void keyboard(unsigned char key, int x, int y) {
11   if (key == 'a') dragMode = !dragMode; // toggle tracking mode
12   if (key == 27)  exit(0);
13   glutPostRedisplay();
14 }
15
16 void mouseMove(int x, int y) {
17   if (dragMode) return;
18   loc.x = x;
19   loc.y = y;
20   glutPostRedisplay();
21 }
22
23 void mouseDrag(int x, int y) {
24   if (!dragMode) return;
25   loc.x = x;
26   loc.y = y;
27   glutPostRedisplay();
28 }
29
30 void handleSpecialKeypress(int key, int x, int y) {
31   if (key == GLUT_KEY_LEFT)  loc.x -= DELTA;
32   if (key == GLUT_KEY_RIGHT) loc.x += DELTA;
33   if (key == GLUT_KEY_UP)    loc.y -= DELTA;
34   if (key == GLUT_KEY_DOWN)  loc.y += DELTA;
```

```
35    glutPostRedisplay();
36 }
37
38 void printInstructions() {
39    printf("flashlight interactions\n");
40    printf("a: toggle mouse tracking mode\n");
41    printf("arrow keys: move ref location\n");
42    printf("esc: close graphics window\n");
43 }
44
45 #endif
```

The stated goal of the flashlight app is to display an image corresponding to the distance to a reference point that can be moved interactively, and we are now ready to define and implement the interactions. The code for interactions.h shown in Listing 4.8 allows the user to move the reference point (i.e., the center of the flashlight beam) by moving the mouse or pressing the arrow keys. Pressing a toggles between tracking mouse motions and tracking mouse drags (with the mouse button pressed), and the esc key closes the graphics window. Here's a quick description of what the code does and how those interactions work:

- Lines 3–6 set the image dimensions, the text displayed in the title bar, and how far (in pixels) the reference point moves when an arrow key is pressed.

- Line 7 sets the initial reference location at $\{W/2,\ H/2\}$, the center of the image.

- Line 8 declares a Boolean variable dragMode that is initialized to false. We use dragMode to toggle back and forth between tracking mouse motions and "click-drag" motions.

- Lines 10–14 specify the defined interactions with the keyboard:

  - Pressing the a key toggles dragMode to switch the mouse tracking mode.

  - The ASCII code 27 corresponds to the Esc key. Pressing Esc closes the graphics window.

  - glutPostRedisplay() is called at the end of each callback function telling to compute a new image for display (by calling display() in main.cpp) based on the interactive input.

- Lines 16–21 specify the response to a mouse movement. When dragMode is toggled, return ensures that no action is taken. Otherwise, the components of the reference location are set to be equal to the x and y coordinates of the mouse before computing and displaying an updated image (via glutPostRedisplay()).

- Lines 23–28 similarly specify the response to a "click-drag." When `dragMode` is `false`, `return` ensures that no action is taken. Otherwise, the reference location is reset to the last location of the mouse while the mouse was clicked.

- Lines 30–36 specify the response to special keys with defined actions. (Note that standard keyboard interactions are handled based on ASCII key codes [6], so special keys like arrow keys and function keys that do not generate standard ASCII codes need to be handled separately.) The `flashlight` app is set up so that depressing the arrow keys moves the reference location `DELTA` pixels in the desired direction.

- The `printInstructions()` function on lines 38–43 consists of print statements that provide user interaction instructions via the console.

While all the code and explanation for the `flashlight` app took about nine pages, let's pause to put things in perspective. While we presented numbered listings totaling about 200 lines, if we were less concerned about readability, the entire code could be written in many fewer lines, so there is not a lot of code to digest. Perhaps more importantly, over half of those lines reside in `main.cpp`, which you should not really need to change at all to create your own apps other than to alter the list of arguments for the `kernelLauncher()` function or to customize the information displayed in the title bar. If you start with the `flashlight` app as a template, you should be able to (and are heartily encouraged to) harness the power of CUDA to create your own apps with interactive graphics by replacing the kernel function with one of your own design and by revising the collection of user interactions implemented in `interactions.h`.

Finally, the Makefile for building the app in Linux is provided in Listing 4.9.

Listing 4.9 `flashlight/Makefile`

```
1 UNAME_S := $(shell uname)
2
3 ifeq ($(UNAME_S), Darwin)
4   LDFLAGS = -Xlinker -framework,OpenGL -Xlinker -framework,GLUT
5 else
6   LDFLAGS += -L/usr/local/cuda/samples/common/lib/linux/x86_64
7   LDFLAGS += -lglut -lGL -lGLU -lGLEW
8 endif
9
10 NVCC = /usr/local/cuda/bin/nvcc
11 NVCC_FLAGS = -g -G -Xcompiler "-Wall -Wno-deprecated-declarations"
12
13 all: main.exe
14
```

```
15 main.exe: main.o kernel.o
16    $(NVCC) $^ -o $@ $(LDFLAGS)
17
18 main.o: main.cpp kernel.h interactions.h
19    $(NVCC) $(NVCC_FLAGS) -c $< -o $@
20
21 kernel.o: kernel.cu kernel.h
22    $(NVCC) $(NVCC_FLAGS) -c $< -o $@
```

Windows users will need to change one build customization and include two pairs of library files: the **OpenGL Utility Toolkit (GLUT)** and the **OpenGL Extension Wrangler (GLEW)**. To keep things simple and ensure consistency of the library version, we find it convenient to simply make copies of the library files (which can be found by searching within the CUDA Samples directory for the filenames freeglut.dll, freeglut.lib, glew64.dll, and glew64.lib), save them to the project directory, and then add them to the project with PROJECT ⇒ Add Existing Item.

The build customization is specified using the Project Properties pages: Right-click on flashlight in the Solution Explorer pane, then select Properties ⇒ Configuration Properties ⇒ C/C++ ⇒ General ⇒ Additional Include Directories and edit the list to include the CUDA Samples' common\inc directory. Its default install location is C:\ProgramData\ NVIDIA Corporation\CUDA Samples\v7.5\common\inc.

Application: Stability

To drive home the idea of using the flashlight app as a template for creating more interesting and useful apps, let's do exactly that. Here we build on flashlight to create an app that analyzes the stability of a linear oscillator, and then we extend the app to handle general single degree of freedom (1DoF) systems, including the van der Pol oscillator, which has more interesting behavior.

The linear oscillator arises from models of a mechanical mass-spring-damper system, an electrical RLC circuit, and the behavior of just about any 1DoF system in the vicinity of an equilibrium point. The mathematical model consists of a single second-order ordinary differential equation (ODE) that can be written in its simplest form (with suitable choice of time unit) as $x'' + 2bx' + x = 0$, where x is the displacement from the equilibrium position, b is the damping constant, and the primes indicate time derivatives. To put things in a handy form for finding solutions, we convert to a system of two first-order ODEs by introducing the velocity y as a new variable and writing the first-order ODEs that give the rate of change of x and y:

$$x' = y$$
$$y' = -x - 2by = f\left(x, y, t, ...\right)$$

As a bit of foreshadowing, everything we do from here generalizes to a wide variety of 1DoF oscillators by just plugging other expressions in for $f(x, y, t, ...)$ on the right-hand side of the y-equation. While we can write analytical solutions for the linear oscillator, here we focus on numerical solutions using finite difference methods that apply to the more general case. Finite difference methods compute values at discrete multiples of the time step dt (so we introduce $t_k = k * dt$, $x_k = x(t_k)$, and $y_k = y(t_k)$ as the relevant variables) and replace exact derivatives by difference approximations; that is, $x' \rightarrow (x_{k+1} - x_k) / dt$, $y' \rightarrow (y_{k+1} - y_k) / dt$. Here we apply the simplest finite difference approach, the explicit Euler method, by substituting the finite difference expressions for the derivatives and solving for the new values at the end of the time step, x_{k+1} and y_{k+1}, in terms of the previous values at the beginning of a time step, x_k and y_k, to obtain:

$$x_{k+1} = x_k + dt*y_k$$
$$y_{k+1} = y_k + dt*\left(-x_k - 2by_k\right)$$

We can then choose an initial state $\{x_o, y_o\}$ and compute the state of the system at successive time steps.

We've just described a method for computing a solution (a sequence of states) arising from a single initial state, and the solution method is completely serial: Entries in the sequence of states are computed one after another.

However, stability depends not on the solution for one initial state but on the solutions for *all* initial states. For a stable equilibrium, all nearby initial states produce solutions that approach (or at least don't get further from) the equilibrium. Finding a solution that grows away from the equilibrium indicates instability. For more information on dynamics and stability, see [7,8].

It is this collective-behavior aspect that makes stability testing such a good candidate for parallelization: By launching a computational grid with initial states densely sampling the neighborhood of the equilibrium, we can test the solutions arising from the surrounding initial states. We'll see that we can compute hundreds of thousands of solutions in parallel and, with CUDA/OpenGL interop, see and interact with the results in real time.

In particular, we'll choose a grid of initial states that regularly sample a rectangle centered on the equilibrium. We'll compute the corresponding solutions and assign shading values based on the fractional change in distance, `dist_r` (for distance ratio) from the equilibrium during the simulation. To display the results, we'll assign each pixel a red channel value proportional to the distance ratio (and clipped to [0, 255]) and a blue channel value proportional to the inverse distance ratio (and clipped). Initial states producing solutions that are attracted to the equilibrium (and suggest stability) are dominated by blue, while initial states that produce solutions being repelled from the equilibrium are dominated by red, and the attracting/repelling transition is indicated by equal parts of blue and red; that is, purple.

Color Adjustment to Enhance Grayscale Contrast

Since it is difficult to see the difference between red (R) and blue (B) when viewing figures converted to grayscale, the figures included here use the green (G) channel to enhance contrast and brightness according to the formula $G = 0.3 + (R - B) / 2$. Full color images produced by the `stability` app are available at www.cudaforengineers.com.

The result shown in the graphics window will then consist of the equilibrium (at the intersection of the horizontal x-axis and the vertical y-axis shown using the green channel) on a field of red, blue, or purple pixels. Figure 4.3 previews a result from the stability application with both attracting and repelling regions.

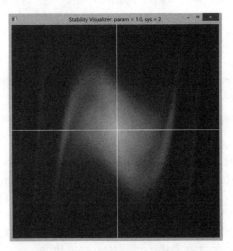

Figure 4.3 Stability map with shading adjusted to show a bright central repelling region and surrounding darker attracting region

We now have a plan for producing a stability image for a single system, but we will also introduce interactions so we can observe how the stability image changes for different parameter values or for different systems.

With the plan for the kernel and the interactions in mind, we are ready to look at the code. As promised, the major changes from the flashlight app involve a new kernel function (and a few supporting functions), as shown in Listing 4.10, and new interactivity specifications, as shown in Listing 4.11.

Listing 4.10 stability/kernel.cu

```
 1 #include "kernel.h"
 2 #define TX 32
 3 #define TY 32
 4 #define LEN 5.f
 5 #define TIME_STEP 0.005f
 6 #define FINAL_TIME 10.f
 7
 8 // scale coordinates onto [-LEN, LEN]
 9 __device__
10 float scale(int i, int w) { return 2*LEN*(((1.f*i)/w) - 0.5f); }
11
12 // function for right-hand side of y-equation
13 __device__
14 float f(float x, float y, float param, float sys) {
15   if (sys == 1) return x - 2*param*y; // negative stiffness
16   if (sys == 2) return -x + param*(1 - x*x)*y; //van der Pol
17   else return -x - 2*param*y;
18 }
19
20 // explicit Euler solver
21 __device__
22 float2 euler(float x, float y, float dt, float tFinal,
23               float param, float sys) {
24   float dx = 0.f, dy = 0.f;
25   for (float t = 0; t < tFinal; t += dt) {
26     dx = dt*y;
27     dy = dt*f(x, y, param, sys);
28     x += dx;
29     y += dy;
30   }
31   return make_float2(x, y);
32 }
33
34 __device__
35 unsigned char clip(float x){ return x > 255 ? 255 : (x < 0 ? 0 : x); }
36
37 // kernel function to compute decay and shading
38 __global__
39 void stabImageKernel(uchar4 *d_out, int w, int h, float p, int s) {
40   const int c = blockIdx.x*blockDim.x + threadIdx.x;
41   const int r = blockIdx.y*blockDim.y + threadIdx.y;
42   if ((c >= w) || (r >= h)) return; // Check if within image bounds
```

```
43    const int i = c + r*w; // 1D indexing
44    const float x0 = scale(c, w);
45    const float y0 = scale(r, h);
46    const float dist_0 = sqrt(x0*x0 + y0*y0);
47    const float2 pos = euler(x0, y0, TIME_STEP, FINAL_TIME, p, s);
48    const float dist_f = sqrt(pos.x*pos.x + pos.y*pos.y);
49    // assign colors based on distance from origin
50    const float dist_r = dist_f/dist_0;
51    d_out[i].x = clip(dist_r*255); // red ~ growth
52    d_out[i].y = ((c == w/2) || (r == h/2)) ? 255 : 0; // axes
53    d_out[i].z = clip((1/dist_r)*255); // blue ~ 1/growth
54    d_out[i].w = 255;
55 }
56
57 void kernelLauncher(uchar4 *d_out, int w, int h, float p, int s) {
58    const dim3 blockSize(TX, TY);
59    const dim3 gridSize = dim3((w + TX - 1)/TX, (h + TY - 1)/TY);
60    stabImageKernel<<<gridSize, blockSize>>>(d_out, w, h, p, s);
61 }
```

Here is a brief description of the code in `kernel.cu`. Lines 1–6 include `kernel.h` and define constant values for thread counts, the spatial scale factor, and the time step and time interval for the simulation. Lines 8–35 define new device functions that will be called by the kernel:

- `scale()` scales the pixel values onto the coordinate range [-LEN, LEN].

- `f()` gives the rate of change of the velocity. If you are interested in studying other 1DoF oscillators, you can edit this to correspond to your system of interest. In the sample code, three different versions are included corresponding to different values of the variable `sys`.

  - The default version with `sys = 0` is the damped linear oscillator discussed above.

  - Setting `sys = 1` corresponds to a linear oscillator with negative effective stiffness (which may seem odd at first, but that is exactly the case near the inverted position of a pendulum).

  - Setting `sys = 2` corresponds to a personal favorite, the van der Pol oscillator, which has a nonlinear damping term.

- `euler()` performs the simulation for a given initial state and returns a `float2` value corresponding to the location of the trajectory at the end of the simulation interval. (Note that the `float2` type allows us to bundle the position and velocity together into a single entity. The alternative approach, passing a pointer to memory allocated to store multiple values as we do to handle larger sets of output from kernel functions, is not needed in this case.)

Lines 34–35 define the same clip() function that we used in the flashlight app, and the definition of the new kernel, stabImageKernel(), starts on line 38. Note that arguments have been added for the damping parameter value, p, and the system specifier, s. The index computation and bounds checking in lines 40–43 is exactly as in distanceKernel() from the flashlight app. On lines 44–45 we introduce {x0, y0} as the scaled float coordinate values (which range from −LEN to LEN) corresponding to the pixel location and compute the initial distance, dist_0, from the equilibrium point at the origin. Line 47 calls euler() to perform the simulation with fixed time increment TIME_STEP over an interval of duration FINAL_TIME and return pos, the state the simulated trajectory has reached at the end of the simulation. Line 50 compares the final distance from the origin and to the initial distance. Lines 51–54 assign shading values based on the distance comparison with blue indicating decay toward equilibrium (a.k.a. a vote in favor of stability) and red indicating growth away from equilibrium (which vetoes other votes for stability). Line 52 uses the green channel to show the horizontal *x*-axis and the vertical *y*-axis which intersect at the equilibrium point.

Lines 57–61 define the revised wrapper function kernelLauncher() with the correct list of arguments and name of the kernel to be launched.

Listing 4.11 stability/interactions.h

```
 1 #ifndef INTERACTIONS_H
 2 #define INTERACTIONS_H
 3 #define W 600
 4 #define H 600
 5 #define DELTA_P 0.1f
 6 #define TITLE_STRING "Stability"
 7 int sys = 0;
 8 float param = 0.1f;
 9 void keyboard(unsigned char key, int x, int y) {
10   if (key == 27)  exit(0);
11   if (key == '0') sys = 0;
12   if (key == '1') sys = 1;
13   if (key == '2') sys = 2;
14   glutPostRedisplay();
15 }
16
17 void handleSpecialKeypress(int key, int x, int y) {
18   if (key == GLUT_KEY_DOWN) param -= DELTA_P;
19   if (key == GLUT_KEY_UP)   param += DELTA_P;
20   glutPostRedisplay();
21 }
22
23 // no mouse interactions implemented for this app
24 void mouseMove(int x, int y) { return; }
25 void mouseDrag(int x, int y) { return; }
26
```

```
27 void printInstructions() {
28    printf("Stability visualizer\n");
29    printf("Use number keys to select system:\n");
30    printf("\t0: linear oscillator: positive stiffness\n");
31    printf("\t1: linear oscillator: negative stiffness\n");
32    printf("\t2: van der Pol oscillator: nonlinear damping\n");
33    printf("up/down arrow keys adjust parameter value\n\n");
34    printf("Choose the van der Pol (sys=2)\n");
35    printf("Keep up arrow key depressed and watch the show.\n");
36 }
37
38 #endif
```

The description of the alterations to `interactions.h`, as shown in Listing 4.11, is also straightforward. To the `#define` statements that set the width `W` and height `H` of the image, we add `DELTA_P` for the size of parameter value increments. Lines 7–8 initialize variables for the system identifier `sys` and the parameter value `param`, which is for adjusting the damping value.

There are a few keyboard interactions: Pressing `Esc` exits the app; pressing number key 0, 1, or 2 selects the system to simulate; and the up arrow and down arrow keys decrease or increase the damping parameter value by `DELTA_P`. There are no planned mouse interactions, so `mouseMove()` and `mouseDrag()` simply `return` without doing anything.

Finally, there are a couple details to take care of in other files:

- `kernel.h` contains the prototype for `kernelLauncher()`, so the first line of the function definition from `kernel.cu` should be copied and pasted (with a colon terminator) in place of the old prototype in `flashlight/kernel.h`.

- A couple small changes are also needed in `main.cpp`:

  - The argument list for the `kernelLauncher()` call in `render()` has changed, and that call needs to be changed to match the syntax of the revised kernel.

  - `render()` is also an appropriate place for specifying information to be displayed in the title bar of the graphics window. For example, the sample code displays an application name ("Stability") followed by the values of `param` and `sys`. Listing 4.12 shows the updated version of `render()` with the title bar information and updated kernel launch call.

Listing 4.12 Updated `render()` function for `stability/main.cpp`

```
 1 void render() {
 2   uchar4 *d_out = 0;
 3   cudaGraphicsMapResources(1, &cuda_pbo_resource, 0);
 4   cudaGraphicsResourceGetMappedPointer((void **)&d_out, NULL,
 5                                     cuda_pbo_resource);
 6   kernelLauncher(d_out, W, H, param, sys);
 7   cudaGraphicsUnmapResources(1, &cuda_pbo_resource, 0);
 8   // update contents of the title bar
 9   char title[64];
10   sprintf(title, "Stability: param = %.1f, sys = %d", param, sys);
11   glutSetWindowTitle(title);
12 }
```

RUNNING THE STABILITY VISUALIZER

Now that we've toured the relevant code, it is time to test out the app. In Linux, the Makefile for building this project is the same as the Makefile for the `flashlight` app that was provided in Listing 4.9. In Visual Studio, the included library files and the project settings are the same as described in `flashlight`. When you build and run the application, two windows should open: the usual command window showing a brief summary of supported user inputs and a graphics window showing the stability results. The default settings specify the linear oscillator with positive damping, which you can verify from the title bar that displays `Stability: param = 0.1, sys = 0`, as shown in Figure 4.4(a). Since all solutions of an unforced, damped linear oscillator are attracted toward the equilibrium, the graphics window should show the coordinate axes on a dark field, indicating stability. Next you might test the down arrow key. A single press reduces the damping value from 0.1 to 0.0 (which you should be able to verify in the title bar), and you should see the field changes from dark to moderately bright, as shown in Figure 4.4(b). The linear oscillator with zero damping is neutrally stable (with sinusoidal oscillations that remain near, but do not approach, the equilibrium). The explicit Euler ODE solver happens to produce small errors that systematically favor repulsion from the origin, but the color scheme correctly indicates that all initial states lead to solutions that roughly maintain their distance from the equilibrium. Another press of the down arrow key changes the damping parameter value to –0.1, and the bright field shown in Figure 4.4(c) legitimately indicates instability.

Now press the 1 key to set `sys = 1` corresponding to a system with negative effective stiffness, and increase the damping value. You should now see the axes

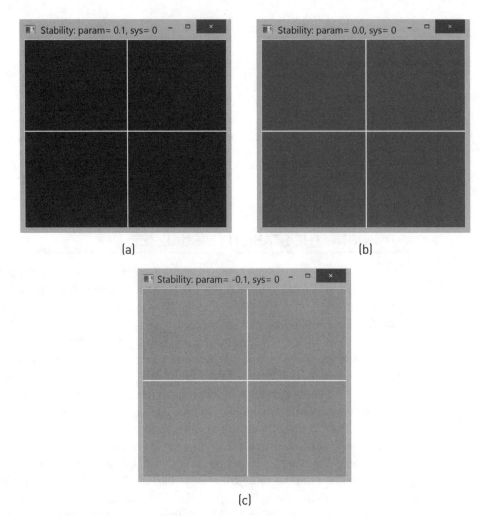

(a)   (b)

(c)

Figure 4.4 Stability visualization for the linear oscillator with different damping parameter values. (a) For param = 0.1, the dark field indicates solutions attracted to a stable equilibrium. (b) For param = 0.0, the moderately bright field indicates neutral stability. (c) For param = -0.1, the bright field indicates solutions repelled from an unstable equilibrium.

on a bright field with a dark sector (and moderately bright transition regions), as shown in Figure 4.5. In this case, some solutions are approaching the equilibrium, but almost all initial conditions lead to solutions that grow away from the equilibrium, which is unstable.

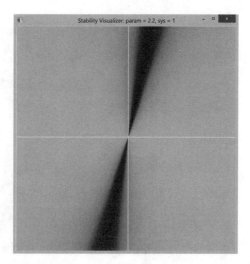

Figure 4.5 Phase plane of a linear oscillator with negative stiffness. A dark sector appears, but the bright field indicates growth away from an unstable equilibrium.

Setting the damping `param = 0.0` and `sys = 2` brings us to the final case in the example, the van der Pol oscillator. With `param = 0.0`, this system is identical to the undamped linear oscillator, so we again see the equilibrium in a moderately bright field. What happens when you press the up arrow key to make the damping positive? The equilibrium is surrounded by a bright region, so nearby initial states produce solutions that are repelled and the equilibrium is unstable. However, the outer region is dark, so initial states further out produce solutions that are attracted inwards. There is no other equilibrium point to go to, so where do all these solutions end up? It turns out that there is a closed, attracting loop near the shading transition corresponding to a stable period motion or "limit cycle" (Figure 4.6).

Note that the results of this type of numerical stability analysis should be considered as advisory. The ODE solver is approximate, and we *only* test a few hundred thousand initial states, so it is highly likely but not guaranteed that we did not miss something.

Before we are done, you might want to press and hold the up arrow key and watch the hundreds of thousands of pixels in the stability visualization change in real time. This is something you are not likely to be able to do without the power of parallel computing.

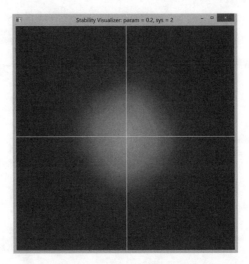

Figure 4.6 Phase plane of the van der Pol oscillator. The bright central region indicates an unstable equilibrium. The dark outer region indicates solutions decaying inwards. These results are consistent with the existence of a stable periodic "limit cycle" trajectory in the moderately bright region.

Summary

In this chapter, we covered the essentials of defining and launching kernels on 2D computational grids. We presented and explained sample code, the `flashlight` app that takes advantage of CUDA/OpenGL interop to implement real-time graphical display and interaction with the results from 2D computational grids. Finally, we showed how to use `flashlight` as a template and perform modifications to make it applicable to a real engineering problem, numerical exploration of dynamic stability.

Suggested Projects

1. Modify the `flashlight` app to be a version of the "hotter/colder" game. Provide an interface for player A to pick a target pixel. Player B then seeks out the target pixel based on the color of the spot, which turns blue (or red) as it is moved farther from (or closer to) the target.

2. Find another 1DoF system of interest and modify the `stability` app to study the nature of its equilibrium.

3. The explicit Euler method is perhaps the simplest and least reliable method for numerical solution of ODEs. Enhance the `stability` app by implementing a more sophisticated ODE solver. A Runge-Kutta method would be a good next step into a major field.

4. The van der Pol limit cycle turns out to be nearly circular for `param = 0.1`. Modify the `stability` app so the shading depends on the difference between the final distance and a new parameter `rad`. Implement interactive control of `rad`, and run the modified app to identify the size of the limit cycle.

References

[1] Microsoft Windows Dev Center. "Direct3D," 2015, https://msdn.microsoft.com/en-us/library/windows/desktop/hh309466(v=vs.85).aspx.

[2] Mason Woo, Jackie Neider, Tom Davis, and Dave Shreiner, *OpenGL Programming Guide: The Official Guide to Learning OpenGL, Version 1.2, Third Edition.* (Reading, MA: Addison-Wesley, 1999).

[3] NVIDIA Corporation. "CUDA C Programming Guide," NVIDIA Developer Zone, CUDA Toolkit Documentation, 2015, http://docs.nvidia.com/cuda/cuda-c-programming-guide/index.html#abstract.

[4] Graham Sellers, Richard S. Wright, Jr., and Nicholas Haemel, *OpenGL Superbible: Comprehensive Tutorial and Reference, Seventh Edition.* (Boston, MA: Addison-Wesley, 2016).

[5] Randi J. Rost et al., *OpenGL Shading Language, Third Edition.* (Boston, MA: Addison-Wesley, 2010).

[6] cppreference.com, "ASCII Chart," 2015, http://en.cppreference.com/w/cpp/language/ascii.

[7] Richard H. Rand. *Lecture Notes on Nonlinear Vibrations*, Cornell University eCommons, May 2012, http://hdl.handle.net/1813/28989.

[8] Steven H. Strogatz, *Nonlinear Dynamics and Chaos, Second Edition.* (Cambridge, MA: Westview Press, 2014).

Chapter 5

Stencils and Shared Memory

Can stencil be used for a grouper? Local max?

In this chapter, we look at applications involving computational threads that, instead of being independent, are *inter*dependent with other threads in their neighborhood on the computational grid. The mathematical models we will implement involve convolution (or correlation) operations in which data from threads in a neighborhood contribute to a linear combination with a constant array of coefficients. In the computing context, the operation is often referred to as **filtering,** and the coefficient array is a filter or **stencil**. Thread interactions can produce bottlenecks associated with multiple threads competing for access to the same data, so CUDA provides some capabilities for alleviating the bottlenecks and enhancing performance. Most CUDA "tricks of the trade" involve special types of memory, and here we will focus on **shared memory**, which supports efficient sharing of information between threads in a block.

We introduce the basic ideas of stencil computations and shared memory in a 1D example that computes the second derivative of a function from uniformly sampled values. We extend stencils and shared memory to 2D and create an app that computes and visualizes steady-state temperature distributions by solving Laplace's equation using Jacobi iteration. (Note that solutions of Laplace's equation also have applications in fluid mechanics, electrostatics, gravity, and complex variables.) We finish up by creating an app to sharpen an image, and we engage in some profiling studies to justify embellishments of the initial implementation.

Thread Interdependence

This chapter marks a significant step forward, and we should take a moment to explicitly state the step we are taking. We finished up Chapter 4, "2D Grids and Interactive Graphics," with a stability app that computes the time histories of an oscillator for a grid of initial states. We introduced a finite difference derivative estimate and used it to relate successive values in the time history computed by each thread. The derivative computation lives within a single thread, and each thread proceeds without reliance on any of the other threads. Each thread has access to its own initial state (based on its index values), but has no access to the state of the simulation in any other thread.

Now we are ready to apply a finite difference operator to compute the derivative of a function whose sampled values are associated with different points on a grid (each associated with a different thread). To be concrete, let's consider computing the numerical solution $u(x)$ of a differential equation. The computation is discretized on a grid of points $x_i = ih$ with uniform spacing h along a line segment, and the derivative gets replaced by the difference between values at neighboring points. The parallel solver launches a 1D computational grid, and each thread has a variable $\mathtt{u}$ to store the computed value of $u_i = u(x_i)$. The coefficients in the finite difference formula now combine the values of variables associated with neighboring threads.

Why make such a big deal of this point? If you try to write a simple kernel that says "compute the difference between the value of a variable in this thread and the value of the same variable in the adjacent grid," that operation is not supported in CUDA. In SIMT parallelism, each thread has access to its own version of each kernel variable, but no access to the versions in other threads. How do we get around such a restriction when we need threads to share information? The "naïve" approach is to allocate arrays in device global memory where each thread can read its input and write its output value of $\mathtt{u}$. We will implement the global array approach and show that it does work, but it turns out to be not terribly efficient. When a large grid is launched, there may be millions of threads trying to read and write values to and from the same arrays, which creates issues with synchronization and memory traffic.

We won't get into all the details right now, but you should be aware of the general principle that the farther data is stored from the processor, the longer it takes to process the data. We have already discussed one application of this principle in Chapter 3, "From Loops to Grids," when we first copied data from host to device. Device memory is closer to the streaming multiprocessors (SMs), so it is a preferred storage location compared to host memory, which requires data transfer across a relatively slow communications bus. Moreover, when we do have to transfer data, we want to do it as few times as possible to reduce the total data transfer time.

We now encounter the second application of the "nearer is faster" principle: There are different memory areas on the GPU, and we would prefer to use storage closer to the SM. Previously, we have encountered global memory (where all device arrays have been stored) and register memory (where the local variables for each thread are stored). Global memory provides the bulk of the device storage capacity, but it is as far from the SMs as you can get on the GPU, so global memory provides universal but relatively slow memory access. (Recall that it is still much faster to access than host memory.) Register memory is as close to the SM as possible, so it offers fast access but its scope is local only to a single thread.

Now we introduce **shared memory,** which aims to bridge the gap in memory speed and access. Shared memory resides adjacent to the SM and provides up to 48KB of storage that can be accessed efficiently by all threads in a block. It is sensible to think of shared memory as CUDA's primary mechanism for efficiently supporting thread cooperation, and in many cases (including many stencil computations) use of shared memory can lead to significant gains in performance. Without further ado, let's get on to our examples.

Computing Derivatives on a 1D Grid

Computations using stencils and shared memory involve a bit of index book-keeping, so we begin with a 1D example to keep the presentation as simple as possible. While our efforts in 1D may not achieve acceleration compared to computation on the CPU, rest assured that a significant payoff will come when we move on to 2D. We again choose a specific example to support a concrete discussion. In particular, we choose to build on the basic finite difference method from Chapter 4, "2D Grids and Interactive Graphics," adapted to dependent variable u and independent variable x sampled at discrete points x_i with uniform spacing h. The forward difference estimate of the first derivative becomes

$$\frac{du}{dx}\left(x_n\right)=\left(u_{i+1}-u_i\right)/h$$

where $u_i = u(x_i) = u(ih)$. A second application of the finite difference formula provides a centered difference formula for computing the second derivative:

$$\frac{d^2u}{dx^2}\left(x_n\right) = \left(u_{i+1} - 2u_i + u_{i-1}\right)/h^2$$

Our first example is quite straightforward: Create an array of sampled values of the function sin(x) and use the centered difference formula to compute an array of values of the second derivative. (Differentiating sin(x) twice just introduces a sign change, so the results will be easy to check.)

Now we are back to the usual question that arises at the start of a new application: How do we divide our overall computing task up into pieces that can be identified with the action of a thread? Again, we keep things simple and choose to have each thread compute one of the derivative values; that is, the thread with index i reads the entries in the input device array d_in necessary to compute the local value of the second derivative (i.e., d_in[i-1], d_in[i], and d_in[i+1]), computes the derivative, and stores the value in the output matrix d_out[i].

IMPLEMENTING dd_1d_global

A global memory implementation of the dd_1d_global (indicating two derivatives in one dimension using global memory) app is shown in Listings 5.1, 5.2, and 5.3.

Let's start by discussing the details of main.cpp, shown in Listing 5.1. The main() function begins by computing the arrays of values for x and u (lines 14–17) and then executes the parallel derivative computation (line 19). The result, stored in the array result_parallel, is then written to the .csv (comma separated values) file results.csv, which can be opened with a spreadsheet or text editor for inspection.

Listing 5.1 dd_1d_global/main.cpp

```
1 #include "kernel.h"
2 #include <math.h>
3 #include <stdio.h>
4
5 int main() {
6     const float PI = 3.1415927;
7     const int N = 150;
8     const float h = 2*PI/N;
9
```

```
10    float x[N] = {0.0};
11    float u[N] = {0.0};
12    float result_parallel[N] = {0.0};
13
14    for (int i = 0; i < N; ++i) {
15      x[i] = 2*PI*i/N;
16      u[i] = sinf(x[i]);
17    }
18
19    ddParallel(result_parallel, u, N, h);
20
21    FILE *outfile = fopen("results.csv", "w");
22    for (int i = 1; i < N - 1; ++i) {
23      fprintf(outfile, "%f,%f,%f,%f\n", x[i], u[i],
24              result_parallel[i], result_parallel[i] + u[i]);
25    }
26    fclose(outfile);
27 }
```

Now let's proceed on to the kernel and launcher code in Listing 5.2. Hopefully, the ddKernel() code looks unsurprising by now. The other function in kernel.cu is the wrapper function ddParallel() that allocates device arrays d_in and d_out (lines 14–15), copies the input data to the device (line 16), launches ddKernel() on line 18, copies the results stored in d_out back to the host (line 20), and frees the device memory (lines 21–22).

Listing 5.2 dd_1d_global/kernel.cu

```
 1 #include "kernel.h"
 2 #define TPB 64
 3
 4 __global__
 5 void ddKernel(float *d_out, const float *d_in, int size, float h) {
 6   const int i = threadIdx.x + blockDim.x*blockIdx.x;
 7   if (i >= size) return;
 8   d_out[i] = (d_in[i - 1] - 2.f*d_in[i] + d_in[i + 1])/(h*h);
 9 }
10
11 void ddParallel(float *out, const float *in, int n, float h) {
12   float *d_in = 0, *d_out = 0;
13
14   cudaMalloc(&d_in, n*sizeof(float));
15   cudaMalloc(&d_out, n*sizeof(float));
16   cudaMemcpy(d_in, in, n*sizeof(float), cudaMemcpyHostToDevice);
17
18   ddKernel<<<(n + TPB - 1)/TPB, TPB>>>(d_out, d_in, n, h);
19
20   cudaMemcpy(out, d_out, n*sizeof(float), cudaMemcpyDeviceToHost);
21   cudaFree(d_in);
22   cudaFree(d_out);
23 }
```

Finally, we look at the contents of `kernel.h`, shown in Listing 5.3. The primary content of the header file is the prototype for the kernel wrapper `ddParallel()`. The remaining lines constitute the include guard.

Listing 5.3 `dd_1d_global/kernel.h`

```
1 #ifndef KERNEL_H
2 #define KERNEL_H
3
4 void ddParallel(float *out, const float *in, int n, float h);
5
6 #endif
```

The Makefile for building the app under Linux is provided in Listing 5.4.

Listing 5.4 `dd_1d_global/Makefile`

```
1 NVCC = /usr/local/cuda/bin/nvcc
2 NVCC_FLAGS = -g -G -Xcompiler -Wall
3
4 all: main.exe
5
6 main.exe: main.o kernel.o
7   $(NVCC) $^ -o $@
8
9 main.o: main.cpp kernel.h
10   $(NVCC) $(NVCC_FLAGS) -c $< -o $@
11
12 kernel.o: kernel.cu kernel.h
13   $(NVCC) $(NVCC_FLAGS) -c $< -o $@
```

Build and execute the `dd_1d_global` app and convince yourself that it works as planned by inspecting the contents of `results.csv`. The columns show the values of x, $\sin(x)$, the second-derivative estimate, and the sum of the result and $\sin(x)$. Values in the last column uniformly close to zero indicate the validity (and accuracy limitations) of the finite difference approximation.

Once correct results are verified, we can turn to efficiency considerations. While we will engage in some profiling when we look at the image-sharpening app at the end of this chapter, for the moment let's note that implementing the stencil computation with global memory involves redundant memory transfers that create unnecessary data traffic. Since each thread reads the input data associated with its own index and those of its neighbors, every element in the input array gets requested three times. (`d_in[i]` gets requested as the right-hand neighbor value, center value, and left-hand neighbor value by threads with index i-1, i, and i+1, respectively.)

Stencil Radius and Redundant Data Access

The number of neighbors on either side covered by the stencil is referred to as the **radius**. In 1D, the level of redundancy for our stencil with second-order accuracy and radius $r = 1$ is $2r + 1 = 3$. The redundancy in N-dimensions is $(2r + 1)^N$, so the issue becomes more significant as the radius and/or the dimensionality increase.

We now move on to a more efficient implementation of the stencil computation using data tiles and shared memory to increase the speed and reduce the redundancy of the memory transactions.

IMPLEMENTING dd_1d_shared

The basic idea of the shared memory approach is to break the large grid up into tiles of data that provide all the input and output required for a computational block. We then create input and/or output arrays to store the tile of data in shared memory, where it provides both fast access (because it is near the SM) and availability to all threads in the block. Here we focus on using shared memory for the input, because that is where the known redundant access issue arises. The goal is to access each piece of input data from global memory only once (to populate the shared memory arrays), after which the data needed by all the threads in the block can be obtained quickly from shared memory.

To keep the bookkeeping simple, a sensible approach is to maintain the usual index i (which we will refer to as the **global index** because it identifies the corresponding element of the array in global memory) and to introduce a new **local index** s_idx to keep track of where things are stored in the shared array. Note that it is not sufficient just to copy the entries corresponding to the threads in the block; we will also need neighboring values that are covered by the stencil when it gets to the edges of the block. We will use the name RAD to indicate the stencil - radius in the code, and we will need to include RAD neighboring array elements at the edges of the block. A common description is that handling a stencil with radius RAD requires that, in addition to one element for each thread in the block, the shared array must also include 2*RAD **halo cells** added at each end to ensure that the shared array includes all of the necessary data. The first thread in the block (with threadIdx.x = 0) needs to leave room for RAD neighbors to its left and therefore get local index s_idx = RAD. The general relation between the local index and thread index is s_idx = threadIdx.x + RAD.

Now that we have a systematic bookkeeping plan, we can get into the implementation details. The good news is that, since the interface to calling the derivative function remains the same, no changes are needed in `main.cpp` or `kernel.h`, which remain exactly as shown in Listings 5.1 and 5.3. We can focus on the shared memory version of the kernel shown in Listing 5.5. Once we've computed the global index `i` and checked that it is in bounds (lines 7–8), we compute the local index `s_idx` (line 10) and declare the shared array `s_in` using the `__shared__` qualifier (line 11).

Listing 5.5 `dd_1d_shared/kernel.cu`

```
 1 #include "kernel.h"
 2 #define TPB 64
 3 #define RAD 1 // radius of the stencil
 4
 5 __global__
 6 void ddKernel(float *d_out, const float *d_in, int size, float h) {
 7   const int i = threadIdx.x + blockDim.x*blockIdx.x;
 8   if (i >= size) return;
 9
10   const int s_idx = threadIdx.x + RAD;
11   extern __shared__ float s_in[];
12
13   // Regular cells
14   s_in[s_idx] = d_in[i];
15
16   // Halo cells
17   if (threadIdx.x < RAD) {
18     s_in[s_idx - RAD] = d_in[i - RAD];
19     s_in[s_idx + blockDim.x] = d_in[i + blockDim.x];
20   }
21   __syncthreads();
22   d_out[i] = (s_in[s_idx-1] - 2.f*s_in[s_idx] + s_in[s_idx+1])/(h*h);
23 }
24
25 void ddParallel(float *out, const float *in, int n, float h) {
26   float *d_in = 0, *d_out = 0;
27   cudaMalloc(&d_in, n*sizeof(float));
28   cudaMalloc(&d_out, n*sizeof(float));
29   cudaMemcpy(d_in, in, n*sizeof(float), cudaMemcpyHostToDevice);
30
31   // Set shared memory size in bytes
32   const size_t smemSize = (TPB + 2*RAD)*sizeof(float);
33
34   ddKernel<<<(n + TPB - 1)/TPB, TPB, smemSize>>>(d_out, d_in, n, h);
35
36   cudaMemcpy(out, d_out, n*sizeof(float), cudaMemcpyDeviceToHost);
37
38   cudaFree(d_in);
39   cudaFree(d_out);
40 }
```

Setting the Size of the Shared Array

If you create your shared array with a fixed size, the array can be created as follows:

```
__shared__ float s_in[34];
```

and no change to the kernel call is needed. Note that the following will produce a compiler error:

```
__shared__ float s_in[blockDim.x + 2*RAD];
```

If you allocate the array dynamically, the declaration requires the keyword `extern` as follows:

```
extern __shared__ float s_in[];
```

And the kernel call requires an optional third argument within the chevrons to specify the size of the shared memory allocation in bytes.

```
const size_t smemSize = (TPB + 2*RAD)*sizeof(float);
ddKernel<<<(n+TPB-1)/TPB, TPB, smemSize>>>(d_out, d_in, n, h);
```

Execution Configuration Parameters

There is also a fourth (optional) execution configuration parameter that specifies the computational stream number. Since we are not using multiple streams for any of the examples in this book, the default value 0 suffices for our purposes. For more details on using multiple streams in CUDA computation, see the "CUDA C Runtime" section's "Streams" subsection in the CUDA C Programming Guide [1] and the *Parallel Forall* blog post "GPU Pro Tip: CUDA 7 Streams Simplify Concurrency" [2].

Once the shared array is allocated, we are ready to transfer the data from global memory to shared memory. The basic plan is that each thread requests the entry in the input array whose index matches the thread's global index and stores that value in the shared array at the entry corresponding to the local index (i.e., `s_in[s_idx] = d_in[i]`, which appears as line 14). The values for the halo cells still need to be obtained and stored, and that job is accomplished by the following snippet:

```
if (threadIdx.x < RAD) {
s_in[s_idx - RAD] = d_in[i - RAD];
s_in[s_idx + blockDim.x] = d_in[i + blockDim.x];
}
```

which allocates the job to threads 0 to RAD-1, each of which read and store a pair of halo values, one at each end of the block. Thread 0 has s_idx = RAD, so

- s_idx-RAD is 0, and the leftmost neighbor, in[i-RAD], gets stored in the leftmost halo cell at the beginning of the shared array.

- s_idx+blockDim.x is blockDim.x and the immediate neighbor to the right, in[i+blockDim.x], gets stored in the leftmost halo cell at the end of the array.

The reading and storage of halo values continues in pairs over the first RAD threads until the shared array is fully populated.

We are almost ready for the last kernel statement (line 22) where the desired finite difference estimate of the second derivative is computed and stored, but first we need to take care of another important bookkeeping item.

Recall that kernel launches are asynchronous. In return for access to the power of massively parallel computing, we give up some control of the order in which things are executed. In this context, it means that we cannot just assume that all of the input data has been loaded into the shared memory array before threads execute the final statement (and possibly use some arbitrary values that happened to be sitting in the memory locations allocated for the shared array). To ensure that all the data has been properly stored, we employ the CUDA function __syncthreads() (line 21), which forces all the threads in the block to complete the previous statements before any thread in the block proceeds further. Synchronization can take time and reduce your acceleration factor, so it should be used as needed, and it is needed here to ensure reliable results.

Once again, build and execute the dd_1d_shared app and convince yourself that it works as planned by inspecting the contents of results.csv. If you are using Linux, the Makefile for this app is the same as the one for dd_1d_global, which is provided in Listing 5.4.

SOLVING LAPLACE'S EQUATION IN 2D: heat_2d

With an efficient method in hand for performing stencil computations that arise from derivatives, we are within reach of some real engineering applications. Here we compute the solution of Laplace's equation, which governs potential fields. While this problem can be interpreted in many contexts, we will discuss the application in terms of solving for the equilibrium temperature distribution $u(x)$ in a region with the temperature specified on the boundary. The basic physics says that the rate of temperature change, $\frac{\partial u}{\partial t}$, is proportional to the net flux of heat per unit volume. The net flux of heat per volume is measured by the divergence of the heat flow field, and the basic diffusion model specifies a heat flow field proportional to the gradient of the temperature distribution. Putting the pieces together gives

$$\frac{\partial u}{\partial t} = \alpha \nabla \cdot \nabla u = \alpha \nabla^2 u = \alpha \left(\frac{\partial^2 u}{\partial x^2} + \frac{\partial^2 u}{\partial y^2} + \frac{\partial^2 u}{\partial z^2} \right)$$

where α is the thermal conductivity and ∇^2 is the Laplacian operator whose expression in 3D Cartesian coordinates is given at the far right.

Now let's focus in on a particular problem that involves equilibrium temperature distributions (which do not vary over time) in a thin plate. The plate lies in the xy-plane with insulated faces, so there is no significant temperature variation across the plate (in the z-direction). The z-derivative on the right-hand side then vanishes, as does the t-derivative on the left-hand side, and the conductivity cancels out leaving 2D Laplace's equation in Cartesian coordinates

$$\frac{\partial^2 u}{\partial x^2} + \frac{\partial^2 u}{\partial y^2} = 0$$

to be solved along with suitable boundary conditions.

We want things to be simple but nontrivial and have a specific context, so let's construct an engineering scenario in which we are analyzing the steady-state temperature distribution in proposed designs for a plate that acts as a vertical support for a circular steam pipe. The plate is constructed from a square with a circular hole (to accommodate the pipe) and chamfers on the top corners. The bottom edge of the plate is in contact with the ground and therefore has temperature t_g (where g stands for ground). Similarly the edge of the hole is at t_s (where s stands for source flowing through the pipe), and the other edges of the plate are in contact with the surrounding air and have temperature t_a. Our mission is to create an app called heat_2d to compute and visualize the steady-state temperature in the plate as we change the following items:

- The location, size, and temperature of the pipe

- The size of the chamfer

- The temperature of the air and ground

The problem consisting of the partial differential equation plus boundary conditions is summarized in Figure 5.1.

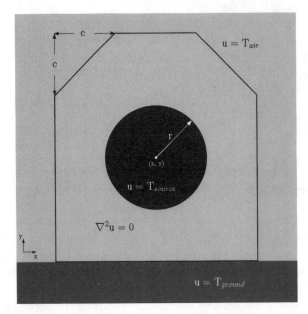

Figure 5.1 Pictorial summary of the equation and boundary conditions to be solved by the `heat_2d` app

Now we discretize for the purposes of numerical solution, and the second derivatives get replaced with our previous finite difference formula with a second index appropriate for a 2D setting:

$$\frac{\partial^2 u}{\partial x^2}\left(x_{i,j}\right) \rightarrow \frac{u_{i+1,j} - 2u_{i,j} + u_{i-1,j}}{h^2}$$

$$\frac{\partial^2 u}{\partial y^2}\left(x_{i,j}\right) \rightarrow \frac{u_{i,j+1} - 2u_{i,j} + u_{i,j-1}}{h^2}$$

Plugging the finite difference expressions into Laplace's equation and solving for $u_{i,j}$ gives

$$u_{i,j} = \left(u_{i-1,j} + u_{i+1,j} + u_{i,j-1} + u_{i,j+1}\right)/4$$

So the discrete sampling of the equilibrium temperature distribution is characterized by the property that each value is the average of the four immediate neighboring values, and we have obtained a new stencil, now in 2D:

$$\left(\frac{1}{4}\right)\begin{bmatrix} 0 & 1 & 0 \\ 1 & -4 & 1 \\ 0 & 1 & 0 \end{bmatrix}$$

This stencil (often referred to as a **5-point stencil** because it includes the central entry plus four neighbors) describes the essential property of steady-state solutions to the differential equation; that is, at equilibrium, the temperature at a grid point should be the average of the temperatures at the immediate neighbor points.

Perhaps the simplest approach to computing a steady-state temperature distribution is to repeatedly average neighboring values by applying the stencil to the array of temperature values. This scheme is known as Jacobi iteration, and its results do converge to a solution of Laplace's equation. (Note that the convergence can be slow for large problems. For a full discussion of this and related methods along with their convergence properties, see Chapter 4 in Leveque's *Finite Difference Methods for Ordinary and Partial Differential Equations* [3].)

While Jacobi iteration converges to a solution of Laplace's equation, it most likely does not converge to the solution that satisfies the desired boundary conditions. We'll handle this with a straightforward adjustment of the kernel. Instead of applying the stencil everywhere, specified boundary condition values are imposed at pixels outside the plate and the stencil is applied only at pixels within the plate.

Having specified the problem and a numerical solution strategy, let's move on to implementation as shown in Listings 5.6, 5.7, 5.8, and 5.9. This app includes interactive graphics, so it was constructed using the flashlight app from Chapter 4, "2D Grids and Interactive Graphics," as a template, and only a few lines of main.cpp in Listing 5.6 should be unfamiliar:

- The render() function repetitively calls a different kernel launcher to be described below.

- The title bar will display the current values for the boundary values: t_s, t_a, and t_g for the temperature of the source, air, and ground, respectively. Note that these values appear as components of a boundary condition data structure defined in kernel.h as described below.

- The main() function starts off by printing a summary of available user interactions, allocating the array to store a 2D grid of temperature values, and calls resetTemperature(), which launches a kernel to initialize the temperature array.

- There is one additional GLUT call to glutIdleFunc() that is relevant because we want our iterative scheme to continue updating between user interactions.

Listing 5.6 heat_2d/main.cpp

```
 1 #include "interactions.h"
 2 #include "kernel.h"
 3 #include <stdio.h>
 4 #include <stdlib.h>
 5 #ifdef _WIN32
 6 #define WINDOWS_LEAN_AND_MEAN
 7 #define NOMINMAX
 8 #include <windows.h>
 9 #endif
10 #ifdef __APPLE__
11 #include <GLUT/glut.h>
12 #else
13 #include <GL/glew.h>
14 #include <GL/freeglut.h>
15 #endif
16 #include <cuda_runtime.h>
17 #include <cuda_gl_interop.h>
18 #define ITERS_PER_RENDER 50
19
20 // texture and pixel objects
21 GLuint pbo = 0;      // OpenGL pixel buffer object
22 GLuint tex = 0;      // OpenGL texture object
23 struct cudaGraphicsResource *cuda_pbo_resource;
24
25 void render() {
26   uchar4 *d_out = 0;
27   cudaGraphicsMapResources(1, &cuda_pbo_resource, 0);
28   cudaGraphicsResourceGetMappedPointer((void **)&d_out, NULL,
29                                  cuda_pbo_resource);
30   for (int i = 0; i < ITERS_PER_RENDER; ++i) {
31     kernelLauncher(d_out, d_temp, W, H, bc);
32   }
33   cudaGraphicsUnmapResources(1, &cuda_pbo_resource, 0);
34   char title[128];
35   sprintf(title, "Temperature Visualizer - Iterations=%4d, "
36                  "T_s=%3.0f, T_a=%3.0f, T_g=%3.0f",
37                  iterationCount, bc.t_s, bc.t_a, bc.t_g);
38   glutSetWindowTitle(title);
39 }
40
41 void draw_texture() {
42   glTexImage2D(GL_TEXTURE_2D, 0, GL_RGBA, W, H, 0, GL_RGBA,
43                GL_UNSIGNED_BYTE, NULL);
44   glEnable(GL_TEXTURE_2D);
```

```
45    glBegin(GL_QUADS);
46    glTexCoord2f(0.0f, 0.0f); glVertex2f(0, 0);
47    glTexCoord2f(0.0f, 1.0f); glVertex2f(0, H);
48    glTexCoord2f(1.0f, 1.0f); glVertex2f(W, H);
49    glTexCoord2f(1.0f, 0.0f); glVertex2f(W, 0);
50    glEnd();
51    glDisable(GL_TEXTURE_2D);
52  }
53
54  void display() {
55    render();
56    draw_texture();
57    glutSwapBuffers();
58  }
59
60  void initGLUT(int *argc, char **argv) {
61    glutInit(argc, argv);
62    glutInitDisplayMode(GLUT_RGBA | GLUT_DOUBLE);
63    glutInitWindowSize(W, H);
64    glutCreateWindow("Temp. Vis.");
65  #ifndef __APPLE__
66    glewInit();
67  #endif
68  }
69
70  void initPixelBuffer() {
71    glGenBuffers(1, &pbo);
72    glBindBuffer(GL_PIXEL_UNPACK_BUFFER, pbo);
73    glBufferData(GL_PIXEL_UNPACK_BUFFER, W*H*sizeof(GLubyte) * 4, 0,
74                GL_STREAM_DRAW);
75    glGenTextures(1, &tex);
76    glBindTexture(GL_TEXTURE_2D, tex);
77    glTexParameteri(GL_TEXTURE_2D, GL_TEXTURE_MIN_FILTER, GL_NEAREST);
78    cudaGraphicsGLRegisterBuffer(&cuda_pbo_resource, pbo,
79                      cudaGraphicsMapFlagsWriteDiscard);
80  }
81
82  void exitfunc() {
83    if (pbo) {
84      cudaGraphicsUnregisterResource(cuda_pbo_resource);
85      glDeleteBuffers(1, &pbo);
86      glDeleteTextures(1, &tex);
87    }
88    cudaFree(d_temp);
89  }
90
91  int main(int argc, char** argv) {
92    cudaMalloc(&d_temp, W*H*sizeof(float));
93    resetTemperature(d_temp, W, H, bc);
94    printInstructions();
95    initGLUT(&argc, argv);
96    gluOrtho2D(0, W, H, 0);
97    glutKeyboardFunc(keyboard);
98    glutMouseFunc(mouse);
99    glutIdleFunc(idle);
```

```
100   glutDisplayFunc(display);
101   initPixelBuffer();
102   glutMainLoop();
103   atexit(exitfunc);
104   return 0;
105 }
```

That about does it for new aspects of `main.cpp`, so let's look at the contents of the header file `kernel.h` shown in Listing 5.7:

- Line 4 forward declares the `uchar4` type. `nvcc` knows how to handle `uchar4` variables, but we need the declaration so the C++ compiler invoked through `nvcc` does not produce an error.

- Lines 6–11 define the `BC` data structure that allows us to include all of the boundary condition information (including the coordinates and radius of the pipe, the size of the chamfer, and the temperatures of the source, the air, and the ground) in a single argument.

- Lines 13–15 are the prototypes for the kernel wrapper functions (i.e., the functions that will be called from `main.cpp`): `kernelLauncher()` and `resetTemperature()`.

Listing 5.7 `heat_2d/kernel.h`

```
 1 #ifndef KERNEL_H
 2 #define KERNEL_H
 3
 4 struct uchar4;
 5 // struct BC that contains all the boundary conditions
 6 typedef struct {
 7   int x, y; // x and y location of pipe center
 8   float rad; // radius of pipe
 9   int chamfer; // chamfer
10   float t_s, t_a, t_g; // temperatures in pipe, air, ground
11 } BC;
12
13 void kernelLauncher(uchar4 *d_out, float *d_temp, int w, int h,
14                     BC bc);
15 void resetTemperature(float *d_temp, int w, int h, BC bc);
16
17 #endif
```

Now that we know the variables in the `BC` structure and the functions that are made available from `kernel.cu`, we are ready to look at details of `interactions.h` as shown in Listing 5.8. Lines 3–11 include headers used in `interactions.h`. Lines 13–19 define relevant parameter values (including the width and height of the computational grid, and increments for changes in position and temperature), and then make necessary declarations for the pointer to the device array that will store the temperature values, the counter that keeps track of iterations since the most recent reset, and a BC structure bc to store the boundary conditions. (bc is initialized so the pipe is in the center of the plate with radius 1/10th the plate width, a chamfer of 150 grid spacings, pipe temperature 212°F, air temperature 70°F, and ground temperature 0°F.)

The keyboard callback function allows the user to reset or terminate the simulation and provides interactive control of all the boundary conditions:

- The z resets the boundary conditions and resets iterationCount to 0.

- The s key changes the pipe temperature.

- The a key changes the air temperature.

- The g key changes the ground temperature.

- The r key changes the pipe radius.

- The c key changes the plate chamfer.

- The Esc key terminates the simulation.

The mouse() callback reads the position of a mouse click and relocates the center of the pipe to the selected location. The other relevant callback is idle(), which increments the iteration count and calls glutPostRedisplay(), which in turn calls render, which calls the kernel launcher. The idle() function keeps the Jacobi iteration scheme updating (and converging toward the desired solution) in the absence of user interaction.

Listing 5.8 heat_2d/interactions.h

```
1  #ifndef INTERACTIONS_H
2  #define INTERACTIONS_H
3  #include "kernel.h"
4  #include <stdio.h>
5  #include <stdlib.h>
6  #ifdef __APPLE__
7  #include <GLUT/glut.h>
8  #else
9  #include <GL/glew.h>
10 #include <GL/freeglut.h>
11 #endif
12 #define MAX(x, y) (((x) > (y)) ? (x) : (y))
13 #define W   640
14 #define H   640
15 #define DT 1.f // source intensity increment
16
```

```
17 float *d_temp = 0;
18 int iterationCount = 0;
19 BC bc = {W/2, H/2, W/10.f, 150, 212.f, 70.f, 0.f}; // Boundary conds
20
21 void keyboard(unsigned char key, int x, int y) {
22   if (key == 'S')   bc.t_s += DT;
23   if (key == 's')   bc.t_s -= DT;
24   if (key == 'A')   bc.t_a += DT;
25   if (key == 'a')   bc.t_a -= DT;
26   if (key == 'G')   bc.t_g += DT;
27   if (key == 'g')   bc.t_g -= DT;
28   if (key == 'R')   bc.rad += DT;
29   if (key == 'r')   bc.rad = MAX(0.f, bc.rad-DT);
30   if (key == 'C')   ++bc.chamfer;
31   if (key == 'c')   --bc.chamfer;
32   if (key == 'z')   resetTemperature(d_temp, W, H, bc);
33   if (key == 27)    exit(0);
34   glutPostRedisplay();
35 }
36
37 void mouse(int button, int state, int x, int y) {
38   bc.x = x, bc.y = y;
39   glutPostRedisplay();
40 }
41
42 void idle(void) {
43   ++iterationCount;
44   glutPostRedisplay();
45 }
46
47 void printInstructions() {
48   printf("Temperature Visualizer:\n"
49          "Relocate source with mouse click\n"
50          "Change source temperature (-/+): s/S\n"
51          "Change air temperature     (-/+): a/A\n"
52          "Change ground temperature  (-/+): g/G\n"
53          "Change pipe radius         (-/+): r/R\n"
54          "Change chamfer             (-/+): c/C\n"
55          "Reset to air temperature      : z\n"
56          "Exit                          : Esc\n");
57 }
58
59 #endif
```

Now we get to the specifics of the utility functions, kernels, and wrapper functions in kernel.cu shown in Listing 5.9. Let's start with the utility functions:

- divUp() is for computing the number of blocks of a specified size to cover a computational grid.

- clip() is used to ensure that color values are of type unsigned char and in the correct range [0, 255].

- `idxClip()` keeps from sampling out of bounds. `idxClip(i, N)` returns an `int` in the interval [0, N – 1] (i.e., the set of legal indices for an array of length N).

- `flatten()` computes the index in a flattened 1D array corresponding to the entry at `col` and `row` in a 2D array (or image) of `width` and `height`. Note that `flatten()` uses `idxClip()` to prevent from trying to access nonexistent array entries when the stencil extends beyond the edge of the grid.

Next come the kernel functions:

- The first, `resetKernel()`, is particularly simple. It starts by using the built-in CUDA index and dimension variables to compute the indices `col` and `row` for each point on the 2D geometric grid. If the pixel lies within the bounds of the graphics window, the flattened index `idx` is computed, and a default value (chosen to be the air temperature) is saved at each point on the grid.

- `tempKernel()` first assigns the default color black (with full opacity) to all pixels, then loads a tile (including the necessary halo) of existing temperature values into shared memory.

- For points outside the domain of the plate, the kernel reapplies the specified boundary values.

- For the points inside the problem domain, the kernel performs one step of Jacobi iteration by applying the stencil computation to compute the updated temperature value and writes the solution to the corresponding location in the global memory array.

- Finally, the updated temperature values are clipped to the interval [0, 255], converted to `unsigned char` values, and coded into color values with cold regions having a strong blue component and hot regions having a strong red component.

The kernel functions are called by wrapper or launcher functions:

- `resetTemperature()` calls the `resetKernel()` with necessary grid and block dimensions.

- `kernelLauncher()` computes the necessary grid dimensions, then launches `tempKernel()` to perform all the necessary computations for averaging, reapplying boundary conditions, and computing of updated color values for display via OpenGL interop. `kernelLauncher()` is called a specified number of times by `render()` in `main.cpp`, so `ITERS_PER_RENDER` Jacobi iterations take place between each screen update. (The screen updates occur imperceptibly fast, and the Jacobi iterations are happening 50 times faster than that even with 400,000 values to compute at each iteration.] Each callback function, including `idle()`, ends with `glutPostRedisplay()`, which calls `display()`, which calls for 50 kernel launches, so the Jacobi iterations proceed until the user intervenes.

Listing 5.9 `heat_2d/kernel.cu`

```
1  #include "kernel.h"
2  #define TX 32
3  #define TY 32
4  #define RAD 1
5
6  int divUp(int a, int b) { return (a + b - 1) / b; }
7
8  __device__
9  unsigned char clip(int n) { return n > 255 ? 255 : (n < 0 ? 0 : n); }
10
11  __device__
12  int idxClip(int idx, int idxMax) {
13    return idx > (idxMax-1) ? (idxMax-1) : (idx < 0 ? 0 : idx);
14  }
15
16  __device__
17  int flatten(int col, int row, int width, int height) {
18    return idxClip(col, width) + idxClip(row, height)*width;
19  }
20
21  __global__
22  void resetKernel(float *d_temp, int w, int h, BC bc) {
23    const int col = blockIdx.x*blockDim.x + threadIdx.x;
24    const int row = blockIdx.y*blockDim.y + threadIdx.y;
25    if ((col >= w ) || (row >= h)) return;
26    d_temp[row*w+col] = bc.t_a;
27  }
28
29  __global__
30  void tempKernel(uchar4 *d_out, float *d_temp, int w, int h, BC bc) {
31    extern __shared__ float s_in[];
32    // global indices
33    const int col = threadIdx.x + blockDim.x * blockIdx.x;
34    const int row = threadIdx.y + blockDim.y * blockIdx.y;
35    if ((col >= w ) || (row >= h)) return;
36    const int idx = flatten(col, row, w, h);
37    // local width and height
38    const int s_w = blockDim.x + 2*RAD;
39    const int s_h = blockDim.y + 2*RAD;
40    // local indices
41    const int s_col = threadIdx.x + RAD;
42    const int s_row = threadIdx.y + RAD;
43    const int s_idx = flatten(s_col, s_row, s_w, s_h);
44    // assign default color values for d_out (black)
45    d_out[idx].x = 0;
```

```
46    d_out[idx].z = 0;
47    d_out[idx].y = 0;
48    d_out[idx].w = 255;
49
50    // Load regular cells
51    s_in[s_idx] = d_temp[idx];
52    // Load halo cells
53    if (threadIdx.x < RAD) {
54      s_in[flatten(s_col - RAD, s_row, s_w, s_h)] =
55        d_temp[flatten(col - RAD, row, w, h)];
56      s_in[flatten(s_col + blockDim.x, s_row, s_w, s_h)] =
57        d_temp[flatten(col + blockDim.x, row, w, h)];
58    }
59    if (threadIdx.y < RAD) {
60      s_in[flatten(s_col, s_row - RAD, s_w, s_h)] =
61        d_temp[flatten(col, row - RAD, w, h)];
62      s_in[flatten(s_col, s_row + blockDim.y, s_w, s_h)] =
63        d_temp[flatten(col, row + blockDim.y, w, h)];
64    }
65
66    // Calculate squared distance from pipe center
67    float dSq = ((col - bc.x)*(col - bc.x) + (row - bc.y)*(row - bc.y));
68    // If inside pipe, set temp to t_s and return
69    if (dSq < bc.rad*bc.rad) {
70      d_temp[idx] = bc.t_s;
71      return;
72    }
73    // If outside plate, set temp to t_a and return
74    if ((col == 0) || (col == w - 1) || (row == 0) ||
75        (col + row < bc.chamfer) || (col - row > w - bc.chamfer)) {
76      d_temp[idx] = bc.t_a;
77      return;
78    }
79    // If point is below ground, set temp to t_g and return
80    if (row == h - 1) {
81      d_temp[idx] = bc.t_g;
82      return;
83    }
84    __syncthreads();
85    // For all the remaining points, find temperature and set colors.
86    float temp = 0.25f*(s_in[flatten(s_col - 1, s_row, s_w, s_h)] +
87                        s_in[flatten(s_col + 1, s_row, s_w, s_h)] +
88                        s_in[flatten(s_col, s_row - 1, s_w, s_h)] +
89                        s_in[flatten(s_col, s_row + 1, s_w, s_h)]);
90    d_temp[idx] = temp;
91    const unsigned char intensity = clip((int)temp);
92    d_out[idx].x = intensity; // higher temp -> more red
93    d_out[idx].z = 255 - intensity; // lower temp -> more blue
94  }
95
96  void kernelLauncher(uchar4 *d_out, float *d_temp, int w, int h,
97                      BC bc) {
98    const dim3 blockSize(TX, TY);
99    const dim3 gridSize(divUp(w, TX), divUp(h, TY));
100   const size_t smSz = (TX+2*RAD)*(TY+2*RAD)*sizeof(float);
```

```
101   tempKernel<<<gridSize, blockSize, smSz>>>(d_out, d_temp, w, h, bc);
102 }
103
104 void resetTemperature(float *d_temp, int w, int h, BC bc) {
105   const dim3 blockSize(TX, TY);
106   const dim3 gridSize(divUp(w, TX), divUp(h, TY));
107   resetKernel<<<gridSize, blockSize>>>(d_temp, w, h, bc);
108 }
```

That completes the implementation discussion, and it is time to build and execute the heat_2d app. Listing 5.10 shows the Makefile for building this app in Linux. For Visual Studio users, the procedure for building and executing the app should be just like what you did for flashlight. If you start the app in its default configuration, you should see a graphics window that looks much like Figure 5.2.

Listing 5.10 heat_2d/Makefile

```
 1 UNAME_S := $(shell uname)
 2
 3 ifeq ($(UNAME_S), Darwin)
 4   LDFLAGS = -Xlinker -framework,OpenGL -Xlinker -framework,GLUT
 5 else
 6   LDFLAGS += -L/usr/local/cuda/samples/common/lib/linux/x86_64
 7   LDFLAGS += -lglut -lGL -lGLU -lGLEW
 8 endif
 9
10 NVCC = /usr/local/cuda/bin/nvcc
11 NVCC_FLAGS = -Xcompiler "-Wall -Wno-deprecated-declarations"
12 INC = -I/usr/local/cuda/samples/common/inc
13
14 all: main.exe
15
16 main.exe: main.o kernel.o
17   $(NVCC) $^ -o $@ $(LDFLAGS)
18
19 main.o: main.cpp kernel.h interactions.h
20   $(NVCC) $(NVCC_FLAGS) $(INC) -c $< -o $@
21
22 kernel.o: kernel.cu kernel.h
23   $(NVCC) $(NVCC_FLAGS) -c $< -o $@
```

Color Adjustment to Enhance Grayscale Contrast

Since it is difficult to see the difference between red (R) and blue (B) when viewing figures converted to grayscale, the figures included here use the green (G) channel to enhance contrast and brightness according to the formula $G = 0.3 + (R - B) / 2$. Full color images produced by the heat_2d app are available at www.cudaforengineers.com

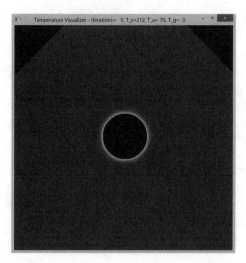

Figure 5.2 Initial configuration of the `heat_2d` app with color scheme adjusted for grayscale visibility

A summary of the supported interactions is printed in the console window, and you are encouraged to adjust the boundary conditions and watch how the temperature evolves in response. You should be able to produce a variety of more interesting distributions, such as the one shown in Figure 5.3.

Figure 5.3 The `heat_2d` app with an edited configuration with the color scheme adjusted for grayscale visibility

There are a couple of points that you should take away from your experience with the heat_2d app. First of all, you should note that when you run heat_2d, you are computing a solution of a partial differential equation on a decent-sized 2D grid (640 × 640 to start, but you should experiment with changing the size) spanning an irregularly shaped domain on a semi-interactive time scale. The iteration count displayed in the title bar will give you a direct look at how fast the iterations are happening (keeping in mind that each iteration actually calls the kernel ITERS_PER_RENDER times).

Note that the stencil sum has been written out by hand in lines 86–89 of Listing 5.9. If you use this kernel for larger stencils (i.e., RAD > 1), you will likely want to replace the stencil sum with a loop structure, so now we move on to another stencil example that allows us to implement a stencil loop structure and do some profiling and performance enhancement.

SHARPENING EDGES IN AN IMAGE: sharpen

Here we employ stencil computations to create a classic image-processing effect: edge sharpening. We present the sharpen app, which takes an input image, applies an edge-sharpening stencil, and writes the sharpened image to an output file that you can open and view with your favorite image viewer. Since reading and writing standard image file formats is required, we introduce a few essentials from CImg, "a small, open source, and modern C++ toolkit for image processing" [4].

Image sharpening is again a stencil operation, and the stencil we are going to use is a 3 × 3 stencil of the following form:

$$\begin{bmatrix} -1 & -1 & -1 \\ -1 & 9 & -1 \\ -1 & -1 & -1 \end{bmatrix}$$

which is the difference between a Dirac delta kernel (a 1 in the middle surrounded by zeroes that would reproduce the input without change) and a smoothing kernel. Thus the sharpening occurs by taking the original image and subtracting a blurred version (an approach that is sometimes referred to as **unsharp masking**). Note that the stencil is now full, so in the shared memory versions, you will see additional code for storing halo values at the corners of the tile as well as at the edges.

This app does not include graphical interaction, so it can be built from as a standard CUDA 7.5 app (with the inclusion of CImg.h). The complete app includes four files: sharpen/main.cpp, shown in Listing 5.11; a header file, shown in Listing 5.12; a Makefile (for Linux users), shown in Listing 5.13; and a kernel file. We present three versions of sharpen/kernel.cu that take advantage of shared memory to varying degrees and provide an opportunity for performance comparison:

- A global version that uses no shared memory arrays (Listing 5.14)

- A shared input version that uses a shared memory array for storing the input data (Listing 5.15)

- A shared input/output version that uses a shared memory array for loading the input data and writing the output data (Listing 5.16)

Listing 5.11 sharpen/main.cpp

```
1  #include "kernel.h"
2  #define cimg_display 0
3  #include "CImg.h"
4  #include <cuda_runtime.h>
5  #include <stdlib.h>
6
7  int main() {
8    cimg_library::CImg<unsigned char> image("butterfly.bmp");
9    const int w = image.width();
10   const int h = image.height();
11
12   // Initialize uchar4 array for image processing
13   uchar4 *arr = (uchar4*)malloc(w*h*sizeof(uchar4));
14
15   // Copy CImg data to array
16   for (int r = 0; r < h; ++r) {
17     for (int c = 0; c < w; ++c) {
18       arr[r*w + c].x = image(c, r, 0);
19       arr[r*w + c].y = image(c, r, 1);
20       arr[r*w + c].z = image(c, r, 2);
21     }
22   }
23
24   sharpenParallel(arr, w, h);
25
26   // Copy from array to CImg data
27   for (int r = 0; r < h; ++r) {
28     for (int c = 0; c < w; ++c) {
29       image(c, r, 0) = arr[r*w + c].x;
30       image(c, r, 1) = arr[r*w + c].y;
31       image(c, r, 2) = arr[r*w + c].z;
32     }
33   }
34
35   image.save_bmp("out.bmp");
36   free(arr);
37   return 0;
38 }
```

Could we use a similar approach to calculate a probability map for a target to do a different type of tracking.

Maybe clutter tracking?

Let's begin with a quick look at notable features of the code for sharpen/main.cpp, shown in Listing 5.11:

- The directive #define cimg_display 0 indicates that the display capability of CImg will not be used; we will just read and write image files to be viewed using other software.

- The first line of main() instantiates a CImg image object for input and output. (Yes, there is some object-oriented C++ going on here, but we are going to stick to the need-to-know aspects so we don't get hung up.). Line 8 declares image with an argument that corresponds to an image file, butterfly.bmp.

- Lines 9–10 set the variables w and h to the width and height of the input image.

- Line 13 declares and allocates a uchar4 array to hold the image data in a C-style array.

- Lines 16–22 copy the image data from the CImg object image into the in array. The first (red) component of the image value in column c and row r, image(c, r, 0), gets stored as the .x component at the corresponding position of in on line 18: in[r*w + c].x = inImage(c, r, 0);. Lines 19–20 store the green and blue components in a similar fashion.

- Line 24 calls the kernel wrapper sharpenParallel() to apply the sharpening stencil to the input data and store the results in out.

- Lines 27–33 copy our output data (stored in the array out) to the CImg object, image.

- Line 35 invokes the .save_bmp method (a function provided with the CImg object) to save the sharpened results in the standard portable bitmap (.bmp) format in a file named out.bmp.

- Line 36 frees the allocated arrays.

There is nothing notable in sharpen/kernel.h or sharpen/Makefile, so we can jump ahead to the kernel implementations.

Listing 5.12 sharpen/kernel.h

```
1 #ifndef KERNEL_H
2 #define KERNEL_H
3
4 struct uchar4;
5
6 void sharpenParallel(uchar4 *arr, int w, int h);
7 #endif
```

Listing 5.13 sharpen/Makefile

```
 1 NVCC = /usr/local/cuda/bin/nvcc
 2 NVCC_FLAGS = -Xcompiler -Wall
 3
 4 all: main.exe
 5
 6 main.exe: main.o kernel.o
 7    $(NVCC) $^ -o $@
 8
 9 main.o: main.cpp kernel.h
10    $(NVCC) $(NVCC_FLAGS) -c $< -o $@
11
12 kernel.o: kernel.cu kernel.h
13    $(NVCC) $(NVCC_FLAGS) -c $< -o $@
```

Now we arrive at our primary focus: the kernel implementations starting with the global memory version in Listing 5.14. We hope that kernel codes are starting to look somewhat familiar so that we can just mention a few notable new aspects:

- Lines 24–27 define the usual row, column, and flat indices. They also do bounds checking.

- Line 28 defines the size (width or height), $fltSz$, of the stencil. We use the prefix flt (as in **filter**) for stencil quantities.

- Lines 31–41 accumulate the stencil contributions as a nested for loop with indices cd and rd, which are the column displacement and row displacement from the central pixel to a specific pixel under the mask.

- Note that the input data is read from the d_in global memory array and written to the d_out global memory array.

Listing 5.14 sharpen/kernel.cu with global memory implementation

```
 1 #include "kernel.h"
 2 #define TX 32
 3 #define TY 32
 4 #define RAD 1
 5
 6 int divUp(int a, int b) { return (a + b - 1) / b; }
 7
 8 __device__
 9 unsigned char clip(int n) { return n > 255 ? 255 : (n < 0 ? 0 : n); }
10
11 __device__
12 int idxClip(int idx, int idxMax) {
13    return idx > (idxMax-1) ? (idxMax-1) : (idx < 0 ? 0 : idx);
14 }
15
```

```
16  __device__
17  int flatten(int col, int row, int width, int height) {
18    return idxClip(col, width) + idxClip(row, height)*width;
19  }
20
21  __global__
22  void sharpenKernel(uchar4 *d_out, const uchar4 *d_in,
23                       const float *d_filter, int w, int h) {
24    const int c = threadIdx.x + blockDim.x * blockIdx.x;
25    const int r = threadIdx.y + blockDim.y * blockIdx.y;
26    if ((c >= w) || (r >= h)) return;
27    const int i = flatten(c, r, w, h);
28    const int fltSz = 2*RAD + 1;
29    float rgb[3] = {0.f, 0.f, 0.f};
30
31    for (int rd = -RAD; rd <= RAD; ++rd) {
32      for (int cd = -RAD; cd <= RAD; ++cd) {
33        int imgIdx = flatten(c + cd, r + rd, w, h);
34        int fltIdx = flatten(RAD + cd, RAD + rd, fltSz, fltSz);
35        uchar4 color = d_in[imgIdx];
36        float weight = d_filter[fltIdx];
37        rgb[0] += weight*color.x;
38        rgb[1] += weight*color.y;
39        rgb[2] += weight*color.z;
40      }
41    }
42    d_out[i].x = clip(rgb[0]);
43    d_out[i].y = clip(rgb[1]);
44    d_out[i].z = clip(rgb[2]);
45  }
46
47  void sharpenParallel(uchar4 *arr, int w, int h) {
48    const int fltSz = 2 * RAD + 1;
49    const float filter[9] = {-1.0, -1.0, -1.0,
50                             -1.0,  9.0, -1.0,
51                             -1.0, -1.0, -1.0};
52
53    uchar4 *d_in = 0, *d_out = 0;
54    float *d_filter = 0;
55
56    cudaMalloc(&d_in, w*h*sizeof(uchar4));
57    cudaMemcpy(d_in, arr, w*h*sizeof(uchar4), cudaMemcpyHostToDevice);
58
59    cudaMalloc(&d_out, w*h*sizeof(uchar4));
60
61    cudaMalloc(&d_filter, fltSz*fltSz*sizeof(float));
62    cudaMemcpy(d_filter, filter, fltSz*fltSz*sizeof(float),
63               cudaMemcpyHostToDevice);
64
65    const dim3 blockSize(TX, TY);
66    const dim3 gridSize(divUp(w, blockSize.x), divUp(h, blockSize.y));
67
68    sharpenKernel<<<gridSize, blockSize>>>(d_out, d_in, d_filter, w, h);
69
70    cudaMemcpy(arr, d_out, w*h*sizeof(uchar4), cudaMemcpyDeviceToHost);
```

```
71    cudaFree(d_in);
72    cudaFree(d_out);
73    cudaFree(d_filter);
74 }
```

The second implementation is shown in Listing 5.15. Notable changes include the following:

- Creation of the shared array s_in on line 24.

- A tile of input data is loaded into the shared array on lines 36–61, including edge halo values on lines 50–60 and corner halo values on lines 40–49.

- The kernel launch on line 102 includes a third execution configuration parameter smSz that specifies the number of bytes of memory to allocate for the shared array.

Listing 5.15 sharpen/kernel.cu for shared memory input array

```
 1 #include "kernel.h"
 2 #define TX 32
 3 #define TY 32
 4 #define RAD 1
 5
 6 int divUp(int a, int b) { return (a + b - 1) / b; }
 7
 8 __device__
 9 unsigned char clip(int n) { return n > 255 ? 255 : (n < 0 ? 0 : n); }
10
11 __device__
12 int idxClip(int idx, int idxMax) {
13   return idx > (idxMax-1) ? (idxMax-1) : (idx < 0 ? 0 : idx);
14 }
15
16 __device__
17 int flatten(int col, int row, int width, int height) {
18   return idxClip(col, width) + idxClip(row, height)*width;
19 }
20
21 __global__
22 void sharpenKernel(uchar4 *d_out, const uchar4 *d_in,
23                     const float *d_filter, int w, int h) {
24   extern __shared__ uchar4 s_in[];
25   const int c = threadIdx.x + blockDim.x * blockIdx.x;
26   const int r = threadIdx.y + blockDim.y * blockIdx.y;
27   if ((c >= w) || (r >= h)) return;
28   const int i = flatten(c, r, w, h);
29   const int s_c = threadIdx.x + RAD;
30   const int s_r = threadIdx.y + RAD;
31   const int s_w = blockDim.x + 2*RAD;
32   const int s_h = blockDim.y + 2*RAD;
33   const int s_i = flatten(s_c, s_r, s_w, s_h);
```

```
34    const int fltSz = 2*RAD + 1;
35
36    // Regular cells
37    s_in[s_i] = d_in[i];
38
39    // Halo cells
40    if (threadIdx.x < RAD && threadIdx.y < RAD) {
41      s_in[flatten(s_c - RAD, s_r - RAD, s_w, s_h)] =
42        d_in[flatten(c - RAD, r - RAD, w, h)];
43      s_in[flatten(s_c + blockDim.x, s_r - RAD, s_w, s_h)] =
44        d_in[flatten(c + blockDim.x, r - RAD, w, h)];
45      s_in[flatten(s_c - RAD, s_r + blockDim.y, s_w, s_h)] =
46        d_in[flatten(c - RAD, r + blockDim.y, w, h)];
47      s_in[flatten(s_c + blockDim.x, s_r + blockDim.y, s_w, s_h)] =
48        d_in[flatten(c + blockDim.x, r + blockDim.y, w, h)];
49    }
50    if (threadIdx.x < RAD) {
51      s_in[flatten(s_c - RAD, s_r, s_w, s_h)] =
52        d_in[flatten(c - RAD, r, w, h)];
53      s_in[flatten(s_c + blockDim.x, s_r, s_w, s_h)] =
54        d_in[flatten(c + blockDim.x, r, w, h)];
55    }
56    if (threadIdx.y < RAD) {
57      s_in[flatten(s_c, s_r - RAD, s_w, s_h)] =
58        d_in[flatten(c, r - RAD, w, h)];
59      s_in[flatten(s_c, s_r + blockDim.y, s_w, s_h)] =
60        d_in[flatten(c, r + blockDim.y, w, h)];
61    }
62    __syncthreads();
63
64    float rgb[3] = {0.f, 0.f, 0.f};
65    for(int rd = -RAD; rd <= RAD; ++rd) {
66      for(int cd = -RAD; cd <= RAD; ++cd) {
67        const int s_imgIdx = flatten(s_c + cd, s_r + rd, s_w, s_h);
68        const int fltIdx = flatten(RAD + cd, RAD + rd, fltSz, fltSz);
69        const uchar4 color = s_in[s_imgIdx];
70        const float weight = d_filter[fltIdx];
71        rgb[0] += weight*color.x;
72        rgb[1] += weight*color.y;
73        rgb[2] += weight*color.z;
74      }
75    }
76    d_out[i].x = clip(rgb[0]);
77    d_out[i].y = clip(rgb[1]);
78    d_out[i].z = clip(rgb[2]);
79 }
80
81 void sharpenParallel(uchar4 *arr, int w, int h) {
82    const int fltSz = 2 * RAD + 1;
83    const float filter[9] = {-1.0, -1.0, -1.0,
84                             -1.0,  9.0, -1.0,
85                             -1.0, -1.0, -1.0};
86
87    uchar4 *d_in = 0, *d_out = 0;
88    float *d_filter = 0;
89
```

```
 90    cudaMalloc(&d_in, w*h*sizeof(uchar4));
 91    cudaMemcpy(d_in, arr, w*h*sizeof(uchar4), cudaMemcpyHostToDevice);
 92
 93    cudaMalloc(&d_out, w*h*sizeof(uchar4));
 94
 95    cudaMalloc(&d_filter, fltSz*fltSz*sizeof(float));
 96    cudaMemcpy(d_filter, filter, fltSz*fltSz*sizeof(float),
 97              cudaMemcpyHostToDevice);
 98
 99    const dim3 blockSize(TX, TY);
100    const dim3 gridSize(divUp(w, TX), divUp(h, TY));
101    const size_t smSz = (TX+2*RAD)*(TY+2*RAD)*sizeof(uchar4);
102    sharpenKernel<<<gridSize, blockSize, smSz>>>(d_out, d_in, d_filter,
103                                                 w, h);
104
105    cudaMemcpy(arr, d_out, w*h*sizeof(uchar4), cudaMemcpyDeviceToHost);
106    cudaFree(d_in);
107    cudaFree(d_out);
108    cudaFree(d_filter);
109 }
```

The third version shown in Listing 5.16 creates a shared memory array for both reading input and writing output. The fact that only one shared array can be created leads to the bit of trickery that appears on lines 35–37 and 106.

Listing 5.16 sharpen/kernel.cu with input and output shared memory arrays

```
 1 #include "kernel.h"
 2 #define TX 32
 3 #define TY 32
 4 #define RAD 1
 5
 6 int divUp(int a, int b) { return (a + b - 1) / b; }
 7
 8 __device__
 9 unsigned char clip(int n) { return n > 255 ? 255 : (n < 0 ? 0 : n); }
10
11 __device__
12 int idxClip(int idx, int idxMax) {
13   return idx > (idxMax-1) ? (idxMax-1) : (idx < 0 ? 0 : idx);
14 }
15
16 __device__
17 int flatten(int col, int row, int width, int height) {
18   return idxClip(col, width) + idxClip(row, height)*width;
19 }
20
21 __global__
22 void sharpenKernel(uchar4 *d_out, const uchar4 *d_in,
23                    const float *d_filter, int w, int h) {
24   const int c = threadIdx.x + blockDim.x * blockIdx.x;
25   const int r = threadIdx.y + blockDim.y * blockIdx.y;
26   if ((c >= w) || (r >= h)) return;
```

```
27    const int i = flatten(c, r, w, h);
28    const int s_c = threadIdx.x + RAD;
29    const int s_r = threadIdx.y + RAD;
30    const int s_w = blockDim.x + 2*RAD;
31    const int s_h = blockDim.y + 2*RAD;
32    const int s_i = flatten(s_c, s_r, s_w, s_h);
33    const int fltSz = 2*RAD + 1;
34
35    extern __shared__ uchar4 s_block[];
36    uchar4 *s_in = s_block;
37    uchar4 *s_out = &s_block[s_w*s_h];
38
39    // Regular cells
40    s_in[s_i] = d_in[i];
41
42    // Halo cells
43    if (threadIdx.x < RAD && threadIdx.y < RAD) {
44      s_in[flatten(s_c - RAD, s_r - RAD, s_w, s_h)] =
45        d_in[flatten(c - RAD, r - RAD, w, h)];
46      s_in[flatten(s_c + blockDim.x, s_r - RAD, s_w, s_h)] =
47        d_in[flatten(c + blockDim.x, r - RAD, w, h)];
48      s_in[flatten(s_c - RAD, s_r + blockDim.y, s_w, s_h)] =
49        d_in[flatten(c - RAD, r + blockDim.y, w, h)];
50      s_in[flatten(s_c + blockDim.x, s_r + blockDim.y, s_w, s_h)] =
51        d_in[flatten(c + blockDim.x, r + blockDim.y, w, h)];
52    }
53    if (threadIdx.x < RAD) {
54      s_in[flatten(s_c - RAD, s_r, s_w, s_h)] =
55        d_in[flatten(c - RAD, r, w, h)];
56      s_in[flatten(s_c + blockDim.x, s_r, s_w, s_h)] =
57        d_in[flatten(c + blockDim.x, r, w, h)];
58    }
59    if (threadIdx.y < RAD) {
60      s_in[flatten(s_c, s_r - RAD, s_w, s_h)] =
61        d_in[flatten(c, r - RAD, w, h)];
62      s_in[flatten(s_c, s_r + blockDim.y, s_w, s_h)] =
63        d_in[flatten(c, r + blockDim.y, w, h)];
64    }
65    __syncthreads();
66
67    float rgb[3] = {0.f, 0.f, 0.f};
68    for(int rd = -RAD; rd <= RAD; ++rd) {
69      for(int cd = -RAD; cd <= RAD; ++cd) {
70        const int s_imgIdx = flatten(s_c + cd, s_r + rd, s_w, s_h);
71        const int fltIdx = flatten(RAD + cd, RAD + rd, fltSz, fltSz);
72        const uchar4 color = s_in[s_imgIdx];
73        const float weight = d_filter[fltIdx];
74        rgb[0] += weight*color.x;
75        rgb[1] += weight*color.y;
76        rgb[2] += weight*color.z;
77      }
78    }
79
80    const int s_outIdx = threadIdx.y*blockDim.x + threadIdx.x;
81    s_out[s_outIdx].x = clip(rgb[0]);
```

```
82      s_out[s_outIdx].y = clip(rgb[1]);
83      s_out[s_outIdx].z = clip(rgb[2]);
84
85      __syncthreads();
86      d_out[i] = s_out[s_outIdx];
87   }
88
89   void sharpenParallel(uchar4 *arr, int w, int h) {
90      const int fltSz = 2 * RAD + 1;
91      const float filter[9] = {-1.0, -1.0, -1.0,
92                               -1.0,  9.0, -1.0,
93                               -1.0, -1.0, -1.0};
94      uchar4 *d_in = 0, *d_out = 0;
95      float *d_filter = 0;
96
97      cudaMalloc(&d_in, w*h*sizeof(uchar4));
98      cudaMemcpy(d_in, arr, w*h*sizeof(uchar4), cudaMemcpyHostToDevice);
99      cudaMalloc(&d_out, w*h*sizeof(uchar4));
100     cudaMalloc(&d_filter, fltSz*fltSz*sizeof(float));
101     cudaMemcpy(d_filter, filter, fltSz*fltSz*sizeof(float),
102               cudaMemcpyHostToDevice);
103
104     const dim3 blockSize(TX, TY);
105     const dim3 gridSize(divUp(w, TX), divUp(h, TY));
106     const size_t smSz = ((TX+2*RAD)*(TY+2*RAD)+(TX*TY))*sizeof(uchar4);
107     sharpenKernel<<<gridSize, blockSize, smSz>>>(d_out, d_in, d_filter,
108                                                  w, h);
109     cudaMemcpy(arr, d_out, w*h*sizeof(uchar4), cudaMemcpyDeviceToHost);
110     cudaFree(d_in);
111     cudaFree(d_out);
112     cudaFree(d_filter);
113  }
```

A single shared array s_block is created of size smSz, but now the kernel launcher sharpenParallel() increases the allocated size, as specified on line 106. The number of uchar4 variables is now set to be the sum of the number of pixels in the input tile, ((TX+2*RAD)*(TY+2*RAD)), and the number of pixels in the output tile (TX*TY). Lines 36 and 37 divide up s_block to create the illusion of separate shared arrays for input and output.

On line 36, uchar4 *s_in = s_block creates a pointer to the beginning of the shared array, and on line 37 uchar4 *s_out = &s_block[s_w*s_h] creates a pointer at the entry beyond what is needed to store the tile of input data. With this set up, we can write the code as if s_in and s_out are separate arrays, and some pointer arithmetic going on in the background makes it all work. On lines 81–83, the output pixel value is written to shared memory, and __syncthreads() is called to make sure all the output values are written to s_out in shared memory before the shared output array contents are copied to d_out in global memory. After the kernel has completed, the results are transferred from d_out back to the host array arr from where CImg can construct and write the output image file.

That completes the tour of the code, and it is time to build and run the app and inspect the results. (Be sure to include a copy of butterfly.bmp and CImg.h in the project directory before compiling the app.) We chose an input image butterfly.bmp that is shown along with the sharpened output image in Figure 5.4. The images show a giant owl butterfly, and sharpening produces noticeable enhancement of the vein structure in the wings.

Test the sharpen app and verify that all three versions produce the same output image. After verifying that the results are consistent, let's compare performance.

We'll generate the performance information using the NVIDIA Visual Profiler (NVVP). A detailed introduction to NVVP can be found in Appendix D, "CUDA Practicalities: Timing, Profiling, Error Handling, and Debugging." Start NVVP, open a New Session, and fill in the entry for File: with the full path to the executable you want to profile. You also need to fill in a Working Directory: giving the path to the folder where the input image is stored if the executable and the image are in different folders.

Profiling Tip

To ward off possible errors, you should insert the line cudaDeviceReset(); at the end of your application (above return 0;) and rebuild before profiling with NVVP.

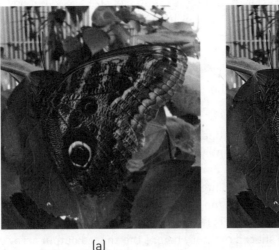

(a)   (b)

Figure 5.4 Images of a giant owl butterfly: (a) original and (b) sharpened

Profiling results of the global memory version of the `sharpen` app are shown in Figure 5.5, where the first warning sign (in both the `Properties` tab at top-right and the `Analysis` tab at the bottom) deals with `Low Global Memory Load Efficiency`, which is our cue that a shared memory implementation may improve memory transfer efficiency.

Profiling results of the shared input array version of the `sharpen` app are shown in Figure 5.6. The Properties tab shows that `Global Store Efficiency` is now 83.7%, up from 59.1%. The kernel `Duration` of 292.232 μs represents a 20% decrease from the previous value of 345.993 μs.

The Results tab no longer shows the `Low Global Memory Load Efficiency` warning, but there is still a `Low Global Memory Store Efficiency`

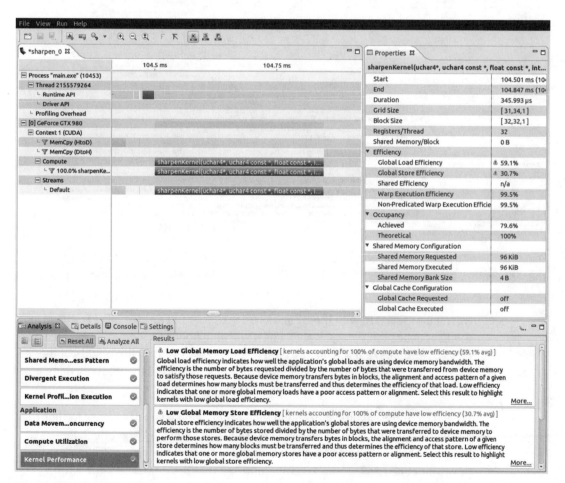

Figure 5.5 Visual Profiler results for the global memory implementation of the `sharpen` app

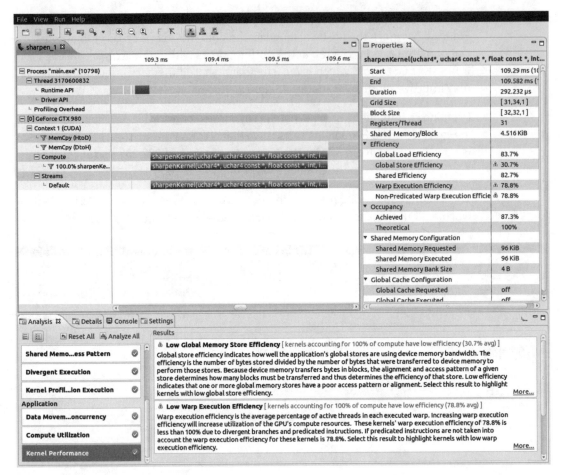

Figure 5.6 Profiling results for the `sharpen` app implementation that loads input data into a shared memory array

warning associated with the `Global Store Efficiency` of 30.7% shown in the Properties tab. There is also a new warning about `Low Warp Execution Efficiency` of 78.8%. This warning has to do with storing the results of the kernel computation, and using shared memory to store the output provides a possible approach for resolving this warning.

Let's look at the results of profiling the kernel using shared memory for both input and output data, as shown in Figure 5.7, to determine the effectiveness of this approach. In the `Analysis` tab, at the bottom of the Visual Profiler window, select `Kernel Performance` and see that the `Results` pane shows a check mark on a green background along with the `No Issues` message.

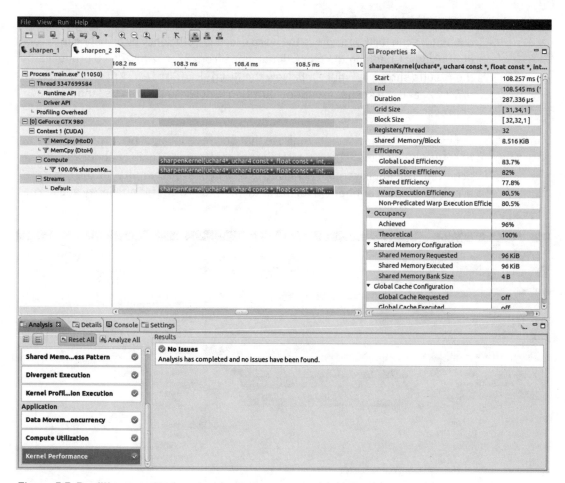

Figure 5.7 Profiling results for `sharpenKernel()` with shared memory for both input and output data

The efficiencies in the Properties tab are now all above warning levels. The duration of kernel execution has also decreased further to 287.336 μs, but this is only about a 2% improvement over the time for the shared input array implementation.

The net result is that, rather than having to do a global memory store for each output element, the system can increase memory store efficiency by bundling multiple elements of the output data into a single memory transaction.

Another warning from the shared input array profiling session involved `Low Warp Execution Efficiency` (78.8%). The shared input/output version raised the warp execution efficiency to 80.5% and eliminated that warning. It turns out that we can further improve the warp execution efficiency by adjusting the block dimensions. Changing the block dimensions from 32 × 32 to 128 × 8 produces the results shown in Figure 5.8. Now the `Warp Execution Efficiency` is up to 92.9%, and the kernel execution duration is down to 281.704 µs (another ~2% improvement).

Overall, the profiling results indicate that between using shared memory and adjusting block dimensions, a total kernel performance gain of about 25% was achieved. The improvement achieved by use of shared memory for the input array was significant both in terms of the memory transfer efficiency and kernel

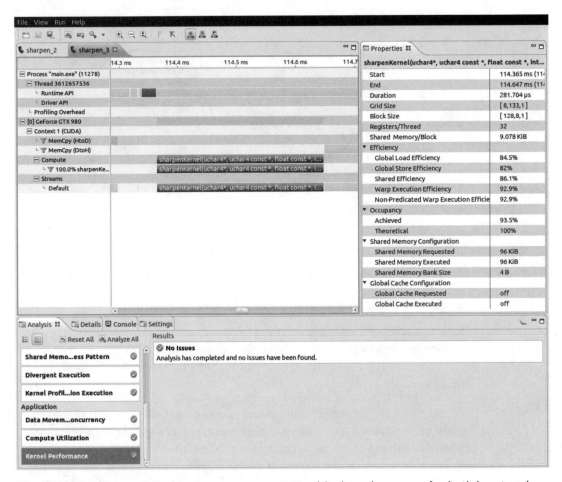

Figure 5.8 Profiling results for `sharpenKernel()` with shared memory for both input and output data and block dimensions of 128 × 8

timing measurements. Using shared memory for the output array produced a significant increase in global store efficiency but only small improvement in kernel duration. In this case, we achieved some small gains by increasing the width of the block. However, tuning the execution configuration parameters is an empirical process; experimentation is required to determine what block dimensions work best for a particular system and input data, and a reasonable way to generate candidate block dimensions is to start by choosing values of `blockDim.x` that are multiples of 32.

Summary

In this chapter, we have looked at the situation in which computational threads, rather than being completely independent, need to cooperate with neighboring threads in the grid. We formulated uniform interaction with neighboring threads as a stencil computation, and we implemented code for three applications: computation of derivatives from sampled values of a function (`dd_1d_global` and `dd_1d_shared`), solving Laplace's equation for steady-state temperature distribution via Jacobi iteration (`heat_2d`), and enhancing edges in an image (`sharpen`). We presented initial implementations using only arrays stored in global memory and then showed how to adjust the implementation to take advantage of shared memory. We finished up by using NVIDIA Visual Profiler (NVVP) to inspect the performance of three different versions of the kernel for the `sharpen` app: one with only global memory arrays, one with a shared input array, and one with a shared input/output array. We saw that, for the specific case of the sample image, execution parameters, and GPU used for execution during profiling, loading the input data into shared memory produced significant improvements in both global load efficiency and kernel duration. Further use of shared memory for storing or transferring the output data produced a significant improvement in global store efficiency, but only a small decrease in kernel duration. Finally, additional small improvements were obtained by adjusting block dimensions.

This points out one of the realities of optimizing code: The performance enhancement may not scale with the time and effort that goes into the optimization. It often pays to stop and think about the expected costs and potential benefits before embarking on a major optimization effort. Remember that SIMT parallelism scales reasonably well, so sometimes the right answer is simply acquiring additional processors. You should also be aware of Amdahl's law, which limits the amount of speedup S that can be achieved by parallelization from 1 to N processors:

$$S(N) = \frac{1}{(1-P) + P/N}$$

where P is the fraction of the total computation that can be parallelized. For example, if 90% of the computing task can be parallelized, then even with infinitely many processors, 10% of the job needs to happen serially and the maximum achievable speedup due to parallelization is 10x.

Suggested Projects

1. Embellish the heat_2d app by

   a. Using the 9-point Laplacian stencil:

   $$\left(\frac{1}{20}\right) \begin{bmatrix} 1 & 4 & 1 \\ 4 & -20 & 4 \\ 1 & 4 & 1 \end{bmatrix}$$

   b. Using a larger Laplacian stencil

   c. Importing an image and segmenting or thresholding it to create a very irregular region on which to impose boundary conditions

2. The heat_2d app provides visualization of the output and an iteration counter, but what would you propose as a reasonable measure of convergence to steady state? What would it take to implement your criterion?

3. Experiment with the sharpen app and see how the following changes affect performance (as measured using Visual Profiler):

   a. Choose sample images of different sizes.

   b. Change the execution parameters (i.e., block size and grid size).

   c. Choose alternate stencils of different sizes.

References

[1]   NVIDIA Corporation. "CUDA C Programming Guide," NVIDIA Developer Zone, CUDA Toolkit Documentation, 2015, http://docs.nvidia.com/cuda/cuda-c-programming-guide/index.html#abstract.

[2]   Mark Harris, "GPU Pro Tip: CUDA 7 Streams Simplify Concurrency." *Parallel Forall* (blog), 2015, http://devblogs.nvidia.com/parallelforall/gpu-pro-tip-cuda-7-streams-simplify-concurrency/.

[3]   Randall J. LeVeque, *Finite Difference Methods for Ordinary and Partial Differential Equations* (Philadelphia, PA: SIAM, 2007).

[4]   David Tschumperlé, The CImg Library, 2015. http://cimg.eu.

Chapter 6

Reduction and Atomic Functions

In this chapter we deal with computations where all of the threads interact to contribute to a single output. Many such computations lead to a pattern known as **reduction**, which involves an input array whose elements are combined until a single output value is obtained. Applications include dot products (a.k.a. inner products or scalar products), image similarity measures, integral properties, and (with slight generalization) histograms.

Threads Interacting Globally

In Chapter 5, "Stencils and Shared Memory," we took the first serious step toward dealing with interaction between computational threads, but stencil computations only involve local interactions between threads that are nearby in the grid. Now we are ready to deal with computations where all of the threads interact to contribute to the output.

As we prepare to move forward from interactions between nearby threads that arise in stencil computations to more general thread interactions, there are a few questions that deserve considered answers before proceeding:

Q: Do reduction computations arise in real applications?

A: Yes, they arise frequently. Dot products may begin with term-wise multiplication, but they end by summing the contributions from each of those products;

every entry contributes to that sum, so the operation is a reduction. Matrices can be thought of as lists of vectors, so matrix-vector and matrix-matrix multiplications involve reductions. Inertial properties (e.g., centroids and moments of inertia) that are obtained by summing contributions from mass elements involve reductions.

Q: Do reductions arise related to any of the applications we have already seen?

A: Again, yes. When we solved for steady-state heat distribution using Jacobi iteration, we just started the iteration and let it run toward steady state. At the end of the chapter, one of the projects asked about stopping criterion: How do you tell that the current state is close to equilibrium so the computation can be terminated? The usual approach is to stop the computation once further iterations do not produce a significant change in the array of temperature values. Determining whether the change is significant requires a measure of the change in the temperature array. Whether you use the L^2-norm (in other words the multidimensional Pythagorean formula where elements are combined by squaring and adding) or the L^∞-norm (where elements are combined by comparing and taking the larger absolute value), all the elements can interact to contribute to the outcome, and the computation required includes a reduction.

Q: If reductions are so common, why is it that the sample code in the CUDA 7.5 Visual Studio template just does an element-wise operation (addition)?

A: The element-wise operation is the part that is easy to parallelize. With no interaction at all between threads, it is sometimes termed **embarrassingly parallel**. Yes, we could change the element-wise operation from addition to multiplication and almost have a dot product; all that is left is to sum the results of the element-wise products, but that turns out to be the more challenging part to parallelize.

Q: If reductions are important, shouldn't there be code libraries that provide reduction implementations that I can use?

A: Yes, there are library implementations of reductions available for your use. In this chapter we provide enough background so you can implement your own reductions. We discuss using libraries for this purpose in Chapter 8, "Using CUDA Libraries," and you can go there directly if you are in urgent need of reduction capabilities.

With the Q&A out of the way, let's jump into implementing some particular reductions starting with the dot product.

Implementing `parallel_dot`

We begin by creating an app called `parallel_dot` to parallelize computation of the dot (or inner or scalar) product of a pair of input vectors. The input vectors, a and b, will be stored as two arrays of equal length N, and the output will be a single scalar quantity (stored in the variable res) equal to the sum of the products of the corresponding elements:

$$res = \sum_{idx=0}^{N-1} a\big[idx\big]*b\big[idx\big]$$

Since every element contributes to res, this is a classic reduction (perhaps *the* classic reduction). Any reduction requires a variable (like res) to accumulate the contributions from all of the threads. In CUDA's SIMT model of parallelism, a variable created in a thread (and stored in a register) is not accessible by any other thread. A variable declared as __shared__ (and stored in shared memory for the block) is not accessible to any thread outside of the block. To escape these limitations, the reduction will need an accumulator variable that is declared outside the kernel and stored in global memory.

A completely naïve approach would have each thread read a pair of corresponding elements from the input arrays in global memory, multiply them together, and add the result to the value stored in the global accumulator variable d_res (the device version of the result that will get copied to res on the host side when we are all done). If you are starting to develop some feel for the CUDA world, the description of that approach should cause, if not fear and loathing, at least mild aversion. Yes, the input data has to be read from global memory once; there is no getting around that. However, there is no good reason that every thread should have to write its result to global memory. The global memory traffic can be greatly reduced by taking a tiled approach in which we break the large input vectors up into block-sized pieces and only update d_res once per block (instead of once per thread). The simplest version of the plan goes as follows:

- Create a shared memory array to store the product of corresponding entries in the tiles of the input arrays.

- Synchronize to ensure that the shared array is completely filled before proceeding.

- Assign one thread (e.g., with `threadIdx.x == 0`) to loop over the shared array (whose data is accessible by any thread in the block) to accumulate the contribution from the block into a register variable `blockSum`.

- Perform one global memory transaction (for the whole block) to add blockSum to the value stored in the global accumulator d_res.

The kernel for a shared memory implementation of the dot product kernel dotKernel() and the wrapper function dotLauncher() are shown in Listing 6.1. As usual, we include the header file and the standard input/output library, and then we define constant values including TPB (the number of threads per block) and ATOMIC, which we will get to shortly. The kernel starts with the usual global and shared index computations and bounds check on lines 8–10. The shared array s_prod is declared on line 12. (The s_ reminds us that the array is shared, and prod indicates that it will hold the product of the corresponding elements of the input arrays.) The entries of the input arrays at the global index position are multiplied, and the product is stored as the local index entry of s_prod on line 13. On line 14, __syncthreads() ensures that s_prod has been fully populated before any thread proceeds further. The way we've set things up, only the first thread (with threadIdx.x == 0) needs to proceed further. It initializes the register variable blockSum = 0 on line 17, then loops over the range of the shared array index incrementing blockSum by the values stored in s_prod on lines 16–20. We've included a print statement on line 21 so you can check the blockSum values and see explicitly that the blocks do not execute in any particular order. While the accumulation within the block can be performed in a more parallel fashion, let's hold off on discussion of such optional embellishments until we've created and tested an initial implementation of parallel_dot.

Finally, on lines 23–26, the block's contribution, blockSum, is added to the value stored in the global accumulator d_res. Note that what really happens here is a read-add-store sequence of operations, and it is coded up to be performed in two very different ways depending on the value of ATOMIC set in the #define directive. With #define ATOMIC 0, regular addition occurs. With #define ATOMIC 1, the function atomicAdd(d_res, blockSum) is called to increase the value of d_res by the amount blockSum. Let's look at the other files needed for the project and then perform test runs to see how things work.

Listing 6.1 parallel_dot/kernel.cu including dotKernel() and the wrapper function dotLauncher()

```
1 #include "kernel.h"
2 #include <stdio.h>
3 #define TPB 64
4 #define ATOMIC 1 // 0 for non-atomic addition
5
6 __global__
7 void dotKernel(int *d_res, const int *d_a, const int *d_b, int n) {
8   const int idx = threadIdx.x + blockDim.x * blockIdx.x;
9   if (idx >= n) return;
```

```
10    const int s_idx = threadIdx.x;
11
12    __shared__ int s_prod[TPB];
13    s_prod[s_idx] = d_a[idx] * d_b[idx];
14    __syncthreads();
15
16    if (s_idx == 0) {
17      int blockSum = 0;
18      for (int j = 0; j < blockDim.x; ++j) {
19        blockSum += s_prod[j];
20      }
21      printf("Block_%d, blockSum = %d\n", blockIdx.x, blockSum);
22      // Try each of two versions of adding to the accumulator
23      if (ATOMIC) {
24        atomicAdd(d_res, blockSum);
25      } else {
26        *d_res += blockSum;
27      }
28    }
29  }
30
31  void dotLauncher(int *res, const int *a, const int *b, int n) {
32    int *d_res;
33    int *d_a = 0;
34    int *d_b = 0;
35
36    cudaMalloc(&d_res, sizeof(int));
37    cudaMalloc(&d_a, n*sizeof(int));
38    cudaMalloc(&d_b, n*sizeof(int));
39
40    cudaMemset(d_res, 0, sizeof(int));
41    cudaMemcpy(d_a, a, n*sizeof(int), cudaMemcpyHostToDevice);
42    cudaMemcpy(d_b, b, n*sizeof(int), cudaMemcpyHostToDevice);
43
44    dotKernel<<<(n + TPB - 1)/TPB, TPB>>>(d_res, d_a, d_b, n);
45    cudaMemcpy(res, d_res, sizeof(int), cudaMemcpyDeviceToHost);
46
47    cudaFree(d_res);
48    cudaFree(d_a);
49    cudaFree(d_b);
50  }
```

The code for the header file `kernel.h` is shown in Listing 6.2. It consists of the include guard along with the prototype for the wrapper function `dotLauncher()` so it can be called from `main()`.

Listing 6.2 `parallel_dot/kernel.h`

```
1  #ifndef KERNEL_H
2  #define KERNEL_H
3
4  void dotLauncher(int *res, const int *a, const int *b, int n);
5
6  #endif
```

The `main.cpp` for the `parallel_dot` app is shown in Listing 6.3. It starts with declarations for `cpu_res` (which stores the CPU reference result), `gpu_res` (which stores the GPU result), and pointers to the input arrays `a` and `b` on lines 9–10. The input array storage is allocated and initialized (with all elements having value 1 to keep things simple) on lines 9–16. The serial reference result is computed and printed to the console on lines 18–21. The kernel wrapper function `dotLauncher()` is called on line 23 and the result of the parallel GPU computation is printed to the console on line 24. We finish up by freeing the memory allocated for the input arrays.

Listing 6.3 `parallel_dot/main.cpp`

```
 1 #include "kernel.h"
 2 #include <stdio.h>
 3 #include <stdlib.h>
 4 #define N 1024
 5
 6 int main() {
 7   int cpu_res = 0;
 8   int gpu_res = 0;
 9   int *a = (int*)malloc(N*sizeof(int));
10   int *b = (int*)malloc(N*sizeof(int));
11
12   //Initialize input arrays
13   for (int i = 0; i < N; ++i) {
14     a[i] = 1;
15     b[i] = 1;
16   }
17
18   for (int i = 0; i < N; ++i) {
19     cpu_res += a[i] * b[i];
20   }
21   printf("cpu result = %d\n", cpu_res);
22
23   dotLauncher(&gpu_res, a, b, N);
24   printf("gpu result = %d\n", gpu_res);
25
26   free(a);
27   free(b);
28   return 0;
29 }
```

The Makefile for compiling the app in Linux is given in Listing 6.4.

Listing 6.4 `parallel_dot/Makefile`

```
 1 NVCC = /usr/local/cuda/bin/nvcc
 2 NVCC_FLAGS = -g -G -Xcompiler -Wall
 3
 4 all: main.exe
 5
```

```
6 main.exe: main.o kernel.o
7    $(NVCC) $^ -o $@
8
9 main.o: main.cpp kernel.h
10    $(NVCC) $(NVCC_FLAGS) -c $< -o $@
11
12 kernel.o: kernel.cu kernel.h
13    $(NVCC) $(NVCC_FLAGS) -c $< -o $@
```

Once again, we've gone through all the code, and it is time to build and execute the app.

The parameter values in the code specify that the input vectors have 1,024 entries (each of which is 1) and there are 64 threads in each block, so when you execute the app, you should get a manageable amount of output: one line for the CPU reference result, one line to give the index and sum for each block, and one line with the GPU result. Moreover, the values should be recognizable: each block should sum to 64 and the final result should be 1,024.

Now, let's change line 4 of parallel_dot/kernel.cu to #define ATOMIC 0. Rebuild the app and run it to see what happens. Your results should resemble the sample output from parallel_dot shown in Figure 6.1, and there a few salient features worth noting. In the first line we see that the CPU correctly computed that the dot product of two vectors each consisting of 1,024 entries of 1 is 1,024. In the next 16 lines, we see that each block of length 64 computed

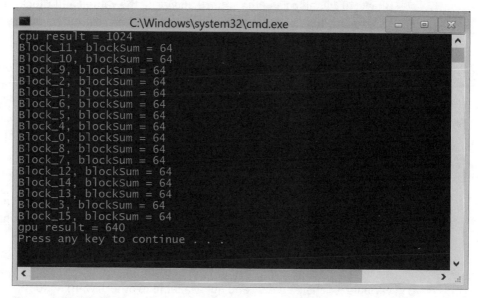

Figure 6.1 Initial output from the parallel_dot app

the correct contribution to the dot product, and we are reminded that the blocks execute in an order over which we have no control. In the next to last line, we get the news that, while each block computed the correct contribution, the global accumulator does not end up with the expected value of 1,024. Instead it ends up, in this case, with 640—that is, 10 × 64 instead of 16 × 64—so it appears that the contributions from six of the blocks got lost. (Note that simply re-executing the app can produce both different block execution orders and different values of gpu_res. Try running your app repeatedly and observing the variety of values returned.)

What exactly is going wrong? Thread 0 in each of the 16 blocks reads a value of d_res from global memory, adds its value of blockSum, and stores the result back into the memory location where d_res is stored. The problem is that the outcome of these operations depends on the sequence in which they are performed, and we do not have control of that sequence.

To be concrete, let's consider just Block_11 (with blockIdx.x == 11) and Block_10 (with blockIdx.x == 10), which happened to be the first two blocks to execute according to the output in Figure 6.1. Block_11 happened to execute first, and its thread 0 read a value of 0 for d_res. That same thread 0 in Block_11 will add its blockSum of 64 and store the value 0 + 64 = 64 back in the memory location of d_res. The thread 0 in Block_10 is also following the same instructions, but not in a way that is synchronized with Block_11. If Block_10 happens to read the value of d_res before Block_11 finishes updating the value, then Block_10 will also read the value 0 and write the value 64. If Block_10 happens to read the value of d_res after Block_11 finishes writing the updated value, then Block_10 reads 64 and writes 128.

This situation, in which the outcome of a computation depends on the order of operations whose sequencing is uncontrollable, is called a **race condition**, and the race conditions result in **undefined behavior**. To cure the race condition problem, we need to take back some control of the order of operations—in this case, to make sure that once a particular thread engages a global accumulator (e.g., to perform a read-modify-write operation sequence), no other thread can engage the global accumulator until the other thread has completed its operation sequence.

CUDA's feature for dealing with race conditions is a group of functions called **atomic functions**. The word *atom* comes from Ancient Greek, meaning uncuttable or indivisible. An atomic function performs a read-modify-write sequence of operations as an indivisible unit by a mechanism that resembles the classic library book lending model. When an atomic operation reads a value, that variable is "checked out" and not available to others wanting to read it. When the modify-write part of the operation sequence is complete, the variable is "returned" to the stacks where it is once again accessible to another reader.

The good news is that atomic operations do provide a cure for our race condition problem. The bad news is that there is a cost: Atomic operations force some serialization and slow things down a bit. This is a good time for another reminder that obtaining incorrect results fast does not constitute computational acceleration. Atomics should be used as needed to get things right, and beyond that, use of atomics should be avoided.

Now that we've proposed atomics as a solution to the race condition problem, let's test it out by reverting to #define ATOMIC 1 on line 4 of parallel_dot/kernel.cu. Rebuild your app and run it, and you should see a result similar to Figure 6.2, which shows the correct result of 1,024. You should run the app several times to convince yourself that the correct answer is produced reliably.

While atomicAdd() served our needs in this case, CUDA offers 10 other atomic functions: atomicSub(), atomicExch(), atomicMin(), atomicMax(), atomicInc(), atomicDec(), atomicCAS() (where **CAS** stands for compare and swap), and the three bitwise functions atomicAnd(), atomicOr(), and atomicXor(). Refer to the CUDA C Programming Guide for details [1].

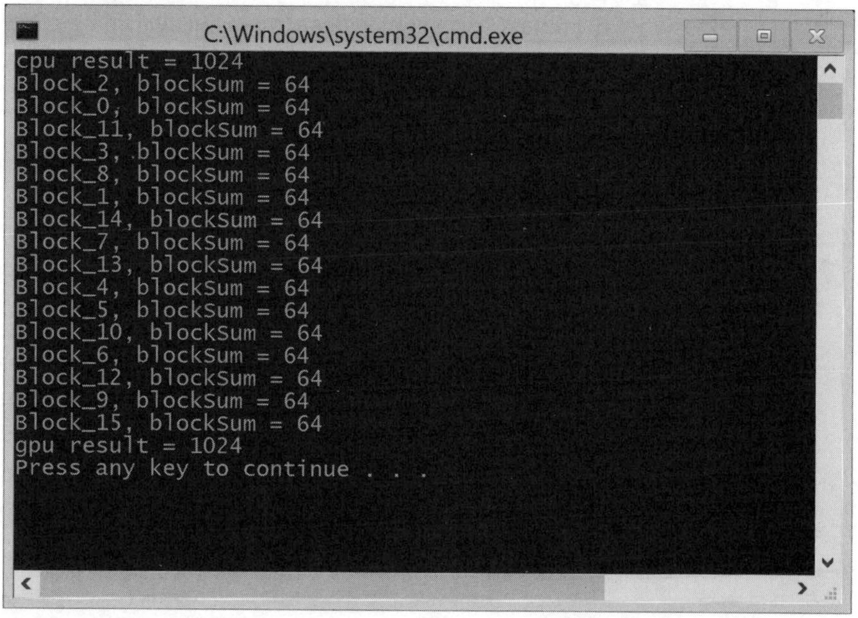

Figure 6.2 Correct output from the parallel_dot app using atomicAdd()

A Floating-Point Caution

Note that standard definition of reduction involves an associative 2-input, 1-output operator that nicely describes how we normally think of addition. However, floating-point addition is only approximately associative; the exact result from summing a `float` array depends on the order of operations, and changing the order of summation can have a big impact when your sum includes terms with large differences in magnitude. This is not a numerical analysis book, so we won't get into all the details (see, e.g., "What Every Computer Scientist Should Know About Floating-Point Arithmetic" by David Goldberg [2]), but this does explain why we chose input arrays of type `int` for our first example.

Computing Integral Properties: `centroid_2d`

In this section we apply atomic operations to perform a reduction in 2D. In particular, we will take as input an image of an object on a white background region. (We'll choose our object to be a state map, but you can apply the app to the images of your choice, and the background region will be referred to as the exterior of the object.) The centroid is simply the average location of a pixel in the object. However, we can also think of the centroid as a weighted average location of all the pixels in the entire image, where the weighting factor is the occupancy function:

$$\chi_{col,row} = \begin{cases} 0, & \{col,row\} \in exterior \\ 1, & \{col,row\} \in interior \end{cases}$$

The column coordinate of the centroid, $\bar{c}$, is obtained as the sum over all the pixels of the weight times the column index divided by the sum of the weights, and similar thinking applies to the row coordinate, $\bar{r}$. (Since we are using $\bar{c}$ and $\bar{r}$ as centroid coordinates, we'll call the column and row indices col and row.) The centroid coordinates are then given by

$$\bar{c} = \frac{\sum_{row}\sum_{col}\chi_{col,row}*col}{\sum_{row}\sum_{col}\chi_{col,row}}, \quad \bar{r} = \frac{\sum_{row}\sum_{col}\chi_{col,row}*row}{\sum_{row}\sum_{col}\chi_{col,row}}$$

where the sums are over all pixels; that is, col from 0 to width-1 and row from 0 to height-1.

The implementation of the centroid_2d app includes the usual kernel, header, and main files, as shown in Listings 6.5, 6.6, and 6.7. Since the app needs to read and write images, the app also includes CImg.h, the header file for the image-processing package introduced with the sharpen app in Chapter 5, "Stencils and Shared Memory."

Let's start by looking at Listing 6.5, which includes code for centroidKernel() and the wrapper function centroidParallel().

Listing 6.5 centroid_2d/kernel.cu

```
1  #include "kernel.h"
2  #include <stdio.h>
3  #include <helper_math.h>
4  #define TPB 512
5
6  __global__
7  void centroidKernel(const uchar4 *d_img, int *d_centroidCol,
8                      int *d_centroidRow, int *d_pixelCount,
9                      int width, int height) {
10   __shared__ uint4 s_img[TPB];
11
12   const int idx = threadIdx.x + blockDim.x * blockIdx.x;
13   const int s_idx = threadIdx.x;
14   const int row = idx/width;
15   const int col = idx - row*width;
16
17   if ((d_img[idx].x < 255 || d_img[idx].y < 255 ||
18       d_img[idx].z < 255) && (idx < width*height)) {
19     s_img[s_idx].x = col;
20     s_img[s_idx].y = row;
21     s_img[s_idx].z = 1;
22   }
23   else {
24     s_img[s_idx].x = 0;
25     s_img[s_idx].y = 0;
26     s_img[s_idx].z = 0;
27   }
28   __syncthreads();
29
30   // for (int s = 1; s < blockDim.x; s *= 2) {
31   //     int index = 2*s*s_idx;
32   //     if (index < blockDim.x) {
33   //         s_img[index] += s_img[index+s];
34   //     }
35   //     __syncthreads();
36   // }
37
38   for (int s = blockDim.x/2; s > 0; s >>= 1) {
39     if (s_idx < s) {
```

```
40         s_img[s_idx] += s_img[s_idx + s];
41      }
42      __syncthreads();
43    }
44
45    if (s_idx == 0) {
46      atomicAdd(d_centroidCol, s_img[0].x);
47      atomicAdd(d_centroidRow, s_img[0].y);
48      atomicAdd(d_pixelCount, s_img[0].z);
49    }
50 }
51
52 void centroidParallel(uchar4 *img, int width, int height) {
53    uchar4 *d_img = 0;
54    int *d_centroidRow = 0, *d_centroidCol = 0, *d_pixelCount = 0;
55    int centroidRow = 0, centroidCol = 0, pixelCount = 0;
56
57    // Allocate memory for device array and copy from host
58    cudaMalloc(&d_img, width*height*sizeof(uchar4));
59    cudaMemcpy(d_img, img, width*height*sizeof(uchar4),
60               cudaMemcpyHostToDevice);
61
62    // Allocate and set memory for three integers on the device
63    cudaMalloc(&d_centroidRow, sizeof(int));
64    cudaMalloc(&d_centroidCol, sizeof(int));
65    cudaMalloc(&d_pixelCount, sizeof(int));
66    cudaMemset(d_centroidRow, 0, sizeof(int));
67    cudaMemset(d_centroidCol, 0, sizeof(int));
68    cudaMemset(d_pixelCount, 0, sizeof(int));
69
70    centroidKernel<<<(width*height + TPB - 1)/TPB, TPB>>>(d_img,
71        d_centroidCol, d_centroidRow, d_pixelCount, width, height);
72
73    // Copy results from device to host.
74    cudaMemcpy(&centroidRow, d_centroidRow, sizeof(int),
75               cudaMemcpyDeviceToHost);
76    cudaMemcpy(&centroidCol, d_centroidCol, sizeof(int),
77               cudaMemcpyDeviceToHost);
78    cudaMemcpy(&pixelCount, d_pixelCount, sizeof(int),
79               cudaMemcpyDeviceToHost);
80
81    centroidCol /= pixelCount;
82    centroidRow /= pixelCount;
83
84    printf("Centroid: {col = %d, row = %d} based on %d pixels\n",
85           centroidCol, centroidRow, pixelCount);
86
87    // Mark the centroid with red lines
88    for (int col = 0; col < width; ++col) {
89      img[centroidRow*width + col].x = 255;
90      img[centroidRow*width + col].y = 0;
91      img[centroidRow*width + col].z = 0;
92    }
93    for (int row = 0; row < height; ++row) {
94      img[row*width + centroidCol].x = 255;
95      img[row*width + centroidCol].y = 0;
```

```
 96        img[row*width + centroidCol].z = 0;
 97    }
 98
 99    // Free the memory allocated
100    cudaFree(d_img);
101    cudaFree(d_centroidRow);
102    cudaFree(d_centroidCol);
103    cudaFree(d_pixelCount);
104 }
```

The kernel definition starts with declaration of a shared array s_img and the usual 1D indices: idx for the array in global memory and s_idx for the array in shared memory. row and col are derived from the 1D index (not from 2D kernel launch parameters) and get used only in assignments in lines 19–20. In fact, a 1D kernel launch is sufficient (and convenient). What changes as we move up to 2D is that we need to accumulate contributions for two coordinates rather than one. We also need the sum of the weights (which in this case is equivalent to the count of interior, nonwhite pixels) in the computation of each coordinate, so we accumulate three sums (contributions to the row sum, contributions to the column sum, and contributions to the pixel count). To accommodate the three sums, we could use three separate arrays, but here we choose to have a single array s_img of type uint4. The first component s_img[].x stores the column contributions; the second component s_img[].y stores the row contributions; and the third component s_img[].z stores the pixel count contributions. (We only need to store three quantities, so we could use uint3, but we choose uint4 because it allows for immediate generalization to 3D centroids and two uint4 variables use 32 bytes of memory, which is a convenient size for efficient memory transactions.)

In lines 17–18 pixel indices and color values are tested. If the pixel index idx lies beyond the input array or the image pixel corresponding to this index is white, it is treated as an outside pixel (and the value 0 is stored in each of the x, y, and z channels). Otherwise, the pixel's contribution is added to the shared memory block. A call to __syncthreads() ensures that all the values to be summed for the block are stored in the shared array before any thread proceeds with summing.

What remains is to sum the contributions in the shared array and increment the global accumulators using atomic operations to avoid race conditions. In the dot product example, we took the very simple and entirely serial approach of choosing a particular thread to compute the sum for the block. We mentioned that more parallel (and more efficient) approaches are available, and in fact, there are a lot of them. In a single, now well-known presentation from 2007, Mark Harris demonstrated seven increasingly efficient (and tricky) embellishments [3]. If you have a GPU with compute capability 3.0 or higher (based on the

Kepler architecture), there is a whole other set of tricks available for efficient reductions, as detailed in a recent post on the *Parallel Forall* blog [4]. Here we are not assuming Kepler architecture, and we limit ourselves to just two of the effective techniques available on pre-Kepler GPUs. Lines 30–36 (which are commented out, but available for you to experiment with) implement a first approach to parallel summation within the block. The basic idea is to have every other thread (corresponding to a **stride** of 2) increment its value at its own index by the value at the neighboring index. After synchronizing threads, we then double the stride to 4 and have every fourth thread increment the value at its index with the value 2 positions higher. We continue synchronizing, doubling the stride, and summing while the stride is less than the block size. Upon termination of the loop, the block sum resides at index 0, and that value can be added to the global accumulator using `atomicAdd()`. This approach makes significant progress by reducing the number of sequential steps required to sum over a block from $O(\texttt{blockDim.x})$ to $O(\log(\texttt{blockDim.x}))$ but comes up short on efficiency of memory access. (For details of big-O notation, see [5].)

Lines 38–43 show an implementation that is more efficient in terms of memory access. It does a similar set of pairwise sums, but instead of summing neighbors and storing the results spaced apart in the array, it sums entries spaced apart in the array and stores the results in neighboring locations. Please see [4] for further refinements. (Note that the sums involve `uint4` variables, and `helper_math.h` is included to provide the definitions of arithmetic on vector variables. Be prepared to take a little extra care at build time to make sure this code gets properly incorporated.)

Lines 52–104 give the implementation of the wrapper function `centroid-Parallel()` that prepares for and calls the kernel launch. We hope that such things are starting to look less surprising, and that there are just a few items worthy of special note. Lines 53–54 declare the pointers to the image data and to the three accumulator variables in global device memory. Line 55 declares the host variables to which the results will be copied. That is followed by various memory operations to allocate and initialize the necessary global memory for the input data and global accumulator variables. Lines 70–71 launch the kernel; as mentioned above, the notable feature is that a 1D kernel launch is all that is required. Lines 74–85 copy the results back to the host and print a summary to the command window. Lines 88–97 use the red channel to create vertical and horizontal axes through the centroid location in the output image, and the kernel concludes by freeing up the allocated memory.

The header file `centroid_2d/kernel.h`, shown in Listing 6.6, consists of the forward declaration of a CUDA built-in vector type and the prototype for the centroidParallel() function that is called in main.cpp, which is shown in Listing 6.7.

Listing 6.6 centroid_2d/kernel.h

```
1  #ifndef KERNEL_H
2  #define KERNEL_H
3
4  struct uchar4;
5
6  void centroidParallel(uchar4 *img, int width, int height);
7
8  #endif
```

The file centroid_2d/main.cpp, shown in Listing 6.7, begins with the usual #include and #define directives and uses the CImg library for importing and exporting images, as we did in Chapter 5, "Stencils and Shared Memory." The centroidParallel() function call is the wrapper function that calls the kernel function centroidKernel(), and once the kernel call is complete, it saves the resulting image.

Listing 6.7 centroid_2d/main.cpp

```
1   #include "kernel.h"
2   #define cimg_display 0
3   #include "CImg.h"
4   #include <cuda_runtime.h>
5
6   int main()
7   {
8     // Initializing input and output images
9     cimg_library::CImg<unsigned char> inImage("wa_state.bmp");
10    cimg_library::CImg<unsigned char> outImage(inImage, "xyzc", 0);
11    int width = inImage.width();
12    int height = inImage.height();
13
14    // Initializing uchar array for image processing
15    uchar4 *imgArray = (uchar4*)malloc(width*height*sizeof(uchar4));
16
17    // Copying CImg data to image array
18    for (int row = 0; row < height; ++row) {
19      for (int col = 0; col < width; ++col) {
20        imgArray[row*width + col].x = inImage(col, row, 0);
21        imgArray[row*width + col].y = inImage(col, row, 1);
22        imgArray[row*width + col].z = inImage(col, row, 2);
23      }
24    }
25
26    centroidParallel(imgArray, width, height);
27
28    // Copying image array to CImg
29    for (int row = 0; row < height; ++row) {
30      for (int col = 0; col < width; ++col) {
```

```
31          outImage(col, row, 0) = imgArray[row*width + col].x;
32          outImage(col, row, 1) = imgArray[row*width + col].y;
33          outImage(col, row, 2) = imgArray[row*width + col].z;
34      }
35   }
36
37   outImage.save("wa_state_out.bmp");
38   free(imgArray);
39 }
```

The `main()` function should present few, if any, new features, aside from spec-ifying an input file corresponding to a map of the State of Washington. You can choose a different input file, but whatever you choose needs to be copied into the project folder. The Makefile for compiling the app in Linux, shown in Listing 6.8, is set up to make sure that the `common/inc` directory from the CUDA Samples is included to provide access to `helper_math.h`.

To successfully build and run the app in Visual Studio, you need to add the input image file to the project using `PROJECT ⇒ Add Existing Item` and make one change in the Project Properties pages. Click on the `sharpen` project in the Solution Explorer and select `PROJECT ⇒ Properties ⇒ Configuration Properties ⇒ C/C++ ⇒ General ⇒ Additional Include Directories` and edit the list to include the CUDA Samples' `common\inc` directory. Its default install location is `C:\ProgramData\ NVIDIA Corporation\CUDA Samples\v7.5\common\inc`.

Once again, we've gone through all the code, and it is time to build and execute the app.

Listing 6.8 `centroid_2d/Makefile`

```
 1 NVCC = /usr/local/cuda/bin/nvcc
 2 NVCC_FLAGS = -g -G -Xcompiler -Wall
 3 INC = -I/usr/local/cuda/samples/common/inc
 4
 5 all: main.exe
 6
 7 main.exe: main.o kernel.o
 8    $(NVCC) $^ -o $@
 9
10 main.o: main.cpp kernel.h
11    $(NVCC) $(NVCC_FLAGS) $(INC) -c $< -o $@
12
13 kernel.o: kernel.cu kernel.h
14    $(NVCC) $(NVCC_FLAGS) $(INC) -c $< -o $@
```

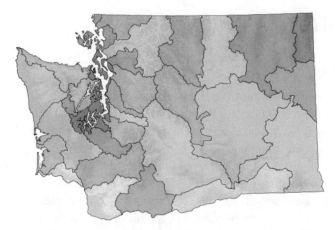

Figure 6.3 Input image showing watershed regions of Washington State. (Map courtesy of United States Geological Survey. http://wa.water.usgs.gov/data/realtime/adr/interactive/index2.html)

The sample input image, a map showing the watershed boundaries in the State of Washington, is shown in Figure 6.3. The results printed to command window indicate that the centroid, based on contributions from 504,244 pixels, is located at column 530 and row 317.

Finally, the output image showing axes through the centroid is shown in Figure 6.4. The computed state centroid lies in southern Chelan County a few miles west of Wenatchee, which agrees nicely with the accepted location.

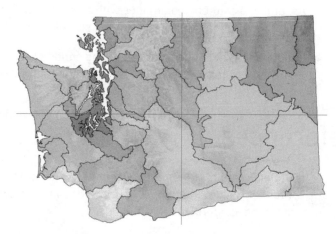

Figure 6.4 Output image with axes locating the centroid

Summary

In this chapter, we took on the problem of computing a reduction in which all the threads in a computational grid can contribute to a result. We started by implementing the dot product, perhaps the ultimate in recognizable applications of reduction. We used shared memory for computing the contribution from a thread block, introduced the issue of race conditions, and presented atomic functions as a means to deal with them. We also extended the reduction implementation to compute image centroids, and saw that a 1D computational grid suffices to handle this problem despite its 2D context. In each case, we implemented the reduction from scratch, but reduction implementations are also provided in standard code libraries including NVIDIA's Thrust library. See Chapter 8, "Using CUDA Libraries," for an alternative implementation of centroid_2d using the Thrust library.

Suggested Projects

1. A common reduction involves finding the maximum or minimum value in a list. Modify the parallel_dot app to create an L_inf app that computes the maximum absolute value of the entries in an array.

2. Explore how the execution time for a reduction varies with the block size chosen for the kernel launch.

3. Assemble a collection of images with a range of sizes, and plot how the centroid computation times vary with the size of the image.

4. Implement a reduction-based stopping condition for the iterations in the heat_2d app from Chapter 5, "Stencils and Shared Memory."

References

[1] NVIDIA Corporation, "CUDA C Programming Guide," NVIDIA Developer Zone, CUDA Toolkit Documentation, 2015, http://docs.nvidia.com/cuda/cuda-c-programming-guide/index.html#abstract.

[2]   David Goldberg, "What Every Computer Scientist Should Know About Floating-Point Arithmetic." *Computing Surveys*, March 1991, http://docs.oracle.com/cd/E19957-01/806-3568/ncg_goldberg.html.

[3]   Mark Harris, *Optimizing Parallel Reduction in CUDA*, NVIDIA. https://docs.nvidia.com/cuda/samples/6_Advanced/reduction/doc/reduction.pdf.

[4]   Justin Luitjens, "Faster Parallel Reductions on Kepler," *Parallel Forall* (blog), 2014. http://devblogs.nvidia.com/parallelforall/faster-parallel-reductions-kepler/.

[5]   Paul E. Black. "Big-O Notation." National Institute of Standards and Technology (NIST), 2012, http://www.nist.gov/dads/HTML/bigOnotation.html.

Chapter 7

Interacting with 3D Data

In this chapter, we move up to apps that involve generating, visualizing, and interacting with data on a 3D grid. A common approach to visualization of any function of three variables starts by sampling the function on a grid, so almost any 3D contour plot produces a 3D data grid at some point in the process. In addition, 3D data grids are produced either experimentally or numerically by a variety of devices and in a wide variety of applications, including the following:

- Volumetric medical scanners such as computed tomography (CT) and positron emission tomography (PET) systems. CT scans are also used for inspection of manufactured parts.

- Direct numerical simulation (DNS) of fluid dynamics, including aerodynamics and hydrodynamics.

- Laser Doppler velocimetry (LDV) experimental measurements of fluid velocity fields.

- Seismic exploration methods in geology and geophysics.

- Ground-penetrating radar systems used in archaeology and civil/environmental engineering.

- Creating physical parts from image stacks using digital light projection (DLP) 3D printing systems.

- Video processing (where the third dimension corresponds to time).

We will begin our 3D experience by launching a parallel computation to sample the values of a function on a 3D grid, and we will see that launching a 3D kernel involves only very minor extensions of what we did to launch 2D kernels in Chapter 4, "2D Grids and Interactive Graphics." Once we can create 3D grids, we move on to consider visualization and interaction. Given the fundamental constraint that your display device (and your vision system) are 2D, we present methods (slicing, volume rendering, and raycasting) to derive 2D images that we can view and interact with by again using the `flashlight` app as a template for CUDA/OpenGL interop. The procedure presented in Chapter 4, "2D Grids and Interactive Graphics," for modifying the `flashlight` template involved three steps:

- In `kernel.cu`, customize the kernel that computes the image to display.

- In `interactions.h`, customize the callback functions that specify the actions associated with input from the keyboard and mouse, and provide the user with an interaction guide.

- In `main.cpp`, modify the name and arguments of the kernel call in the `render()` function, and add a statement to display some useful information in the graphics window title bar.

Here we will do the same thing and add one additional modification: calling for the launch of the 3D kernel to generate the data set to be visualized. By the end of the chapter you will be producing screen images of the kind illustrated in Figure 7.1, but with more interesting data sets.

With that plan in mind, let's get right to coding things, starting with the 3D kernel launch.

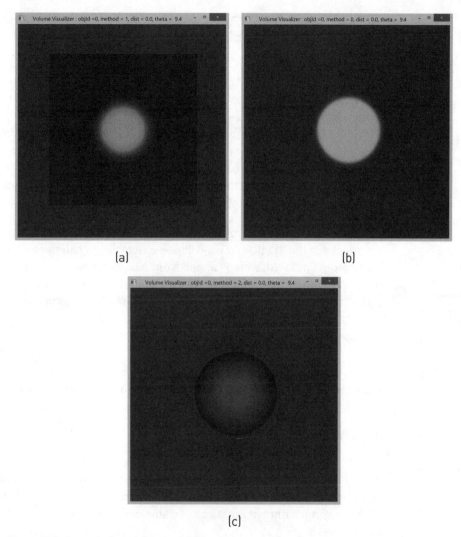

Figure 7.1 Sample images of a 3D distance field (inside a bounding box) produced using the visualization methods provided by `vis_3d`: (a) slicing, (b) volume rendering, and (c) raycasting

Launching 3D Computational Grids: dist_3d

The approach to 3D grids involves a small extension of that for 2D grids, so we will present the idea with similar context and language. In Chapter 4, "2D Grids and Interactive Graphics," we used the context of image processing where the meaningful indices were c for the column number and r for row number of a pixel in image. As we move from 2D to 3D, we expand our context from a single image composed of 2D rectangular pixels (short for picture elements) to an image stack composed of 3D **voxels** (short for volume elements).

In addition to the row and column indices, we need a new integer variable to index the images in the stack, and we will use s (which you can think of as being short for **stratum** or **stack**), which ranges from 0 to D-1, where D is the **depth** of the stack. We compute the row and column indices exactly as before (using the x and y components of CUDA's built-in dimension and index variables blockDim, blockIdx, and threadIdx), and the stratum index is computed based on the z components:

```
int s = blockIdx.z * blockDim.z + threadIdx.z;
```

Since each row of each image has w voxels and each stratum has w*h voxels, the index for storing voxel data in the 1D output array becomes:

```
int i = c + r*w + s*w*h;
```

We also need 3D grid launch parameters, so in addition to TX and TY (which specify the number of threads across a block in the width and height directions), we introduce TZ, the number of threads spanning a block in the depth direction. All three components of the dim3 variable are now used to define the number of threads per block:

```
dim3 blockSize(TX, TY, TZ);
```

and all three dimensions of the grid are divided up to specify gridSize as

```
dim3 gridSize(divUp(W, TX), divUp(H, TY), divUp(D, TZ));
```

where the divUp() function performs the usual trick to ensure that the number of blocks is rounded up so the entire grid is covered by threads.

Listing 7.1 shows the pieces assembled to create an app that computes a 3D grid of distances from a reference point. (We have again started with the simple example of computing a grid of values corresponding to distances from a reference point. However, we will use this kernel almost verbatim, replacing `distance()` with a function that computes a shading value, in the 3D visualization app.)

Listing 7.1 `dist_3d/kernel.cu`, the app that performs parallel computation of a 3D grid of distances from a reference point

```
1  #define W 32
2  #define H 32
3  #define D 32
4  #define TX 8 // number of threads per block along x-axis
5  #define TY 8 // number of threads per block along y-axis
6  #define TZ 8 // number of threads per block along z-axis
7
8  int divUp(int a, int b) { return (a + b - 1)/b; }
9
10 __device__
11 float distance(int c, int r, int s, float3 pos) {
12   return sqrtf((c - pos.x)*(c - pos.x) + (r - pos.y)*(r - pos.y) +
13                (s - pos.z)*(s - pos.z));
14 }
15
16 __global__
17 void distanceKernel(float *d_out, int w, int h, int d, float3 pos) {
18   const int c = blockIdx.x * blockDim.x + threadIdx.x; // column
19   const int r = blockIdx.y * blockDim.y + threadIdx.y; // row
20   const int s = blockIdx.z * blockDim.z + threadIdx.z; // stack
21   const int i = c + r*w + s*w*h;
22   if ((c >= w) || (r >= h) || (s >= d)) return;
23   d_out[i] = distance(c, r, s, pos); // compute and store result
24 }
25
26 int main() {
27   float *out = (float*)calloc(W*H*D, sizeof(float));
28   float *d_out = 0;
29   cudaMalloc(&d_out, W*H*D*sizeof(float));
30   const float3 pos = {0.0f, 0.0f, 0.0f}; // set reference position
31   const dim3 blockSize(TX, TY, TZ);
32   const dim3 gridSize(divUp(W, TX), divUp(H, TY), divUp(D, TZ));
33   distanceKernel<<<gridSize, blockSize>>>(d_out, W, H, D, pos);
34   cudaMemcpy(out, d_out, W*H*D*sizeof(float), cudaMemcpyDeviceToHost);
35   cudaFree(d_out);
36   free(out);
37   return 0;
38 }
```

We hope that you now find the majority of this code to be familiar looking and readable, but there are a few things that arise in the 3D setting and are worth pointing out:

- We use `calloc` to create the host array `out` rather than attempting static array creation by `float out[W*H*D] = {0.0};` because the storage needed for a 3D grid of nontrivial size is likely to produce a stack overflow error.

- Note that block size specifications `TX`, `TY`, and `TZ` have smaller values. That is because there is a hard limit of 1,024 threads in a single block (for GPUs with compute capability between 2.0 and 5.2), so an 8 × 8 × 8 block has a viable number of threads (512), but a 16 × 16 × 16 block would require 4,096 threads and cannot be successfully launched. Generally, there is no special reason for blocks to be cubic, and you may find performance advantages in choosing blocks for which `blockDim.x` is a multiple of 32; for example, `dim3 gridSize(32, 4, 4)` is viable and may offer practical advantages.

- The reference position, `pos`, now has type `float3`, and the column, row, and stratum indices of the corresponding voxel, `pos.x`, `pos.y`, and `pos.z`, appear in the 3D Pythagorean equation.

- Bounds checking is done in all directions, and threads beyond the extent of the grid simply return without performing any computation:

```
if ((c >= w) || (r >= h) || (s >= d)) return;
```

That covers the basics of a 3D kernel launch, so it is time to build and execute the `dist_3d` app and then use the debugging tools to convince yourself the output is as desired. (See Suggested Project 1 at the end of the chapter for more detailed suggestions.) Note that the Makefile needed for building this project in Linux is exactly the same as the one you used for the `dist_2d` app.

Viewing and Interacting with 3D Data: vis_3d

As noted at the beginning of this chapter, current display technology is typically 2D, so we will focus our discussion of viewing and interaction on deriving 2D images that convey meaningful information about the 3D data set. The 2D display and interaction can then be accomplished using the `flashlight` app as our template for OpenGL interop. So while the 3D data set is computed by launching a

3D kernel, our viewing of and interaction with images will involve a 2D kernel launch to compute shading data for the pixels in a 2D image.

Need-to-Know?

You may well ask what it is about the visualization issue that qualifies as need-to-know. Admittedly, very little new CUDA-specific material appears in this section. However, a big part of our goal here is to communicate the relevance and useful-ness of CUDA to the broader engineering community, and this is perhaps the best opportunity to do so. If you have ever started up a 3D contour plot in your favorite software package and been frustrated by the time required to see the results (or the lag to update the display when you change the viewing direction), then this is a need-to-know opportunity to experience the power of GPU-based parallel com-puting with graphics interoperability.

To establish how images are produced from a 3D data set, we adopt a basic model that mimics what actually happens in x-ray or fluoroscopic imaging. There is a point source that emits rays that pass through the 3D data set and arrive at a planar sensor consisting of a 2D array of pixels. We'll adopt radiology-style language and refer to the 3D data values as **densities** and the 2D array of pixel values as **intensities**. Each pixel's intensity value is determined by the density values encountered along the ray (or directed line segment) from the source to the location of that pixel. The distinction between different viewing methods lies in the details of how the shading value gets computed from the density data along the ray, and we will look at three distinct approaches:

- Slicing: We choose a plane that cuts through the data stack and compute the shading based on the density value where the ray hits the plane (or display a background value if the ray misses the plane).

- Volume rendering: We compute the shading value based on integrating the density contributions along the ray as it passes through the data stack.

- Raycasting: We consider the density function as an implicit model of a 3D object and choose a threshold value corresponding to the object's surface. We find where the ray first hits the object's surface (i.e., where the density reaches the threshold value) and compute the shading based on the prop-erties of the density function at the surface point. We'll stick with the simple model of Lambertian reflectance for which the shading depends on the angle between the view direction and the surface normal. (The components of the normal correspond to derivatives of the density and are computed using finite difference approximations.)

Now we arrive at the fundamental question in any parallel computing exercise: How do we identify pieces of our overall mission with the job of a single computational thread? Here we continue with the model employed in the `flashlight` app by assuming that each thread computes the intensity value for a single pixel. (This approach is chosen for clarity of exposition. You may be able to enhance performance by having each thread perform the computation for multiple rays and/or multiple pixels.)

Each of the methods listed above involves a computation along the part of the ray that passes through the box containing the data stack, so let's begin our look at implementation with the ray-box intersection test. Rather than reinventing the wheel, let's take advantage of a small chunk of existing code that does exactly this task and can be readily found in the `volumeRender` app in the 2_Graphics folder in the CUDA Samples, which in turn refer to a set of SIGGRAPH notes [1]. All we really need is a slightly modified form of the function `intersectBox()` and the simple data structure `Ray` that it employs to represent a directed line segment, as shown in Listing 7.2. The ray structure has two `float3` components: The `.o` component is the starting point of the ray, and the `.d` component is the direction of the ray.

Listing 7.2 The `Ray` structure, the linear interpolation function `paramRay()`, and the ray-box intersection test `intersectBox()`

```
typedef struct {
  float3 o, d; // origin and direction
} Ray;

__device__ float3 paramRay(Ray r, float t) { return r.o + t*(r.d); }

// intersect ray with a box from volumeRender SDK sample
__device__ bool intersectBox(Ray r, float3 boxmin, float3 boxmax,
  float *tnear, float *tfar) {
  // compute intersection of ray with all six bbox planes
  const float3 invR = make_float3(1.0f)/r.d;
  const float3 tbot = invR*(boxmin - r.o), ttop = invR*(boxmax - r.o);
  // re-order intersections to find smallest and largest on each axis
  const float3 tmin = fminf(ttop, tbot), tmax = fmaxf(ttop, tbot);
  // find the largest tmin and the smallest tmax
  *tnear = fmaxf(fmaxf(tmin.x, tmin.y), fmaxf(tmin.x, tmin.z));
  *tfar = fminf(fminf(tmax.x, tmax.y), fminf(tmax.x, tmax.z));
  return *tfar > *tnear;
}
```

A directed line segment from point p_0 to p_1 can be described by the parametric ray formula $p(t) = p_0 + t * (p_0 - p_1)$ with t varying over the interval [0,1]. In terms of a `Ray` structure (let's call it `pixRay`), p_0 gets stored in `pixRay.o` and $(p_1 - p_0)$

gets stored in `pixRay.d`. We can declare and initialize the ray from the source point (a `float3` variable named `source`) to a pixel location (a `float3` variable named `pix`) with the following code snippet:

```
Ray pixRay;
pixRay.o = source;
pixRay.d = pix - source;
```

The box containing the data, more specifically an **axis-aligned bounding box (AABB)**, is specified by the lower-left-front corner (given by `float3 boxmin`) and the upper-right-back corner (given by `float3 boxmax`). Inputs to the `intersectBox()` function include the ray description, `pixRay`; an AABB (described by `boxmin` and `boxmax`); and the pointers to two locations that can store `float` variables `tnear` and `tfar` (the parameter values at which the ray enters and exits the box). Note that the return type of `intersectBox()` is `bool`. A return value of `false` indicates that the ray-box intersection test failed (i.e., the ray missed the box). If the ray hits the box, the value `true` is returned, and the entry and exit parameter values get stored in `tnear` and `tfar`. We can then perform linear interpolation along `pixRay` using the `paramRay()` function with parameter values `tnear` and `tfar` to find the points `near` and `far` where the ray enters and leaves the box.

Our plan for computing a shading value for a pixel then goes as follows:

- Compute the coordinates of `pix` and declare/initialize `pixRay`.

- Perform the ray-box intersection test:

  - If the ray misses the box, display a background shading value.

  - If the ray hits the box, create a clipped ray (called `boxRay`) that extends from `near` to `far`, and call a specialized rendering function to compute the shading based on `boxRay`, the image stack of density data, and other necessary inputs.

Now we are ready to look at the details of the shading functions. We'll present code snippets for each function, then assemble them with code based on `flashlight` to produce full listings for all the files in the `vis_3d` app.

SLICING

We'll start with slice visualization because it involves the simplest computation along the ray. A slice plane is chosen to reveal a section through the density image stack. If the clipped ray, `boxRay`, intersects the slice plane, the shading value returned is determined by the density value at the ray-plane intersection point. If boxRay does not intersect the slice plane, then a background shading value is returned. (We have chosen this background color to be different from the general background displayed at pixels whose ray misses the box entirely so that the outline of the data box is visible.)

Note that the ray-plane intersection point will most likely not lie precisely on a grid point, so interpolation will be needed to estimate the density at a nongrid point based on values at nearby grid points.

To simplify the coordinate transformation bookkeeping, let's choose to work in a reference frame attached to the 3D image stack. More specifically, let's put the origin at the center of the central voxel and align the axes with the voxel index directions so that a voxel row lies parallel to the x-axis and a voxel column lies parallel to the y-axis (so an image in the stack lies parallel to the xy-plane). The z-direction corresponds to changing stratum (i.e., moving between images in the stack). In this frame, the value at position $\{x, y, z\} = \{0, 0, 0\}$ is associated with the voxel having indices $\{c_o, r_o, s_o\} = \{\lfloor W/2 \rfloor, \lfloor H/2 \rfloor, \lfloor D/2 \rfloor\}$. (Note that these are intended as integer division operations so the bracketed quantities are rounded down and $\{c_o, r_o, s_o\}$ have integer values.) We can then transform from spatial coordinates to image stack coordinates by a simple translation:

$$c = x + c_o$$
$$r = y + r_o$$
$$s = z + s_o$$

We then need to determine the density value at a position corresponding to pos. If the components of pos have integer values that correspond to the indices of a voxel $\{c, r, s\}$, then the value of interest can be retrieved from the density array dens. If pos corresponds to a position inside the box but not on the grid of data points, then we'll return a value obtained by trilinear interpolation between the values at the surrounding grid points. The integer parts of the coordinates provide the indices of the lower-left-front grid point of the voxel, and the fractional parts, which are the components of the remainder, enable interpolation between the values at the corners of the voxel.

The actual code for determining the density value (by accessing the neighboring grid values and performing the trilinear interpolation) is shown in Listing 7.3. Index increments along the coordinate directions are provided by dx, dy, and dz to help locate the density values at the corners of the surrounding voxel whose name is dens concatenated with a 3-digit binary number identifying a corner of the voxel (e.g., dens000 is the value at lower-left-front corner, and dens111 is the value at the upper-right-back corner). The formula at the end is simply what results from successive linear interpolations along the coordinate directions. It may be a bit long, but we will get to reuse it when implementing the other visualization methods that follow.

Listing 7.3 Computing the density values from a 3D grid of data (or image stack) by clipping beyond the data box and interpolating within the data box

```
__device__ int clipWithBounds(int n, int n_min, int n_max) {
  return n > n_max ? n_max : (n < n_min ? n_min : n);
}

__device__ float density(float *d_vol, int3 volSize, float3 pos) {
  int3 index = posToVolIndex(pos, volSize);
  int i = index.x, j = index.y, k = index.z;
  const int w = volSize.x, h = volSize.y, d = volSize.z;
  const float3 rem = fracf(pos);
  index = make_int3(clipWithBounds(i, 0, w - 2),
    clipWithBounds(j, 0, h - 2), clipWithBounds(k, 0, d - 2));
  // directed increments for computing the gradient
  const int3 dx = {1, 0, 0}, dy = {0, 1, 0}, dz = {0, 0, 1};
  // values sampled at surrounding grid points
  const float dens000 = d_vol[flatten(index, volSize)];
  const float dens100 = d_vol[flatten(index + dx, volSize)];
  const float dens010 = d_vol[flatten(index + dy, volSize)];
  const float dens001 = d_vol[flatten(index + dz, volSize)];
  const float dens110 = d_vol[flatten(index + dx + dy, volSize)];
  const float dens101 = d_vol[flatten(index + dx + dz, volSize)];
  const float dens011 = d_vol[flatten(index + dy + dz, volSize)];
  const float dens111 = d_vol[flatten(index + dx + dy + dz, volSize)];
  // trilinear interpolation
  return (1 - rem.x)*(1 - rem.y)*(1 - rem.z)*dens000 +
    (rem.x)*(1 - rem.y)*(1 - rem.z)*dens100 +
    (1 - rem.x)*(rem.y)*(1 - rem.z)*dens010 +
    (1 - rem.x)*(1 - rem.y)*(rem.z)*dens001 +
    (rem.x)*(rem.y)*(1 - rem.z)*dens110 +
    (rem.x)*(1 - rem.y)*(rem.z)*dens101 +
    (1 - rem.x)*(rem.y)*(rem.z)*dens011 +
    (rem.x)*(rem.y)*(rem.z)*dens111;
}
```

With clipping and interpolation in hand, the `sliceShader()` function is pretty straightforward. The code is shown in Listing 7.4 along with some supporting functions:

- `planeSDF()` gives the signed distance from a point to a plane specified by a normal vector (`float3 norm`) and a distance from the origin (`float dist`).

- `rayPlaneIntersect()` performs the ray-plane intersection test. If `planeSDF()` returns values with opposite signs at the ray endpoints, then the ray intersects the plane, `rayPlaneIntersect()` returns `true`, and the intersection parameter value `at` is stored in `t`. If the plane does not cut the ray, `rayPlaneIntersect()` returns `false`.

Listing 7.4 `sliceShader()` along with supporting functions `planeSDF()` and `rayPlaneIntersect()`

```
__device__ float planeSDF(float3 pos, float3 norm, float d) {
  return dot(pos, normalize(norm)) - d;
}

__device__
bool rayPlaneIntersect(Ray myRay, float3 n, float dist, float *t) {
  const float f0 = planeSDF(paramRay(myRay, 0.f), n, dist);
  const float f1 = planeSDF(paramRay(myRay, 1.f), n, dist);
  bool result = (f0*f1 < 0);
  if (result) *t = (0.f - f0) / (f1 - f0);
  return result;
}

__device__ uchar4 sliceShader(float *d_vol, int3 volSize, Ray boxRay,
  float gain, float dist, float3 norm) {
  float t;
  uchar4 shade = make_uchar4(96, 0, 192, 0); // background value
  if (rayPlaneIntersect(boxRay, norm, dist, &t)) {
    float sliceDens = density(d_vol, volSize, paramRay(boxRay, t));
    shade = make_uchar4(48, clip(-10.f * (1.0f + gain) * sliceDens),
                        96, 255);
  }
  return shade;
}
```

The inputs to the `sliceShader()` function include the following:

- A pointer to the array of density data named `float *d_vol` to remind us that it should be a pointer to a device array

- The dimensions of the image stack, `int3 volSize`

- The `Ray`, `boxRay`

- A float variable `gain` that enables adjusting the shading intensity

- The distance `float dist` and normal vector `float3 norm` specifying the slice plain

The `sliceShader()` function simply invokes the ray-plane intersection test and either returns a default value `boxBackground` (if the test fails) or computes the green color component as a function of the density at `slicePoint` where the ray intersects the plane, according to

```
shade.y = clip(-10.f * (1.0f + gain) * sliceDens);
```

where `sliceDens` is the density value at `slicePt`, `gain` is a multiplier for adjusting the intensity, and `clip()` converts the result to a `uchar` in the allowed range of 0 to 255.

VOLUME RENDERING

The basic idea behind volume rendering is to determine the pixel shading value by integrating the density contributions along `boxRay`. The implementation is shown in Listing 7.5. Here again we use the green channel, so we choose a starting shade with red and blue components. We'll approximate the integral as a finite sum with `numSteps` terms each corresponding to a parameter increment `dt` and a spatial distance `len`. We initialize an accumulation variable (`accum = 0.f;`), then step along `boxRay` incrementing `accum` when the density value is beyond a value `threshold`. The last two lines in the `for` loop update the current position and density value. When we have finished traversing `boxRay`, `accum` is clipped to an allowed `uchar` value for storage in the green color component of the pixel.

Listing 7.5 `volumeRenderShader()`

```
__device__ uchar4 volumeRenderShader(float *d_vol, int3 volSize,
  Ray boxRay, float threshold, int numSteps) {
  uchar4 shade = make_uchar4(96, 0, 192, 0); // background value
  const float dt = 1.f/numSteps;
  const float len = length(boxRay.d)/numSteps;
  float accum = 0.f;
  float3 pos = boxRay.o;
  float val = density(d_vol, volSize, pos);
  for (float t = 0.f; t<1.f; t += dt) {
    if (val - threshold < 0.f) accum += (fabsf(val - threshold))*len;
    pos = paramRay(boxRay, t);
    val = density(d_vol, volSize, pos);
  }
  if (clip(accum) > 0.f) shade.y = clip(accum);
  return shade;
}
```

RAYCASTING

To determine a raycast pixel shading value, we search along the ray to find the threshold density value and compute the shading based on the local surface normal vector. The code for implementing the `raycastShader()` is shown in Listing 7.6. Inputs to `rayCastShader()` include the following:

- A pointer to the device array where the image stack data is stored

- The dimensions of the data stack (`int3 volSize`)

- The ray clipped to the bounding box (`Ray boxRay`)

- The threshold distance value for the surface (`float dist`)

Listing 7.6 `raycastShader()`

```
__device__ uchar4 rayCastShader(float *d_vol, int3 volSize,
  Ray boxRay, float dist) {
  uchar4 shade = make_uchar4(96, 0, 192, 0);
  float3 pos = boxRay.o;
  float len = length(boxRay.d);
  float t = 0.0f;
  float f = density(d_vol, volSize, pos);
  while (f > dist + EPS && t < 1.0f) {
    f = density(d_vol, volSize, pos);
    t += (f - dist) / len;
    pos = paramRay(boxRay, t);
    f = density(d_vol, volSize, pos);
  }
  if (t < 1.f) {
    const float3 ux = make_float3(1, 0, 0), uy = make_float3(0, 1, 0),
                 uz = make_float3(0, 0, 1);
    float3 grad = {(density(d_vol, volSize, pos + EPS*ux) -
                    density(d_vol, volSize, pos))/EPS,
                   (density(d_vol, volSize, pos + EPS*uy) -
                    density(d_vol, volSize, pos))/EPS,
                   (density(d_vol, volSize, pos + EPS*uz) -
                    density(d_vol, volSize, pos))/EPS};
    float intensity = -dot(normalize(boxRay.d), normalize(grad));
    shade = make_uchar4(255*intensity, 0, 0, 255);
  }
  return shade;
}
```

The `raycastShader()` function returns a color value of type `uchar4`. The computation starts with a `while` loop that steps along `boxRay` until exiting the bounding box (so that `t < 1.0f` is no longer satisfied) or coming closer than a specified tolerance value (`EPS`) of the surface threshold distance `dist`.

Rootfinding, Length Scales, and Signed Distance Functions

The process of locating a point where a function takes on a given value is generally referred to as "rootfinding." This is another big topic that can be the subject of at least an entire chapter of a book [2] and is widely considered to be problematic. Indeed, computing roots reliably in general can be problematic. If the function value can change significantly on arbitrarily small scales, there may be no safe way to choose a step size for a root search.

Here, we do not face such problems. Our data set has a fundamental length scale set by the voxel spacing, and choosing a step size that is small compared to the voxel spacing ensures that no features are missed that can be captured by data sampled at that scale.

In the special case of signed distance functions, we can do even better. Evaluating the function (and subtracting the surface threshold value) gives the distance to the closest surface point, so we can safely take a step of that size. If we step in the right direction we will just reach the surface and locate the desired root. If we step in any other direction we will safely arrive at a point short of the surface where we can repeat the process knowing that no roots have been missed. The net result is that the ray-surface intersection can be found to within our chosen tolerance in just a few steps.

If the while loop terminates due to the ray exiting the bounding box, a default shading value (background color) is returned. Alternatively, if the while loop exit is due to encountering the threshold density value (indicating that the ray hit the surface), we compute the gradient at the surface point (a.k.a. the surface normal vector) and determine the shading value (which we choose to store in the green channel) based on the dot product of the gradient and the ray direction.

The components of the gradient grad are the derivatives of the density function along the coordinate directions. The float3 variables ux, uy, and uz provide displacements in the coordinate directions, and the formulas for computing grad.x, grad.y, and grad.z correspond to the finite difference technique introduced in Chapter 4, "2D Grids and Interactive Graphics," applied along each coordinate direction.

The dot product of normalized versions of boxRay.d and grad produces the cosine of the angle between the ray and normal which corresponds to the shading for the Lambertian radiance model used to approximate the appearance of matte surfaces.

Shading Models, Ray Tracing, and Computer Graphics

This is another big topic. There is an entire literature on modeling of surface appearance and lighting of scenes. For discussions of ray tracing (which accounts for the fact that rays can be reflected and refracted) and radiance models (which treat each object as both an emitter and absorber of radiation), and numerous other details of computer graphics, check out the classic reference [3].

CREATING THE vis_3d APP

Now that we've been through all of the shading functions, let's put the pieces together and look at the complete code for the vis_3d app. We are once again building on the flashlight app from Chapter 4, "2D Grids and Interactive Graphics." We start with the same set of files and build instructions, and make the following modifications:

- vis_3d/main.cpp, shown in Listing 7.7, includes only a few changes from flashlight/main.cpp:

  - A revised list of arguments in the call of kernelLauncher() on lines 29–30.

  - A revised string for presenting information in the title bar of the graphics window is constructed on lines 33–35.

  - A call to volumeKernelLauncher() on line 91 to create the 3D data to be visualized.

  - The new createMenu() callback function appears on line 94 and enables a pop-up menu for selecting the object/function to visualize.

- vis_3d/interactions.h, shown in Listing 7.8, sets the geometry-related constants and window size, prints the user instructions, and defines the revised user interactions including the pop-up menu contents and associated actions.

- vis_3d/kernel.h, shown in Listing 7.9, includes definitions of the data types not known to the C/C++ compiler and the prototypes for volumeKernel-Launcher(), which launches the 3D grid and kernelLauncher() that launches the 2D grid for rendering.

- vis_3d/kernel.cu, shown in Listing 7.10, includes the definitions of the kernel launcher functions and the kernel functions themselves.

In this case, the kernels call a list of device functions, including supporting functions; paramRay(), scrIdxToPos(), and intersectBox(), along with func(), for creating the 3D data grids; yRotate() for changing the view; and the three shading functions. To keep vis_3d/kernel.cu from becoming overly long, we created a separate vis_3d/device_funcs.cu file to hold the definitions and a CUDA header file vis_3d/device_funcs.cuh that can be included to make the function prototypes available.

Listing 7.7 vis_3d/main.cpp

```cpp
1  #include "interactions.h"
2  #include "kernel.h"
3  #include <stdio.h>
4  #include <stdlib.h>
5  #ifdef _WIN32
6  #define WINDOWS_LEAN_AND_MEAN
7  #define NOMINMAX
8  #include <windows.h>
9  #endif
10 #ifdef __APPLE__
11 #include <GLUT/glut.h>
12 #else
13 #include <GL/glew.h>
14 #include <GL/freeglut.h>
15 #endif
16 #include <cuda_runtime.h>
17 #include <cuda_gl_interop.h>
18
19 // texture and pixel objects
20 GLuint pbo = 0;      // OpenGL pixel buffer object
21 GLuint tex = 0;      // OpenGL texture object
22 struct cudaGraphicsResource *cuda_pbo_resource;
23
24 void render() {
25    uchar4 *d_out = 0;
26    cudaGraphicsMapResources(1, &cuda_pbo_resource, 0);
27    cudaGraphicsResourceGetMappedPointer((void **)&d_out, NULL,
28                                          cuda_pbo_resource);
29    kernelLauncher(d_out, d_vol, W, H, volumeSize, method, zs, theta,
30                   threshold, dist);
31    cudaGraphicsUnmapResources(1, &cuda_pbo_resource, 0);
32    char title[128];
33    sprintf(title, "Volume Visualizer : objId =%d, method = %d,"
34                   " dist = %.1f, theta =  %.1f", id, method, dist,
35                   theta);
36    glutSetWindowTitle(title);
37 }
38
39 void draw_texture() {
40    glTexImage2D(GL_TEXTURE_2D, 0, GL_RGBA, W, H, 0, GL_RGBA,
41         GL_UNSIGNED_BYTE, NULL);
42    glEnable(GL_TEXTURE_2D);
43    glBegin(GL_QUADS);
```

```
44    glTexCoord2f(0.0f, 0.0f); glVertex2f(0, 0);
45    glTexCoord2f(0.0f, 1.0f); glVertex2f(0, H);
46    glTexCoord2f(1.0f, 1.0f); glVertex2f(W, H);
47    glTexCoord2f(1.0f, 0.0f); glVertex2f(W, 0);
48    glEnd();
49    glDisable(GL_TEXTURE_2D);
50  }
51
52  void display() {
53    render();
54    draw_texture();
55    glutSwapBuffers();
56  }
57
58  void initGLUT(int *argc, char **argv) {
59    glutInit(argc, argv);
60    glutInitDisplayMode(GLUT_RGBA | GLUT_DOUBLE);
61    glutInitWindowSize(W, H);
62    glutCreateWindow("Volume Visualizer");
63  #ifndef __APPLE__
64    glewInit();
65  #endif
66  }
67
68  void initPixelBuffer() {
69    glGenBuffers(1, &pbo);
70    glBindBuffer(GL_PIXEL_UNPACK_BUFFER, pbo);
71    glBufferData(GL_PIXEL_UNPACK_BUFFER, W*H*sizeof(GLubyte) * 4, 0,
72                 GL_STREAM_DRAW);
73    glGenTextures(1, &tex);
74    glBindTexture(GL_TEXTURE_2D, tex);
75    glTexParameteri(GL_TEXTURE_2D, GL_TEXTURE_MIN_FILTER, GL_NEAREST);
76    cudaGraphicsGLRegisterBuffer(&cuda_pbo_resource, pbo,
77                                 cudaGraphicsMapFlagsWriteDiscard);
78  }
79
80  void exitfunc() {
81    if (pbo) {
82      cudaGraphicsUnregisterResource(cuda_pbo_resource);
83      glDeleteBuffers(1, &pbo);
84      glDeleteTextures(1, &tex);
85    }
86    cudaFree(d_vol);
87  }
88
89  int main(int argc, char** argv) {
90    cudaMalloc(&d_vol, NX*NY*NZ*sizeof(float)); // 3D volume data
91    volumeKernelLauncher(d_vol, volumeSize, id, params);
92    printInstructions();
93    initGLUT(&argc, argv);
94    createMenu();
95    gluOrtho2D(0, W, H, 0);
96    glutKeyboardFunc(keyboard);
97    glutSpecialFunc(handleSpecialKeypress);
98    glutDisplayFunc(display);
```

```
 99    initPixelBuffer();
100    glutMainLoop();
101    atexit(exitfunc);
102    return 0;
103  }
```

Next, let's move on to specifying the user interactions; that is, editing the callback functions in the `interactions.h`, which is shown in Listing 7.8. The file begins by defining constants (including image dimensions, image stack dimensions, and block sizes) and variables (including parameters for object dimensions, viewing distance, viewing direction, shading method, threshold value, and slicing plane normal and distance).

The new callback function `mymenu()` uses a `switch()` statement to set the image specification `id` to the integer `value` (which is generated by right-clicking, to open a context menu, and then releasing the mouse with the cursor on a menu item). The final line of `mymenu()` passes `id` as an argument to `volumeKernelLauncher()`. The data for the 3D grid or image stack is computed live (based on functions in `device_funcs.cu` to be described below) after each selection from the object menu.

The next callback function `keyboard()` performs specified actions according to the value of the `unsigned char key` generated by a keypress. Zoom is controlled by the + and – keys (by essentially moving `source`). The d/D key moves the slicing plane, and z resets to default values. The viewing mode is selected by v for volume render, r for raycast, and f for slicing (because f happens to reside between v and r on the QWERTY keyboard layout).

Finally, `handleSpecialFunctionKeypress()` specifies actions based on the `int` value generated by pressing special function keys (which do not generate `unsigned char` values). The left arrow and right arrow change the value of `theta` that will get passed into a transformation in `kernel.cu` to rotate the viewing direction (by transforming the values of `source` and `pix`). The up arrow and down arrow keys change the value of `threshold` that will be passed to the shading functions to change the surface threshold value or the position of the slicing plane.

Listing 7.8 `vis_3d/interactions.h`

```
1 #ifndef INTERACTIONS_H
2 #define INTERACTIONS_H
3 #include "kernel.h"
4 #include <stdio.h>
5 #include <stdlib.h>
6 #ifdef __APPLE__
```

```
 7 #include <GLUT/glut.h>
 8 #else
 9 #include <GL/glew.h>
10 #include <GL/freeglut.h>
11 #endif
12 #include <vector_types.h>
13 #define W   600
14 #define H   600
15 #define DELTA  5 // pixel increment for arrow keys
16 #define NX 128
17 #define NY 128
18 #define NZ 128
19
20 int id = 1;  // 0 = sphere, 1 = torus, 2 = block
21 int method = 2; // 0 = volumeRender, 1 = slice, 2 = raycast
22 const int3 volumeSize = {NX, NY, NZ}; // size of volumetric data grid
23 const float4 params = {NX/4.f, NY/6.f, NZ/16.f, 1.f};
24 float *d_vol; // pointer to device array for storing volume data
25 float zs = NZ; // distance from origin to source
26 float dist = 0.f, theta = 0.f, threshold = 0.f;
27
28 void mymenu(int value) {
29   switch (value) {
30   case 0: return;
31   case 1: id = 0; break; // sphere
32   case 2: id = 1; break; // torus
33   case 3: id = 2; break; // block
34   }
35   volumeKernelLauncher(d_vol, volumeSize, id, params);
36   glutPostRedisplay();
37 }
38
39 void createMenu() {
40   glutCreateMenu(mymenu);          // Object selection menu
41   glutAddMenuEntry("Object Selector", 0); // menu title
42   glutAddMenuEntry("Sphere", 1);       // id = 1 -> sphere
43   glutAddMenuEntry("Torus", 2);      // id = 2 -> torus
44   glutAddMenuEntry("Block", 3);      // id = 3 -> block
45   glutAttachMenu(GLUT_RIGHT_BUTTON);    // right-click for menu
46 }
47
48 void keyboard(unsigned char key, int x, int y) {
49   if (key == '+') zs -= DELTA; // move source closer (zoom in)
50   if (key == '-') zs += DELTA; // move source farther (zoom out)
51   if (key == 'd') --dist; // decrease slice distance
52   if (key == 'D') ++dist; // increase slice distance
53   if (key == 'z') zs = NZ, theta = 0.f, dist = 0.f; // reset values
54   if (key == 'v') method = 0; // volume render
55   if (key == 'f') method = 1; // slice
56   if (key == 'r') method = 2; // raycast
57   if (key == 27) exit(0);
58   glutPostRedisplay();
59 }
60
61 void handleSpecialKeypress(int key, int x, int y)  {
```

```
62    if (key == GLUT_KEY_LEFT) theta -= 0.1f; // rotate left
63    if (key == GLUT_KEY_RIGHT) theta += 0.1f; // rotate right
64    if (key == GLUT_KEY_UP) threshold += 0.1f; // inc threshold (thick)
65    if (key == GLUT_KEY_DOWN) threshold -= 0.1f; // dec threshold (thin)
66    glutPostRedisplay();
67 }
68
69 void printInstructions() {
70    printf("3D Volume Visualizer\n"
71          "Controls:\n"
72          "Volume render mode                          : v\n"
73          "Slice render mode                           : f\n"
74          "Raycast mode                                : r\n"
75          "Zoom out/in                                 : -/+\n"
76          "Rotate view                                 : left/right\n"
77          "Decr./Incr. Offset (intensity in slice mode): down/up\n"
78          "Decr./Incr. distance (only in slice mode)   : d/D\n"
79          "Reset parameters                            : z\n"
80          "Right-click for object selection menu\n");
81 }
82
83 #endif
```

That takes care of the currently implemented interactions (although you are encouraged to experiment with creating additional interactions that you find useful or interesting), and we can move on to the code in kernel.cu. The prototypes for its public "wrapper" functions, volumeKernelLauncher() and kernelLauncher(), reside in kernel.h, shown in Listing 7.9, and the implementation of kernel.cu is shown in Listing 7.10. volumeKernelLauncher() calls volumeKernel() to launch a 3D grid to compute an image stack of data describing an object, and kernelLauncher() calls renderKernel() to launch a 2D grid to compute pixel shading values.

Listing 7.9 vis_3d/kernel.h

```
 1 #ifndef KERNEL_H
 2 #define KERNEL_H
 3
 4 struct uchar4;
 5 struct int3;
 6 struct float4;
 7
 8 void kernelLauncher(uchar4 *d_out, float *d_vol, int w, int h,
 9   int3 volSize, int method, int zs, float theta, float threshold,
10   float dist);
11 void volumeKernelLauncher(float *d_vol, int3 volSize, int id,
12                           float4 params);
13 #endif
```

Listing 7.10 `vis_3d/kernel.cu`

```
 1 #include "kernel.h"
 2 #include "device_funcs.cuh"
 3 #include <helper_math.h>
 4 #define TX_2D 32
 5 #define TY_2D 32
 6 #define TX 8
 7 #define TY 8
 8 #define TZ 8
 9 #define NUMSTEPS 20
10
11 __global__
12 void renderKernel(uchar4 *d_out, float *d_vol, int w, int h,
13   int3 volSize, int method, float zs, float theta, float threshold,
14   float dist) {
15   const int c = blockIdx.x*blockDim.x + threadIdx.x;
16   const int r = blockIdx.y*blockDim.y + threadIdx.y;
17   const int i = c + r * w;
18   if ((c >= w) || (r >= h)) return; // Check if within image bounds
19   const uchar4 background = {64, 0, 128, 0};
20   float3 source = {0.f, 0.f, -zs};
21   float3 pix = scrIdxToPos(c, r, w, h, 2*volSize.z-zs);
22   // apply viewing transformation: here rotate about y-axis
23   source = yRotate(source, theta);
24   pix = yRotate(pix, theta);
25   // prepare inputs for ray-box intersection
26   float t0, t1;
27   const Ray pixRay = {source, pix - source};
28   float3 center = {volSize.x/2.f, volSize.y/2.f, volSize.z/2.f};
29   const float3 boxmin = -center;
30   const float3 boxmax = {volSize.x - center.x, volSize.y - center.y,
31                          volSize.z - center.z};
32   // perform ray-box intersection test
33   const bool hitBox = intersectBox(pixRay, boxmin, boxmax, &t0, &t1);
34   uchar4 shade;
35   if (!hitBox) shade = background; // miss box => background color
36   else {
37     if (t0 < 0.0f) t0 = 0.f; // clamp to 0 to avoid looking backward
38     // bounded by points where the ray enters and leaves the box
39     const Ray boxRay = {paramRay(pixRay, t0),
40                         paramRay(pixRay, t1) - paramRay(pixRay, t0)};
41     if (method == 1) shade =
42       sliceShader(d_vol, volSize, boxRay, threshold, dist, source);
43     else if (method == 2) shade =
44       rayCastShader(d_vol, volSize, boxRay, threshold);
45     else shade =
46       volumeRenderShader(d_vol, volSize, boxRay, threshold, NUMSTEPS);
47   }
48   d_out[i] = shade;
49 }
50
51 __global__
52 void volumeKernel(float *d_vol, int3 volSize, int id, float4 params) {
53   const int w = volSize.x, h = volSize.y, d = volSize.z;
```

```
54    const int c = blockIdx.x * blockDim.x + threadIdx.x; // column
55    const int r = blockIdx.y * blockDim.y + threadIdx.y; // row
56    const int s = blockIdx.z * blockDim.z + threadIdx.z; // stack
57    const int i = c + r * w + s * w * h;
58    if ((c >= w) || (r >= h) || (s >= d)) return;
59    d_vol[i] = func(c, r, s, id, volSize, params); // compute and store
60  }
61
62  void kernelLauncher(uchar4 *d_out, float *d_vol, int w, int h,
63    int3 volSize, int method, int zs, float theta, float threshold,
64    float dist) {
65    dim3 blockSize(TX_2D, TY_2D);
66    dim3 gridSize(divUp(w, TX_2D), divUp(h, TY_2D));
67    renderKernel<<<gridSize, blockSize>>>(d_out, d_vol, w, h, volSize,
68      method, zs, theta, threshold, dist);
69  }
70
71  void volumeKernelLauncher(float *d_vol, int3 volSize, int id,
72    float4 params) {
73    dim3 blockSize(TX, TY, TZ);
74    dim3 gridSize(divUp(volSize.x, TX), divUp(volSize.y, TY),
75      divUp(volSize.z, TZ));
76    volumeKernel<<<gridSize, blockSize>>>(d_vol, volSize, id, params);
77  }
```

The volumeKernelLauncher() gets called (and volumeKernel() executes) once at initiation and again whenever a new object is selected from the pop-up context menu while kernelLauncher() gets called (and renderKernel() executes) at every screen refresh. volumeKernel() is identical to distanceKernel() from the dist_3d app (except that here we evaluate a function func() instead of a Pythagorean formula), so let's focus our attention on the other kernel.

renderKernel() begins with the usual index computations and bounds checking. The source and pixel locations are then computed as follows. The source is chosen to be at {0.f, 0.f, -zs}, and the screen is centered on and perpendicular to the z-axis at a distance spacing (set to twice the depth of the image stack). The kinematics implementation allows the viewing system (source and screen) to be translated along the viewing axis (by changing zs) and rotated about the y-axis (by changing theta) as prescribed by lines 20–24. The coordinate system used is aligned on the principal axes of the image stack and with the center of the stack (float3 center) at the origin. Lines 29–30 construct the inputs for the ray-box intersection test at line 33. If the ray misses the box, a background color is returned. If the ray hits the box, we construct boxRay on line 39 to describe the portion of the ray inside the box and pass boxRay as an argument to one of the shading functions based on the value of method.

The launcher functions and shaders rely on a collection of supporting device functions whose code is collected into `vis_3d/device_funcs.cu` (and the associated header file `vis_3d/device_funcs.cuh`), as shown in Listings 7.11 and 7.12.

Listing 7.11 `vis_3d/device_funcs.cuh`

```
 1 #ifndef DEVICEFUNCS_CUH
 2 #define DEVICEFUNCS_CUH
 3
 4 typedef struct {
 5   float3 o, d; // origin and direction
 6 } Ray;
 7
 8 __host__ int divUp(int a, int b);
 9 __device__ float3 yRotate(float3 pos, float theta);
10 __device__ float func(int c, int r, int s, int id, int3 volSize,
11   float4 params);
12 __device__ float3 paramRay(Ray r, float t);
13 __device__ float3 scrIdxToPos(int c, int r, int w, int h, float zs);
14 __device__ bool intersectBox(Ray r, float3 boxmin, float3 boxmax,
15   float *tnear, float *tfar);
16 __device__ uchar4 sliceShader(float *d_vol, int3 volSize, Ray boxRay,
17   float threshold, float dist, float3 norm);
18 __device__ uchar4 volumeRenderShader(float *d_vol, int3 volSize,
19   Ray boxRay, float dist, int numSteps);
20 __device__ uchar4 rayCastShader(float *d_vol, int3 volSize,
21   Ray boxRay, float dist);
22
23 #endif
```

Listing 7.12 `vis_3d/device_funcs.cu`

```
 1 #include "device_funcs.cuh"
 2 #include <helper_math.h>
 3 #define EPS 0.01f
 4
 5 __host__ int divUp(int a, int b) { return (a + b - 1) / b; }
 6
 7 __device__
 8 unsigned char clip(int n) { return n > 255 ? 255 : (n < 0 ? 0 : n); }
 9
10 __device__ int clipWithBounds(int n, int n_min, int n_max) {
11   return n > n_max ? n_max : (n < n_min ? n_min : n);
12 }
13
14 __device__ float3 yRotate(float3 pos, float theta) {
15   const float c = cosf(theta), s = sinf(theta);
16   return make_float3(c*pos.x + s*pos.z, pos.y, -s*pos.x + c*pos.z);
17 }
18
19 __device__ float func(int c, int r, int s, int id, int3 volSize,
20                       float4 params) {
21   const int3 pos0 = {volSize.x/2, volSize.y/2, volSize.z/2};
```

```
22   const float dx = c - pos0.x, dy = r - pos0.y, dz = s - pos0.z;
23   // sphere
24   if (id == 0) { return sqrtf(dx*dx + dy*dy + dz*dz) - params.x; }
25   else if (id == 1) { // torus
26     const float r = sqrtf(dx*dx + dy*dy);
27     return sqrtf((r - params.x)*(r - params.x) + dz*dz) - params.y;
28   }
29   else { // block
30     float x = fabsf(dx) - params.x, y = fabsf(dy) - params.y,
31           z = fabsf(dz) - params.z;
32     if (x <= 0 && x <= 0 && z <= 0) return fmaxf(x, fmaxf(y, z));
33     else {
34       x = fmaxf(x, 0), y = fmaxf(y, 0), z = fmaxf(z, 0);
35       return sqrtf(x*x + y*y + z*z);
36     }
37   }
38 }
39
40 __device__ float3 scrIdxToPos(int c, int r, int w, int h, float zs) {
41   return make_float3(c - w/2, r - h/2, zs);
42 }
43
44 __device__ float3 paramRay(Ray r, float t) { return r.o + t*(r.d); }
45
46 __device__ float planeSDF(float3 pos, float3 norm, float d) {
47   return dot(pos, normalize(norm)) - d;
48 }
49
50 __device__
51 bool rayPlaneIntersect(Ray myRay, float3 n, float dist, float *t) {
52   const float f0 = planeSDF(paramRay(myRay, 0.f), n, dist);
53   const float f1 = planeSDF(paramRay(myRay, 1.f), n, dist);
54   bool result = (f0*f1 < 0);
55   if (result) *t = (0.f - f0) / (f1 - f0);
56   return result;
57 }
58
59 // Intersect ray with a box from volumeRender SDK sample.
60 __device__ bool intersectBox(Ray r, float3 boxmin, float3 boxmax,
61   float *tnear, float *tfar) {
62   // Compute intersection of ray with all six bbox planes.
63   const float3 invR = make_float3(1.0f)/r.d;
64   const float3 tbot = invR*(boxmin - r.o), ttop = invR*(boxmax - r.o);
65   // Re-order intersections to find smallest and largest on each axis.
66   const float3 tmin = fminf(ttop, tbot), tmax = fmaxf(ttop, tbot);
67   // Find the largest tmin and the smallest tmax.
68   *tnear = fmaxf(fmaxf(tmin.x, tmin.y), fmaxf(tmin.x, tmin.z));
69   *tfar = fminf(fminf(tmax.x, tmax.y), fminf(tmax.x, tmax.z));
70   return *tfar > *tnear;
71 }
72
73 __device__ int3 posToVolIndex(float3 pos, int3 volSize) {
74   return make_int3(pos.x + volSize.x/2, pos.y + volSize.y/2,
75                    pos.z +  volSize.z/2);
76 }
77
```

```
78  __device__ int flatten(int3 index, int3 volSize) {
79    return index.x + index.y*volSize.x + index.z*volSize.x*volSize.y;
80  }
81
82  __device__ float density(float *d_vol, int3 volSize, float3 pos) {
83    int3 index = posToVolIndex(pos, volSize);
84    int i = index.x, j = index.y, k = index.z;
85    const int w = volSize.x, h = volSize.y, d = volSize.z;
86    const float3 rem = fracf(pos);
87    index = make_int3(clipWithBounds(i, 0, w - 2),
88      clipWithBounds(j, 0, h - 2), clipWithBounds(k, 0, d - 2));
89    // directed increments for computing the gradient
90    const int3 dx = {1, 0, 0}, dy = {0, 1, 0}, dz = {0, 0, 1};
91    // values sampled at surrounding grid points
92    const float dens000 = d_vol[flatten(index, volSize)];
93    const float dens100 = d_vol[flatten(index + dx, volSize)];
94    const float dens010 = d_vol[flatten(index + dy, volSize)];
95    const float dens001 = d_vol[flatten(index + dz, volSize)];
96    const float dens110 = d_vol[flatten(index + dx + dy, volSize)];
97    const float dens101 = d_vol[flatten(index + dx + dz, volSize)];
98    const float dens011 = d_vol[flatten(index + dy + dz, volSize)];
99    const float dens111 = d_vol[flatten(index + dx + dy + dz, volSize)];
100   // trilinear interpolation
101   return (1 - rem.x)*(1 - rem.y)*(1 - rem.z)*dens000 +
102     (rem.x)*(1 - rem.y)*(1 - rem.z)*dens100 +
103     (1 - rem.x)*(rem.y)*(1 - rem.z)*dens010 +
104     (1 - rem.x)*(1 - rem.y)*(rem.z)*dens001 +
105     (rem.x)*(rem.y)*(1 - rem.z)*dens110 +
106     (rem.x)*(1 - rem.y)*(rem.z)*dens101 +
107     (1 - rem.x)*(rem.y)*(rem.z)*dens011 +
108     (rem.x)*(rem.y)*(rem.z)*dens111;
109 }
110
111 __device__ uchar4 sliceShader(float *d_vol, int3 volSize, Ray boxRay,
112   float gain, float dist, float3 norm) {
113   float t;
114   uchar4 shade = make_uchar4(96, 0, 192, 0); // background value
115   if (rayPlaneIntersect(boxRay, norm, dist, &t)) {
116     float sliceDens = density(d_vol, volSize, paramRay(boxRay, t));
117     shade = make_uchar4(48, clip(-10.f * (1.0f + gain) * sliceDens),
118                         96, 255);
119   }
120   return shade;
121 }
122
123 __device__ uchar4 volumeRenderShader(float *d_vol, int3 volSize,
124   Ray boxRay, float threshold, int numSteps) {
125   uchar4 shade = make_uchar4(96, 0, 192, 0); // background value
126   const float dt = 1.f/numSteps;
127   const float len = length(boxRay.d)/numSteps;
128   float accum = 0.f;
129   float3 pos = boxRay.o;
130   float val = density(d_vol, volSize, pos);
131   for (float t = 0.f; t<1.f; t += dt) {
132     if (val - threshold < 0.f) accum += (fabsf(val - threshold))*len;
133     pos = paramRay(boxRay, t);
```

```
134      val = density(d_vol, volSize, pos);
135    }
136    if (clip(accum) > 0.f) shade.y = clip(accum);
137    return shade;
138 }
139
140 __device__ uchar4 rayCastShader(float *d_vol, int3 volSize,
141    Ray boxRay, float dist) {
142    uchar4 shade = make_uchar4(96, 0, 192, 0);
143    float3 pos = boxRay.o;
144    float len = length(boxRay.d);
145    float t = 0.0f;
146    float f = density(d_vol, volSize, pos);
147    while (f > dist + EPS && t < 1.0f) {
148      f = density(d_vol, volSize, pos);
149      t += (f - dist) / len;
150      pos = paramRay(boxRay, t);
151      f = density(d_vol, volSize, pos);
152    }
153    if (t < 1.f) {
154      const float3 ux = make_float3(1, 0, 0), uy = make_float3(0, 1, 0),
155                   uz = make_float3(0, 0, 1);
156      float3 grad = {(density(d_vol, volSize, pos + EPS*ux) -
157                      density(d_vol, volSize, pos))/EPS,
158                     (density(d_vol, volSize, pos + EPS*uy) -
159                      density(d_vol, volSize, pos))/EPS,
160                     (density(d_vol, volSize, pos + EPS*uz) -
161                      density(d_vol, volSize, pos))/EPS};
162      float intensity = -dot(normalize(boxRay.d), normalize(grad));
163      shade = make_uchar4(255*intensity, 0, 0, 255);
164    }
165    return shade;
166 }
```

Splitting Kernel Code into Multiple Files Means "Generate Relocatable Device Code"

We have chosen to split the CUDA code for the vis_3d app into multiple files (to try to keep them to a manageable size). This decision requires **separate compilation** and generation of **relocatable device code**. Versions of CUDA prior to 5.0 did not allow this; all kernel code had to be included in a single file for compilation.

Now "separate compilation" is supported, but you need to set the nvcc compiler flag that generates relocatable device code with --relocatable-device-code=true or the shorthand version -rdc=true.

To set the rdc compiler flag in Visual Studio, open the project's Property Pages (by right-clicking on the project in the Property Manager pane or selecting Property Pages from the view menu), then selecting Configuration Properties ⇒ CUDA C/C++ ⇒ Common ⇒ Generate Relocatable Device Code ⇒ Yes (-rdc=true), as shown in Figure 7.2.

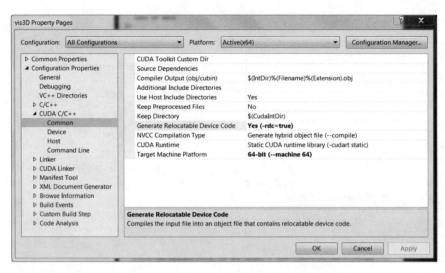

Figure 7.2 Visual Studio property page showing `Generate Relocatable Device Code` set to `Yes(-rdc=true)` to allow kernel code in multiple files

Linux users will find that the appropriate compiler flag is included on line 11 of `vis_3d/Makefile`, as shown in Listing 7.13.

Listing 7.13 `vis_3d/Makefile`

```
 1 UNAME_S := $(shell uname)
 2
 3 ifeq ($(UNAME_S), Darwin)
 4   LDFLAGS = -Xlinker -framework,OpenGL -Xlinker -framework,GLUT
 5 else
 6   LDFLAGS += -L/usr/local/cuda/samples/common/lib/linux/x86_64
 7   LDFLAGS += -lglut -lGL -lGLU -lGLEW
 8 endif
 9
10 NVCC = /usr/local/cuda/bin/nvcc
11 NVCC_FLAGS=-Xcompiler "-Wall -Wno-deprecated-declarations" -rdc=true
12 INC = -I/usr/local/cuda/samples/common/inc
13
14 all: main.exe
15
16 main.exe: main.o kernel.o device_funcs.o
17   $(NVCC) $^ -o $@ $(LDFLAGS)
18
19 main.o: main.cpp kernel.h interactions.h
20   $(NVCC) $(NVCC_FLAGS) -c $< -o $@
21
22 kernel.o: kernel.cu kernel.h device_funcs.cuh
23   $(NVCC) $(NVCC_FLAGS) $(INC) -c $< -o $@
24
```

```
25 device_funcs.o: device_funcs.cu device_funcs.cuh
26    $(NVCC) $(NVCC_FLAGS) $(INC) -c $< -o $@
```

With that final detail covered, the time has come to compile and run the `vis_3d` app. You should be able to do live interactions with data sets of reasonable size. A laptop with a GeForce GT 640M handles a 600 × 600 image of a 512 × 512 × 512 stack at interactive rates. (Larger 3D data sets can start to run into the limits of device memory, so you might want to estimate the size of the largest data set your GPU will accommodate.) Right-click on the graphics window to open a pop-up menu and select an object to visualize. View the object with each of the shading options and experiment with changing view directions and other parameters.

Screenshot images of `vis_3d` visualizations of a 3D image stack of distance data for a torus are shown in Figures 7.3, 7.4, and 7.5.

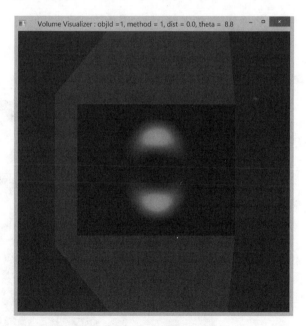

Figure 7.3 Screenshot of `vis_3d` slice visualization of the 3D distance stack for a torus

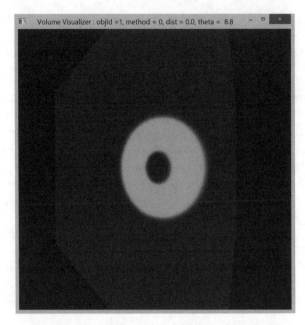

Figure 7.4 Screenshot of `vis_3d` volume rendering visualization of the 3D distance stack for a torus

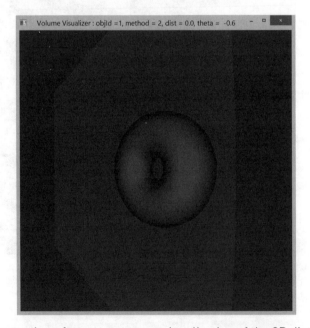

Figure 7.5 Screenshot of `vis_3d` raycast visualization of the 3D distance stack for a torus

Summary

In this chapter, we've seen how to launch 3D computational kernels and how to achieve real-time interaction with 3D data grids (or image stacks) using three different visualization techniques: slicing, volume rendering, and raycasting. We hope you now feel empowered to embark on your own CUDA-powered 3D interactive projects. Here are some suggestions to help get you going.

Suggested Projects

1. Modify the `dist_3d` app to begin by computing the corresponding values on the CPU. Compare the results from CPU and GPU and verify that they agree. Time the CPU and GPU computations, and compare and contrast the execution times for various grid sizes.

2. Extend `raycastShader()` to handle more general data sets by implementing an alternative rootfinding technique.

3. Enhance `volumeRenderShader()` by implementing a higher-order integration routine such as the trapezoidal rule (which averages the values at the ends of a step along the ray instead of just taking the value at one end).

4. Figure out how to import data, and view it interactively with `vis_3d`. The next time you go for a CT or MRI, request a copy of your data and visualize it.

5. Implement full 3D kinematic interaction (rather than just rotation about a single axis).

6. Implement an eikonal equation solver to create signed distance grids from segmented image stacks. (For details, see [4].)

References

[1] G. Scott Owen, "Ray - Box Intersection." (1998) http://www.siggraph.org/education/materials/HyperGraph/raytrace/rtinter3.htm.

[2] William H. Press, Saul A. Teukolsky, William T. Vetterling, and Brian P. Flannery, *Numerical Recipes: The Art of Scientific Computing*. (New York, NY: Cambridge University Press, 1992).

[3] John F. Hughes, Andries van Dam, Morgan McGuire, David F. Sklar, James D. Foley, Steven K. Feiner, and Kurt Akeley, *Computer Graphics: Principles and Practice, Third Edition*. (Boston, MA: Addison-Wesley, 2014).

[4] J. A. Sethian, *Level Set Methods and Fast Marching Methods: Evolving Interfaces in Computational Geometry, Fluid Mechanics, Computer Vision, and Materials Science*. (New York, NY: Cambridge University Press, 1999).

Chapter 8

Using CUDA Libraries

In this penultimate chapter, we take a look at some of the software libraries that are available to provide you with access to CUDA capabilities without having to write all the code yourself. As we tour the libraries, we will explicitly identify some common parallel programming patterns and look at examples illustrating how the libraries make those patterns available for your use. Before we are done, you will see library-based alternative implementations of apps for image processing and computing distances, dot products, and centroids, along with new examples involving Monte Carlo estimation of pi (π), computing distance in image space, and solving systems of linear equations.

Custom versus Off-the-Shelf

Up to this point, we have focused our efforts mostly on how to create custom apps from scratch using the CUDA API and extensions of the C language. However, there are certain kinds of circumstances in which it makes sense to consider using an existing code base that you did not create yourself:

- You need a particular functionality that you cannot access readily yourself without getting involved in a morass of details. We have already run into this situation twice:

  - Interactive graphics: Writing code that interfaces with what is displayed on your monitor actually involves dealing with the specifics of your system and your display device. Using an existing graphics library (such as OpenGL, which we used in previous chapters) provides the necessary layer of abstraction so that interactive graphics can be implemented independent of hardware-specific details.

- Image files: Rather than get into the details of various image file formats, we used the CImg library to import and export data from image files in the projects involving graphics file I/O.

- You have a significant concern for code reliability and maintainability; you want access to routines that have been written by experts and thoroughly tested; and you want to make sure that the important functional aspects of the code are updated in the future to ensure a long, useful lifetime.

We can now identify situations in which existing code libraries can be useful, but we should also acknowledge that there is some cost involved in using them—even the ones that are free of charge. The cost is the time and effort that you need to invest each time you learn to use a new library, but you should not let that deter you too much. As you gain experience, it becomes easier to learn to use new libraries.

We are going to take a quick tour of some relevant CUDA-powered libraries, so you can get some exposure to what it takes to make use of them. When it comes to weighing the costs and benefits, there are a couple things worth keeping in mind:

- Parallel patterns: Clearly, the cost-benefit analysis is influenced by how often we can make use of particular coding tools, and parallel programming constructs that arise in a wide variety of applications are referred to as "parallel patterns." Patterns also provide a useful context for creating and communicating the structure of the apps that we design and create. Libraries become particularly useful when they provide ready access to common parallel patterns, so we will make explicit note of pattern capabilities that we encounter as we tour the libraries. McCool, Robison, and Reinders [1] identified the following set of parallel patterns: superscalar sequences and task graphs, selection, map, gather, stencil, partition, reduce, scan, and pack. In this chapter alone, we will encounter about half of these.

- Foundational knowledge of CUDA: If libraries are so great, why have we dedicated so much of our focus so far to writing our own apps in CUDA C? Has that effort gone to waste? We believe that there is very little need to worry about the effort spent learning CUDA C going to waste. Even if you end up as a heavy user of CUDA-powered libraries (or access the power of CUDA through other languages), your experience creating apps in CUDA C should serve you well. You will have some direct idea of what is going on "under the hood" in the libraries you use, and that will put you in a better to position to understand the limitations and utilize the strengths of those libraries and languages.

Having now set the context, let's start our tour of some CUDA-powered libraries. Since there are already enough CUDA-powered libraries to make a

comprehensive tour impractical, our goals here are to touch on a few libraries, provide illustrative examples of their use, and identify access to parallel
patterns.

Thrust

The CUDA Toolkit Thrust documentation [2] provides a nice, concise description
of what Thrust is all about:

> Thrust is a C++ template library for CUDA based on the **Standard Template
> Library (STL)**. Thrust allows you to implement high performance parallel applica-
> tions with minimal programming effort through a high-level interface that is fully
> interoperable with CUDA C.

> Thrust provides a rich collection of data parallel primitives such as scan, sort, and
> reduce, which can be composed together to implement complex algorithms with
> concise, readable source code. By describing your computation in terms of these
> high-level abstractions, you provide Thrust with the freedom to select the most
> efficient implementation automatically. As a result, Thrust can be utilized in rapid
> prototyping of CUDA applications, where programmer productivity matters most,
> as well as in production, where robustness and absolute performance are crucial.

Further information about Thrust is available at the Thrust project website [3].

Since Thrust bills itself as the C++ template library for CUDA, we should take
a moment to describe its basis, the Standard Template Library. Throughout
this book, we have been mostly using C style where function definitions are
type-specific, so a function definition applies only to a single list of argument
types. C++ provides additional flexibility by allowing functions to act on generic
data types using C++ features called **templates** and overloading (which allows
a single function name to represent different operations on different input
types). C++ supports variable templates, class templates, and function templates (which will be most relevant to the discussion in this section). Recall
that C++ is derived from C, and we have been compiling C with what is really a
C++ compiler, so our development tools fully support the use of such C++
features.

The C++ standard library includes a variety of **containers** for dealing with collections of variables of a given type, and the container that will be of primary use
for our purposes is the vector, which is a sequence container with automatic
resizing capability [4].

Since the standard library is not the only software library that would define something named `vector`, **namespaces** (essentially prefix identifiers) are used to resolve name conflicts. In particular, everything in the C++ standard library has a full name that begins with `std::`, so a vector declaration starts with `std::vector`. (Alternatively, you can put the statement `using namespace std;` in your code file to import the whole `std` namespace. While this may offer some convenience, it can also sacrifice clarity, so we will use full names, including the namespace prefix, in most cases.)

Thrust is the template library for CUDA and uses the namespace `thrust`. Instead of the `std::vector` container, Thrust offers `thrust::host_vector` and `thrust::device_vector`. Individual elements of Thrust vectors can be accessed using the C-style square bracket notation or with C++-style **iterators.**

Using syntax based on vectors and iterators, Thrust provides built-in capabilities for allocating and freeing memory and for creating, populating, copying, and operating on vectors (without the necessity for any explicit calls of `cudaMalloc()`, `cudaMemcpy()`, or `cudaFree()`). Thrust also provides commands for performing a wide variety of parallel patterns, including selection, map, reduce, scan, and partition, along with other common operations such as sorting and comparing vectors. While we will be focusing on executing Thrust code on the GPU using CUDA, Thrust also includes "backend" implementations for OpenMP and threading building blocks (TBB), so Thrust code can be portable between GPU and multicore CPU systems [5,6,7].

Thrust for
C++ implementation
of a Tracker?

Thrust provides a layer of abstraction that eliminates the need to write custom kernels, but that extra layer of abstraction can also make debugging somewhat more challenging, and some C++-specific knowledge is required.

COMPUTING NORMS WITH `inner_product()`

With that little bit of background, let's jump into some Thrust examples. We'll start with a simple example that uses exclusively built-in Thrust functionality and work our way up to adding some customization.

Listing 8.1 shows Thrust code for parallel computation of the length or norm of a vector corresponding to the square root of the scalar obtained by dotting the vector with itself (also known as the *n*-dimensional Pythagorean formula).

$$\left\| v \right\| = \sqrt{\sum_{i=0}^{N-1}\left(v_i\right)^2} = \sqrt{v \cdot v}$$

The dot or inner product computation involves multiplying each entry by itself and summing the results, so both the map and reduce patterns occur during the computation.

Listing 8.1 `norm/kernel.cu`, computing the norm of a vector using Thrust

```
 1 #include <thrust/device_vector.h>
 2 #include <thrust/inner_product.h>
 3 #include <math.h>
 4 #include <stdio.h>
 5 #define N (1024*1024)
 6
 7 int main() {
 8   thrust::device_vector<float> dvec_x(N, 1.f);
 9   float norm = sqrt(thrust::inner_product(dvec_x.begin(),
10     dvec_x.end(), dvec_x.begin(), 0.0f));
11   printf("norm = %.0f\n", norm);
12   return 0;
13 }
14
```

Lines 1–4 include the header files for the Thrust features used in this short code (along with the math and input/output libraries), and line 5 defines the length N of the vector. The `main()` function starts with declaration of a `device_vector` named `dvec_x` to contain N variables of type `float` all set to 1.0. Lines 9–10 compute the inner product of `dvec_x` with itself and take the square root to produce the norm. The arguments of `thrust::inner_product` include starting and ending iterators for the first and the starting iterator for the second input vectors (obtained with the `device_vector`'s member functions, `.begin()` and `.end()` in this case) and the initial value in the reduction following element-wise multiplication. After printing out the value of `norm`, `main()` returns 0 and terminates. You should compile and run the code, then verify that it produces the correct result; each of the entries has value 1, so each square has value 1, the inner product is N, and the norm is $\sqrt{N}$ or, in this case, 1,024. The Makefile for building this program is provided in Listing 8.2

Thrust Code Must Be Placed in a CUDA File

Note that you must put your Thrust code in a `.cu` file to get it to compile!

Listing 8.2 `norm/Makefile`

```
1 NVCC = /usr/local/cuda/bin/nvcc
2 NVCC_FLAGS = -g -G -Xcompiler -Wall
3
4 main.exe: kernel.cu
5   $(NVCC) $(NVCC_FLAGS) $^ -o $@
```

Now we are ready for the important question: How are you supposed to know about `inner_product` and its syntax? Finding good sample codes is one way to start, but when you push beyond the limits of sample codes, you will need access to the full documentation for Thrust. Both sample programs and the full API documentation are available online on the Thrust project website [3].

The documentation tab on the website also includes a link to the Thrust wiki [8], which provides lots of other useful items including the Quick Start Guide, FAQs, and documentation on error handling and debugging.

You are encouraged to explore the Thrust web pages, but right now let's return to our immediate goal of finding information on the `inner_product` and its syntax. Go to http://thrust.github.io/ and select `Documentation` ⇒ `Thrust API (Doxygen)` to bring up a page listing the Thrust modules beginning with iterators and algorithms. We are looking for the algorithm to perform an inner product, and (again thanks to our CUDA background) we know that a reduction is involved. After perhaps a bit of hunting around, we select `Algorithms` ⇒ `Reductions` ⇒ `Transformed Reductions` and find documentation, as shown in Figure 8.1. Such documentation tends to create an information-dense environment, but with a little practice you'll become adept at finding what you need.

In this case, the `Returns` section (along with the two lines of text below the shaded heading) confirm that this algorithm does perform the inner product operation we are looking for. The `Parameters` section describes the list of inputs, and the box at the bottom provides a code snippet illustrating usage.

Using Thrust with Arrays (Instead of Vectors)

For better or worse, the sample on this documentation page happens to use regular C arrays as inputs instead of Thrust vectors, so the iterators are not explicitly seen, and some pointer arithmetic is used instead. Recall that the name of an array is a pointer to the start of the array, so `vec1`, the name of the first array, serves as the iterator specifying the start of the first array, referred to as `first1`. (Likewise, `vec2` is the value for the iterator `first2` that appears as the third argument.) The second argument, `last1`, is an iterator indicating the end of `vec1`. In the sample code, this value is concocted using pointer arithmetic: `vec1` points to the start of an array of length 3, so `vec1+3` points to the end of the array 3 elements later. If you use vectors, you will have the `begin()` and `end()` member functions at your disposal that return iterators, and you will not have to engage directly in pointer arithmetic.

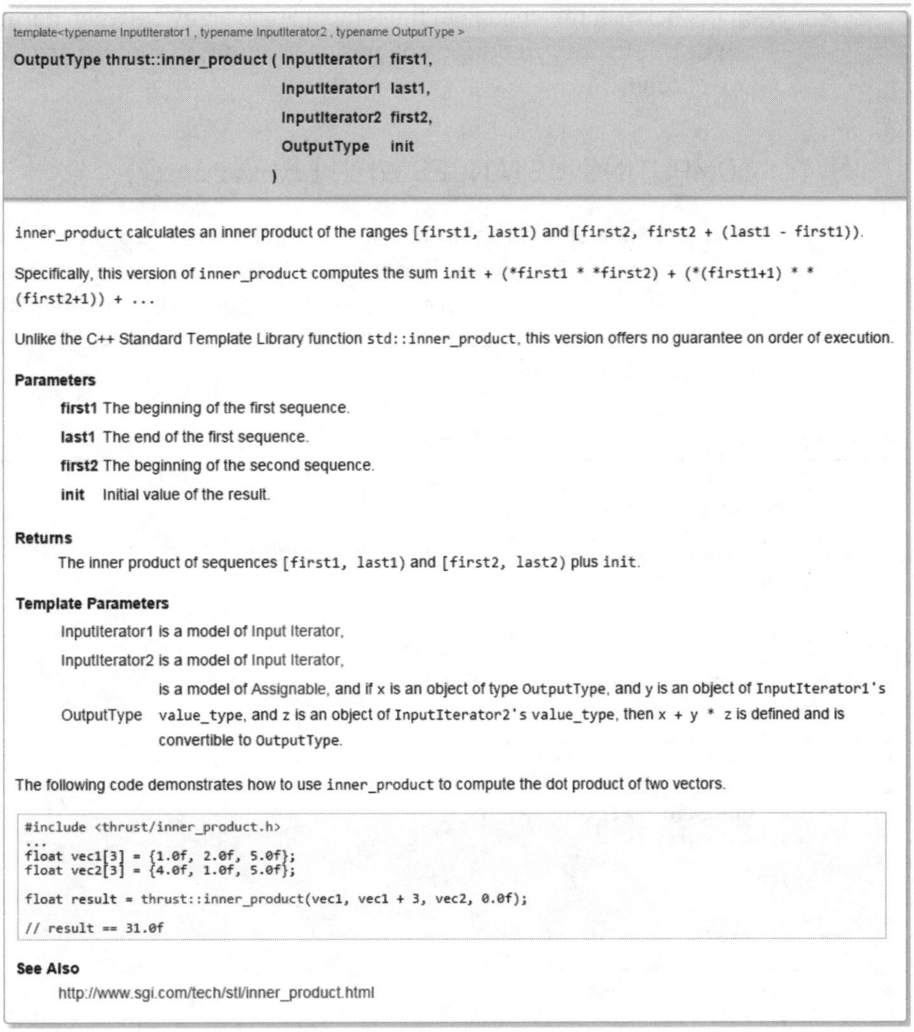

```
template<typename InputIterator1 , typename InputIterator2 , typename OutputType >

OutputType thrust::inner_product ( InputIterator1  first1,

                                   InputIterator1  last1,

                                   InputIterator2  first2,

                                   OutputType    init

                                 )
```

`inner_product` calculates an inner product of the ranges [first1, last1) and [first2, first2 + (last1 - first1)).

Specifically, this version of inner_product computes the sum init + (*first1 * *first2) + (*(first1+1) * * (first2+1)) + ...

Unlike the C++ Standard Template Library function std::inner_product, this version offers no guarantee on order of execution.

Parameters

> **first1** The beginning of the first sequence.
>
> **last1** The end of the first sequence.
>
> **first2** The beginning of the second sequence.
>
> **init** Initial value of the result.

Returns

> The inner product of sequences [first1, last1) and [first2, last2) plus init.

Template Parameters

> InputIterator1 is a model of Input Iterator,
>
> InputIterator2 is a model of Input Iterator,
>
> OutputType   is a model of Assignable, and if x is an object of type OutputType, and y is an object of InputIterator1's value_type, and z is an object of InputIterator2's value_type, then x + y * z is defined and is convertible to OutputType.

The following code demonstrates how to use inner_product to compute the dot product of two vectors.

```
#include <thrust/inner_product.h>
...
float vec1[3] = {1.0f, 2.0f, 5.0f};
float vec2[3] = {4.0f, 1.0f, 5.0f};

float result = thrust::inner_product(vec1, vec1 + 3, vec2, 0.0f);

// result == 31.0f
```

See Also

> http://www.sgi.com/tech/stl/inner_product.html

Figure 8.1 Documentation for `thrust::inner_product`

It is worth noting that we have just identified an efficient solution to an earlier problem. In the `heat_2d` app in Chapter 5, "Stencils and Shared Memory," we implemented Jacobi iteration to converge toward a steady-state temperature distribution. After setting up the boundary conditions, we started the iteration and just let it continue to run. At the end of that chapter, we posed the challenge of creating a convergence criterion to provide a quantitative basis for knowing when the iteration can be stopped. In Chapter 6, "Reduction and Atomic Functions," we noted that a reasonable stopping criterion could be based on the norm of the change of the temperature array between iterations, and `thrust::inner_product` enables us to compute such a norm with a single line of code.

COMPUTING DISTANCES WITH `transform()`

Next let's look at a Thrust implementation of a `dist_1d_thrust` app similar to distance apps in Chapter 3, "From Loops to Grids." The app once again computes distances from a reference point to a sequence of points uniformly spaced on a line segment. The code for the app is shown in Listing 8.3, and we'll go through it line by line.

Listing 8.3 `dist_1d_thrust/kernel.cu`

```
 1 #include <thrust/device_vector.h>
 2 #include <thrust/host_vector.h>
 3 #include <thrust/sequence.h>
 4 #include <thrust/transform.h>
 5 #include <math.h>
 6 #include <stdio.h>
 7 #define N 64
 8
 9 using namespace thrust::placeholders;
10
11 // Define transformation SqrtOf()(x) -> sqrt(x)
12 struct SqrtOf {
13   __host__ __device__
14   float operator()(float x) {
15     return sqrt(x);
16   }
17 };
18
19 int main() {
20   const float ref = 0.5;
21   thrust::device_vector<float> dvec_x(N);
22   thrust::device_vector<float> dvec_dist(N);
23   thrust::sequence(dvec_x.begin(), dvec_x.end());
24   thrust::transform(dvec_x.begin(), dvec_x.end(),
25                     dvec_x.begin(), _1 / (N - 1));
26   thrust::transform(dvec_x.begin(), dvec_x.end(),
27                     dvec_dist.begin(), (_1 - ref)*(_1 - ref));
28   thrust::transform(dvec_dist.begin(), dvec_dist.end(),
29                     dvec_dist.begin(), SqrtOf());
30   thrust::host_vector<float> h_x = dvec_x;
31   thrust::host_vector<float> h_dist = dvec_dist;
32   for (int i = 0; i < N; ++i) {
33     printf("x=%3.3f, dist=%3.3f\n", h_x[i], h_dist[i]);
34   }
35   return 0;
36 }
```

Lines 1–4 specify the include files for the Thrust features we'll use. The other included header files are math.h and stdio.h.

At this point, let's jump ahead to describe the contents of main() and return to discuss the intervening code. Line 20 sets the reference location ref to 0.5, to be consistent with our earlier examples; then we get right into using Thrust. (Note that this implementation is chosen for clarity of presentation, not optimal performance. An optimized version would likely combine or fuse multiple steps into a single, more complicated statement that would be counterproductive to our current purpose, so we'll save the discussion of fusion for later in this chapter.)

Lines 21–22 create Thrust device vectors to hold the input values and the output distances. Lines 23–25 fill the input vector dvec_x with values uniformly spaced on the interval [0, 1] in two steps: sequence(d_x.begin(), d_x.end()) fills the vector with the sequence of values 0.0, 1.0, ..., $N - 1$. To produce the desired values on [0,1], we need to divide each element by $N - 1$. We can perform the division (another occurrence of the map pattern) using thrust::transform, whose arguments include the first and last iterators for the input vector, the first iterator for the output vector, and the transformation. Since dvec_x is both the input and output vector, the first three arguments are dvec_x.begin(), dvec_x.end(), and dvec_x.begin(). The tricky part is the last argument that specifies the transformation. A function cannot be passed directly as an argument, so something more sophisticated is needed.

In this case, the transformation involves only a standard arithmetic operation, and we can create a passable description of the transformation using Thrust's placeholder feature. The placeholder syntax uses an underscore followed by a digit to refer to an argument based on its position in the argument list, and standard arithmetic operations are indicated as usual. Thus we can now decipher the fourth argument of thrust::transform. The expression _1/(N-1) says that the transformation output should consist of the first input (an element of the first input vector) divided by ($N - 1$). (Note that the input vector is declared to be of type float, so floating point division is performed.) Placeholders have a specific namespace, thrust::placeholders, and that's why we have the using namespace directive in line 9.

In lines 26–27, we use placeholder notation again. (dvec_x[i]-ref)* (dvec_x[i]-ref) is the square of the distance from the reference point to the ith grid point, so thrust::transform(dvec_x.begin(), dvec_x.end(), dvec_dist.begin(), (_1 - ref)*(_1 - ref)) fills the output device vector dvec_dist with the squared distances. Now we need to compute the square root of each entry, but sqrt() is not a standard arithmetic operation; its definition resides in the standard math library. The transformation we need here is beyond what can be done with placeholders, and a **function object**, or **functor**, is required.

How much more complicated is it to define a functor rather than a function? Not a lot; let's look at the details. We could create our own custom function (let's call it SqrtOf()) and have it compile for both CPU and GPU to call the sqrt() function included in the math library with the following code:

```
__host__ __device__
float SqrtOf(float x)
{
   return sqrt(x);
}
```

Creating the functor version requires only a few changes:

1. Instead of defining a function named SqrtOf, create a struct (a public class in C++ terminology) of that name by wrapping struct SqrtOf{ }; around the definition of the SqrtOf function.

2. In the function definition, replace SqrtOf with operator().

By making those changes to the function definition, you should have created the functor version appearing in lines 12–17.

Thinking About Functors

If it helps, you can think of the functor as follows. What we really did was to create a struct named SqrtOf that includes an alternative (or **overloaded**) definition of the function call operator (written as parentheses). While parentheses in other contexts group arguments or indicate precedence order, we created an alternative definition (that calls sqrt()) for SqrtOf(); that is, parentheses following the struct name SqrtOf.

That covers the code we skipped, and what remains of main() involves copying the results back to the host and printing them to the command window for inspection. Note that creating each host vector filled with the values from the corresponding device vector takes a single line (lines 30, 31), the memory for all of the vectors get freed automatically (without explicit calls to free() or cudaFree()), and the results printed to the command window agree with those obtained using our earlier distance apps. Finally, the Makefile for building is the same as norm's, which was provided in Listing 8.2.

Lambda expressions (lambda functions), a convenient feature of C++11, make passing functions into other functions cleaner and more readable. Lambda expressions can be used to replace functors and other anonymous functions. CUDA 7.5 recently introduced device lambda expressions as an experimental feature. Thus, now (although experimentally), we can use lambda expressions in our Thrust algorithms. Listing 8.4 shows the dist_1d_thrust application using lambdas.

Listing 8.4 dist_1d_thrust/kernel.cu with device lambda expressions

```
 1 #include <thrust/host_vector.h>
 2 #include <thrust/device_vector.h>
 3 #include <thrust/sequence.h>
 4 #include <thrust/transform.h>
 5 #include <math.h>
 6 #include <stdio.h>
 7 #define N 64
 8
 9 int main() {
10   const float ref = 0.5;
11   thrust::device_vector<float> dvec_x(N);
12   thrust::device_vector<float> dvec_dist(N);
13   thrust::sequence(dvec_x.begin(), dvec_x.end());
14   thrust::transform(dvec_x.begin(), dvec_x.end(), dvec_x.begin(),
15     []__device__(float x){ return x / (N-1); });
16   thrust::transform(dvec_x.begin(), dvec_x.end(), dvec_dist.begin(),
17     [=]__device__(float x){ return (x-ref)*(x-ref); });
18   thrust::transform(dvec_dist.begin(), dvec_dist.end(),
19     dvec_dist.begin(), []__device__(float x){ return sqrt(x); });
20   thrust::host_vector<float> h_x = dvec_x;
21   thrust::host_vector<float> h_dist = dvec_dist;
22   for (int i = 0; i < N; ++i) {
23     printf("x=%.3f, dist=%.3f\n", h_x[i], h_dist[i]);
24   }
25   return 0;
26 }
```

The Makefile is given in Listing 8.5. Visual Studio users need to enter the compiler flag --expt-extended-lambda in the Additional Options box in Configuration Properties ⇒ CUDA C/C++ ⇒ Command Line.

Listing 8.5 dist_1d_thrust/Makefile for experimental lambda feature compatibility

```
1 NVCC = /usr/local/cuda/bin/nvcc
2 NVCC_FLAGS = -g -G -Xcompiler -Wall --std=c++11 --expt-extended-lambda
3
4 main.exe: kernel.cu
5   $(NVCC) $(NVCC_FLAGS) $^ -o $@
```

The code can also be made shorter (and typically more efficient) by **fusion**; that is, merging the functionality of multiple steps of parallel code. A fused version of the functor implementation of the 1D distance app, `dist_1d_fused`, is shown in Listing 8.6.

Listing 8.6 `dist_1d_fused/kernel.cu`, a fused Thrust implementation of `dist_1d`

```
 1 #include <thrust/device_vector.h>
 2 #include <thrust/host_vector.h>
 3 #include <thrust/iterator/counting_iterator.h>
 4 #include <thrust/transform.h>
 5 #include <math.h>
 6 #include <stdio.h>
 7 #define N 64
 8
 9 // DistanceFrom(ref,n)(x)->sqrt((x/(n-1)-ref)*(x/(n-1)-ref))
10 struct DistanceFrom {
11   DistanceFrom(float ref, int n) : mRef(ref), mN(n) {}
12
13   __host__ __device__
14   float operator()(const float &x) {
15     float scaledX = x / (mN - 1);
16     return std::sqrt((scaledX - mRef)*(scaledX - mRef));
17   }
18   float mRef;
19   int mN;
20 };
21
22 int main() {
23   const float ref = 0.5;
24   thrust::device_vector<float> dvec_dist(N);
25   thrust::transform(thrust::counting_iterator<float>(0),
26     thrust::counting_iterator<float>(N), dvec_dist.begin(),
27     DistanceFrom(ref, N));
28
29   thrust::host_vector<float> hvec_dist = dvec_dist;
30   float *ptr = thrust::raw_pointer_cast(&hvec_dist[0]); // debugging
31   for (int i = 0; i < N; ++i) {
32     printf("x[%d]=%.3f, dist=%.3f\n", i, 1.f*i/(N - 1), hvec_dist[i]);
33   }
34   return 0;
35 }
```

Note that the entire computation is accomplished via a single call of `thrust::transform` in lines 25–27. The first two arguments are the starting and stopping values for a `counting_iterator` that serves as a virtual input sequence generator. The third argument gives the starting iterator for the output vector, and the last argument specifies the functor `DistanceFrom()` to be applied. While the counting iterator does the equivalent of storing a regular sequence of values in an input array, the functor does the rest of the work:

It takes two arguments specifying the reference point and the array length, computes the coordinate value on [0, 1] corresponding to each iterator value, computes the distance from `ref`, and stores the result in `dvec_dist`. (The apparently stray pointer declaration on line 30 is a means for making the output data visible using debugging tools, as will be explained in detail at the end of this section.)

ESTIMATING PI WITH `generate()`, `transform()`, AND `reduce()`

Another well-known example that illustrates the convenience of Thrust involves Monte Carlo estimation of π. The plan is simple: Generate coordinates for a large number N of points lying in the unit square [0,1] x [0,1] and count the number N_1 of those points that lie in the first quadrant of the unit circle, as illustrated in Figure 8.2. The working assumption is that random points in 2D are uniformly distributed in the area, so the ratio of the point counts should approach the area ratio for large N. The area of a quadrant of a circle with radius $r = 1$ is $\frac{1}{4}\pi r^2 = \frac{\pi}{4}$, and the unit square has area 1 x 1 = 1, so the area ratio is $\frac{\pi}{4}$. The bottom line is that $\frac{N_1}{N} \approx \frac{\pi}{4}$, so we obtain our Monte Carlo estimate of π by computing $4\frac{N_1}{N}$.

The full Thrust implementation, shown in Listing 8.7, starts with the usual `#include` statements for the Thrust functions we will use, the math library, and the input output library.

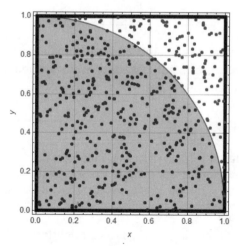

Figure 8.2 For large numbers of points randomly distributed on the unit square, the fraction of the random points that lie within the first quadrant of the unit circle approaches the area ratio $\frac{\pi}{4}$.

Listing 8.7 `thrustpi/kernel.cu`, a simple Thrust implementation of Monte Carlo estimation of π

```
 1 #include <thrust/host_vector.h>
 2 #include <thrust/device_vector.h>
 3 #include <thrust/reduce.h>
 4 #include <thrust/generate.h>
 5 #include <thrust/transform.h>
 6 #include <math.h>
 7 #include <stdio.h>
 8 #define N (1 << 20)
 9
10 using namespace thrust::placeholders;
11
12 int main(void)
13 {
14   thrust::host_vector<float> hvec_x(N);
15   thrust::host_vector<float> hvec_y(N);
16   thrust::generate(hvec_x.begin(), hvec_x.end(), rand);
17   thrust::generate(hvec_y.begin(), hvec_y.end(), rand);
18   thrust::device_vector<float> dvec_x = hvec_x;
19   thrust::device_vector<float> dvec_y = hvec_y;
20   thrust::transform(dvec_x.begin(), dvec_x.end(), dvec_x.begin(),
21     _1 / RAND_MAX);
22   thrust::transform(dvec_y.begin(), dvec_y.end(), dvec_y.begin(),
23     _1 / RAND_MAX);
24   thrust::device_vector<float>dvec_inCircle(N);
25   thrust::transform(dvec_x.begin(), dvec_x.end(), dvec_y.begin(),
26     dvec_inCircle.begin(), (_1*_1 + _2*_2)<1);
27   float pi =
28     thrust::reduce(dvec_inCircle.begin(), dvec_inCircle.end())*4.f/N;
29   printf("pi = %f\n", pi);
30   return 0;
31 }
```

Line 8 specifies a value to plug in for `N`. Line 10 specifies the `thrust::placeholders` namespace to avoid needing prefixes before the underscores in the placeholder expressions.

Bit Shift Operations

Note that `<<` does *not* mean "much less than"; here it is a bit shift operator, so `1<<20` means take the binary representation of the integer 1 and move the bits 20 places to the left (in other words, $2^{20} = 1,048,576$).

The approach in `main()` is as straightforward as possible:

1. Create host vectors `hvec_x` and `hvec_y` to hold the x and y coordinates of `N` points (lines 14–15).

2. Use `thrust::generate` to populate `hvec_x` and `hvec_y` with random numbers (lines 16–17). (Note that this uses the integer random number generator on the host.)

3. Create device vectors `dvec_x` and `dvec_y` with copies of the values of the random data generated on the host (lines 18–19).

4. Divide the random integers by `RAND_MAX` (the largest integer the random number generator can produce) using `thrust::transform` (with a placeholder transformation) to produce random floats on [0,1] (lines 20–23).

5. Create a device vector `dvec_inCircle` to store 0 if the point lies outside the unit circle, or 1 if the point lies within the unit circle (i.e., if $x^2 + y^2 < 1$, or, in placeholder terminology, `(_1*_1+_2*_2)<1`) (lines 24–26).

6. Compute the number of points in the circle (by applying `thrust::reduce` to `dvec_inCircle`), multiply by `4.f/N` to obtain the estimate of π, and print the result to the command window (lines 28–29).

The Makefile for building this app is the same as `norm`'s, which was provided in Listing 8.2. You should compile and run the app to verify that it produces a reasonable numerical value. Hopefully, the takeaway from this example is that you can pretty quickly put some basic pieces together to implement parallel computations without having to do any explicit parallel programming. Listing 8.8 shows a revision of the π estimator using lambda expressions that not only fuses the transform and reduce steps, but also obviates the need for the device vector `dvec_inCircle`.

Listing 8.8 `thrustpi/kernel.cu`, fused Thrust implementation of Monte Carlo estimation of π

```
 1 #include <thrust/host_vector.h>
 2 #include <thrust/device_vector.h>
 3 #include <thrust/generate.h>
 4 #include <thrust/count.h>
 5 #include <stdio.h>
 6 #define N (1 << 20)
 7
 8 int main() {
 9   thrust::host_vector<float> hvec_x(N), hvec_y(N);
10   thrust::generate(hvec_x.begin(), hvec_x.end(), rand);
11   thrust::generate(hvec_y.begin(), hvec_y.end(), rand);
12   thrust::device_vector<float> dvec_x = hvec_x;
13   thrust::device_vector<float> dvec_y = hvec_y;
14   int insideCount =
15     thrust::count_if(thrust::make_zip_iterator(thrust::make_tuple(
16       dvec_x.begin(), dvec_y.begin())), thrust::make_zip_iterator(
17       thrust::make_tuple(dvec_x.end(), dvec_y.end())),
```

```
18        [] __device__(const thrust::tuple<float, float> &el) {
19            return (pow(thrust::get<0>(el)/RAND_MAX, 2) +
20                    pow(thrust::get<1>(el)/RAND_MAX, 2)) < 1.f; });
21    printf("pi = %f\n", insideCount*4.f/N);
22    return 0;
23 }
```

All the parallel computation occurs in a single fused statement on lines 14–20. The combination of `thrust::make_tuple` and `thrust::make_zip_iterator` pair up the x and y coordinates to be operated on by the lambda expression on lines 18–20. The lambda expression accesses the values from `dvec_x` and `dvec_y` (with `thrust::get<0>` and `thrust::get<1>` respectively) and tests if the distance from the origin is less than the value of the argument; i.e., `1.0f`. No vector is needed to store the result; they are summed directly by `thrust::count_if`. Note that this application can be built with the Makefile shown in Listing 8.5.

As a further demonstration of fusion, we present a Thrust implementation to replace `centroid_2d/kernel.cu` in the `centroid_2d` app from Chapter 6, "Reduction and Atomic Functions." The Thrust implementation is shown in Listing 8.9, and it is worth noting that this code is much shorter than the previous version.

Listing 8.9 `centroid_2d/kernel.cu` with Thrust

```
 1 #include "kernel.h"
 2 #include <helper_math.h>
 3 #include <thrust/device_vector.h>
 4 #include <thrust/iterator/counting_iterator.h>
 5 #include <thrust/iterator/zip_iterator.h>
 6 #include <thrust/transform_reduce.h>
 7 #include <thrust/tuple.h>
 8 #include <stdio.h>
 9
10 struct PixelFunctor {
11    PixelFunctor(int width) : mWidth(width) {}
12    template <typename T>
13    __host__ __device__ int3 operator()(const T &el) {
14        const int idx = thrust::get<0>(el);
15        const uchar4 pixel = thrust::get<1>(el);
16        const int r = idx / mWidth;
17        const int c = idx - r*mWidth;
18        int pixVal = (pixel.x < 255 || pixel.y < 255 || pixel.z < 255);
19        return make_int3(pixVal*c, pixVal*r, pixVal);
20    }
21    int mWidth;
22 };
23
24 void centroidParallel(uchar4 *img, int width, int height) {
```

```
25  thrust::device_vector<uchar4> invec(img, img + width*height);
26  thrust::counting_iterator<int> first(0), last(invec.size());
27  int3 res = thrust::transform_reduce(thrust::make_zip_iterator(
28    thrust::make_tuple(first, invec.begin())),
29    thrust::make_zip_iterator(thrust::make_tuple(last, invec.end())),
30    PixelFunctor(width), make_int3(0, 0, 0), thrust::plus<int3>());
31
32  int centroidCol = res.x / res.z;
33  int centroidRow = res.y / res.z;
34  printf("Centroid: {col = %d, row = %d} based on %d pixels\n",
35         centroidCol, centroidRow, res.z);
36
37  for (int c = 0; c < width; ++c) {
38    img[centroidRow*width + c].x = 255;
39    img[centroidRow*width + c].y = 0;
40    img[centroidRow*width + c].z = 0;
41  }
42
43  for (int r = 0; r < height; ++r) {
44    img[r*width + centroidCol].x = 255;
45    img[r*width + centroidCol].y = 0;
46    img[r*width + centroidCol].z = 0;
47  }
48 }
```

There is a lot more to learn about Thrust, but let's just cover one more need-to-know issue before moving on: What do you do when you have data in a Thrust device vector that you want to pass to a CUDA kernel? Conversely, if you have data in a device array, how do you operate on it with a Thrust function? It turns out that both maneuvers can be achieved as follows:

- **Passing CUDA device array as argument to a Thrust function.** Create a device array as usual by declaring a pointer and allocating device memory:

```
float *ptr;
cudaMalloc(&ptr, N * sizeof(float));
```

Thrust provides `thrust::device_pointer` as a means to create a pointer that can be passed to Thrust functions as follows:

```
thrust::device_ptr<float>dev_ptr(ptr);
```

The device pointer can then be passed to Thrust algorithms:

```
thrust::fill(dev_ptr, dev_ptr+N, 1.0f);
```

Remember to include the header files and to free the device memory (`cudaFree(ptr);`) when you are done.

- **Passing a Thrust device vector as argument to a CUDA API function or kernel.**
  A CUDA kernel function accepts pointers to arrays as arguments, but does
  not immediately know what to do with a Thrust device vector. The solution
  is provided by `thrust::raw_pointer_cast`, which turns out to be a very
  descriptive name. (Remember to include the header file!) Once you've created
  a device vector (e.g., `thrust::device_vector<float>dvec_x(N);`),
  you can then create a regular pointer as follows:

```
float* ptrToX = thrust::raw_pointer_cast(&dvec_x[0]);
```

and the raw pointer is suitable for use as a kernel argument.

Related Windows Debugging Note

While thrust vectors are not set up to be directly viewable in the debugger, if you
cast a raw pointer to a Thrust `host_vector`, you can enter the pointer name
followed by a comma and the number of elements of interest in a Watch window
to inspect the values. For example, the pointer created on line 30 of Listing 8.6
provides a way to view the results from inside Visual Studio. Compile the app in
debug mode and place a break point after line 35. Start debugging, open a Watch
window, and enter `ptr`, 64 to view the distance values stored in `hvec_dist`.

We hope that is enough of an introduction to provide you with a productive start
in Thrust, and we'll move on to look at some other useful libraries.

cuRAND

You may have noticed that when we estimated π using Thrust, we generated
the random point coordinates on the host (and initially stored the random coordinates in host vectors). If you want to parallelize that part of the computation,
you need to know about cuRAND, the CUDA Random Number Generation
library.

The general description of the cuRAND library [9] explains its "flexible usage
model" which means that there is a host API for bulk generation of random
numbers (using functions called from the host but executed in parallel on the
GPU) and an inline implementation that can be called from within a kernel. Our
example for estimating π followed the bulk generation model, where we produce a large collection of random numbers and then use them in the ensuing

computation, so we will use the cuRAND host API to replace our previous approach to generating the random point coordinates. The revised code for estimating π using cuRAND is shown in Listing 8.10, which adds the cuRAND header file, `curand.h`, to the included files.

Listing 8.10 `thrustpi/kernel.cu` based on random coordinates generated with the cuRAND library

```
1  #include <curand.h>
2  #include <thrust/device_vector.h>
3  #include <thrust/count.h>
4  #include <math.h>
5  #include <stdio.h>
6  #define N (1 << 20)
7
8  int main() {
9    curandGenerator_t gen;
10   curandCreateGenerator(&gen, CURAND_RNG_PSEUDO_DEFAULT);
11   curandSetPseudoRandomGeneratorSeed(gen, 42ULL);
12   thrust::device_vector<float>dvec_x(N);
13   thrust::device_vector<float>dvec_y(N);
14   float *ptr_x = thrust::raw_pointer_cast(&dvec_x[0]);
15   float *ptr_y = thrust::raw_pointer_cast(&dvec_y[0]);
16   curandGenerateUniform(gen, ptr_x, N);
17   curandGenerateUniform(gen, ptr_y, N);
18   curandDestroyGenerator(gen);
19   int insideCount =
20     thrust::count_if(thrust::make_zip_iterator(thrust::make_tuple(
21       dvec_x.begin(), dvec_y.begin())), thrust::make_zip_iterator(
22       thrust::make_tuple(dvec_x.end(), dvec_y.end())),
23       []__device__(const thrust::tuple<float, float> &el) {
24         return (pow(thrust::get<0>(el), 2) +
25                 pow(thrust::get<1>(el), 2)) < 1.f; });
26   printf("pi = %f\n", insideCount*4.f/N);
27   return 0;
28 }
```

Lines 9–11 comprise the setup for using cuRAND including the following:

- Declaring a `curandGenerator_t` object named gen on line 9. (You can think of `curandGenerator_t` as the type created by cuRAND for referring to random number generators.)

- Creating a specific random number generator with arguments corresponding to the address of gen and choice of a specific generator. `CURAND_RNG_PSEUDO_DEFAULT` selects the default pseudorandom number generator (which is slightly simpler in that it does not require a state input) (line 10).

- Seeding the random number generator on line 11. The arguments to curandSetPseudoRandomGeneratorSeed() include the generator and the seed value. 42ULL indicates the unsigned long long int with value 42.

Next comes the creation of the device vectors dvec_x and dvec_y on lines 12–13. Note that cuRAND lets us generate the random coordinate values on the GPU, so there is no need now for the host vectors hvec_x and hvec_y that we used previously.

We are now presented with our first opportunity to use Thrust's pointer casting capabilities. We are going to use the cuRAND function curandGenerate-Uniform() to generate a collection of uniformly distributed random numbers, and curandGenerateUniform() expects as arguments a curandGenerator_t object (to generate the random values), a pointer to a device array (where the values will be stored), and the number of values to generate. To store the random values in device arrays, we create pointers, ptr_x and ptr_y, to the initial element in each device vector using thrust::raw_pointer_cast() on lines 14–15. The random values are computed with curandGenerateUniform() and stored in the device vectors, dvec_x and dvec_y, via their cast pointers, ptr_x and ptr_y, on lines 16–17. Having finished with generating the random values, we free up the resources used by cuRAND with curandDestroyGenerator() on line 18. The rest of the code is as before, and the Makefile to build it is shown in Listing 8.11. In Visual Studio, link cuRAND by opening the project's property pages, selecting Linker ⇒ Input ⇒ Additional Dependencies ⇒ Edit, and adding curand.lib.

Listing 8.11 thrustpi/Makefile for building with cuRAND capability

```
1 NVCC = /usr/local/cuda/bin/nvcc
2 NVCC_FLAGS = -g -G -Xcompiler -Wall --std=c++11 --expt-extended-lambda
3 LIBS = -lcurand
4
5 main.exe: kernel.cu
6    $(NVCC) $(NVCC_FLAGS) $^ -o $@ $(LIBS)
```

Build and run the code to see how it works. Again, this example aims for clarity of presentation. For another version that aims for tighter Thrust/cuRAND coupling and greater efficiency, see [9].

NPP

The NVIDIA Performance Primitives library (NPP) is a collection of parallel functions that can be used for image, video, and signal processing [10]. As of version 7.5, NPP claims to deliver about 5–10x performance improvement compared to CPU implementations, and its ~1900 "processing primitives" for images and ~600 primitives for signal processing offer even more significant opportunities for accelerating code development. Here we use NPP to create a library-based implementation of the `sharpen` app from Chapter 5, "Stencils and Shared Memory," but before getting into the details of the code, a short aside about library files is needed.

Linking Library Files

Using code libraries sometimes requires inclusion of header files and/or linking with object files. A general discussion of how to do this in Visual Studio is given at the end of Appendix D, "CUDA Practicalities: Timing, Profiling, Error Handling, and Debugging." Here we give the specifics for NPP. Windows users need to tell the system to link in the libraries `nppc.lib` along with `nppi.lib` and `npps.lib`, which have the image-processing and signal-processing functions, respectively). In Visual Studio, you can do this by opening the project's property pages and selecting `Linker ⇒ Input`. You can then click on `Additional Dependencies`, select `Edit`, and add the necessary libraries to the list so that they appear, as shown in Figure 8.3.

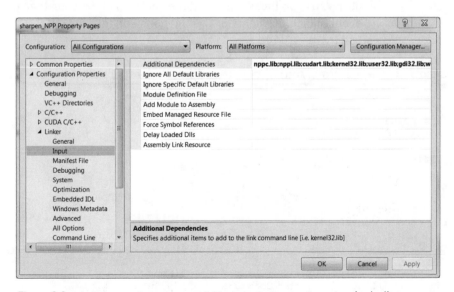

Figure 8.3 `Linker ⇒ Input ⇒ Additional Dependencies` including `nppc.lib` and `nppi.lib`

Linux users have the option of static linking, and if you do static linking, you also need to link in the cuLIBOS library. In our Makefiles, we provide a static linking approach, and Listing 8.12 gives a sample Makefile to link the cuLIBOS and NPP libraries.

Listing 8.12 `sharpen_npp/Makefile`

```
1 NVCC = /usr/local/cuda/bin/nvcc
2 NVCC_FLAGS = -g -G -Xcompiler -Wall
3 LIBS += -lnppi_static -lnppc_static -lculibos
4
5 all: main.exe
6
7 main.exe: main.cpp
8     $(NVCC) $(NVCC_FLAGS) $^ -o $@ $(LIBS)
```

If you are wondering how you are supposed to know such things, you have a couple resources at your disposal. Entering "CUDA NPP additional dependencies" into a search engine succeeded in producing useful information for dealing with this issue. However, this may be a situation where the CUDA Samples really become valuable. If you have a working CUDA Sample that uses the library of interest, you can open its property pages and inspect the various settings including the additional dependencies.

sharpen_npp

Listing 8.13 shows our reimplementation of the `sharpen` app using NPP. Note that in this version there is no `kernel.cu`, and everything is implemented in a single `main.cpp` file. We present the contents of the code then discuss how to go about finding the right library functions and figuring out the syntax for calling them.

Listing 8.13 `sharpen_npp/main.cpp`, the NPP-powered version of the `sharpen` app

```
 1 #define cimg_display 0
 2 #include "CImg.h"
 3 #include <cuda_runtime.h>
 4 #include <npp.h>
 5 #include <stdlib.h>
 6 #define kNumCh 3
 7
 8 void sharpenNPP(Npp8u *arr, int w, int h) {
 9   Npp8u *d_in = 0, *d_out = 0;
10   Npp32f *d_filter = 0;
11   const Npp32f filter[9] = {-1.0, -1.0, -1.0,
12                             -1.0,  9.0, -1.0,
13                             -1.0, -1.0, -1.0};
14
15   cudaMalloc(&d_out, kNumCh*w*h*sizeof(Npp8u));
16   cudaMalloc(&d_in, kNumCh*w*h*sizeof(Npp8u));
17   cudaMalloc(&d_filter, 9*sizeof(Npp32f));
```

```
18   cudaMemcpy(d_in, arr, kNumCh*w*h*sizeof(Npp8u),
19               cudaMemcpyHostToDevice);
20   cudaMemcpy(d_filter, filter, 9*sizeof(Npp32f),
21               cudaMemcpyHostToDevice);
22   const NppiSize oKernelSize = {3, 3};
23   const NppiPoint oAnchor = {1, 1};
24   const NppiSize oSrcSize = {w, h};
25   const NppiPoint oSrcOffset = {0, 0};
26   const NppiSize oSizeROI = {w, h};
27
28   nppiFilterBorder32f_8u_C3R(d_in, kNumCh*w*sizeof(Npp8u), oSrcSize,
29     oSrcOffset, d_out, kNumCh*w*sizeof(Npp8u), oSizeROI, d_filter,
30     oKernelSize, oAnchor, NPP_BORDER_REPLICATE);
31
32   cudaMemcpy(arr, d_out, kNumCh*w*h*sizeof(Npp8u),
33               cudaMemcpyDeviceToHost);
34   cudaFree(d_in);
35   cudaFree(d_out);
36   cudaFree(d_filter);
37 }
38
39 int main() {
40   cimg_library::CImg<unsigned char> image("butterfly.bmp");
41   const int w = image.width();
42   const int h = image.height();
43   Npp8u *arr = (Npp8u*)malloc(kNumCh*w*h*sizeof(Npp8u));
44
45   for (int r = 0; r < h; ++r) {
46     for (int c = 0; c < w; ++c) {
47       for (int ch = 0; ch < kNumCh; ++ch) {
48         arr[kNumCh*(r*w + c) + ch] = image(c, r, ch);
49       }
50     }
51   }
52
53   sharpenNPP(arr, w, h);
54
55   for (int r = 0; r < h; ++r) {
56     for (int c = 0; c < w; ++c) {
57       for (int ch = 0; ch < kNumCh; ++ch) {
58         image(c, r, ch) = arr[kNumCh*(r*w + c) + ch];
59       }
60     }
61   }
62   image.save_bmp("out.bmp");
63   free(arr);
64   return 0;
65 }
```

The code starts, as usual, with some #include directives for the CUDA run-time, the CImg library (to be used once again for image input and output), and the NPP header file along with two #define directives: We will not be using CImg for graphics display so cimg_display is set to 0, and kNumCh is set to 3 to specify the number of color channels in the image data.

The bulk of the computation, applying the stencil using NPP library functions, is performed by sharpenNPP() on lines 8–37. The function starts off in a way that should look familiar: declaration of pointers to two device arrays of type Npp8u (unsigned char) for d_in and d_out and one array of type Npp32f (float) for d_filter to hold the floating point stencil coefficients as defined on lines 11–13. Lines 15–21 allocate the memory for the device arrays and copy the input image data to the device. Lines 22–26 set the parameters for NPP algorithm that applies the stencil:

- oKernelSize sets the dimensions of the stencil to be 3 × 3.

- oAnchor sets the alignment point at indices {1, 1} so the 9 in the middle of the stencil is aligned with the current pixel.

- oSrcSize sets the dimensions of the image to be processed.

- oSrcOffset sets the pixel indices at which to start applying the stencil. {0, 0} starts the process at the first pixel.

- oSizeROI sets the pixel extent of the rectangular region of interest (ROI). The specified values set the ROI to match the entire image.

The main work of the app occurs in the single NPP algorithm call on lines 28–30:

```
nppiFilterBorder32f_8u_C3R(d_in, kNumCh*w*sizeof(Npp8u), oSrcSize,
    oSrcOffset, d_out, kNumCh*w*sizeof(Npp8u), oSizeROI, d_filter,
    oKernelSize, oAnchor, NPP_BORDER_REPLICATE);
```

The function name nppiFilterBorder32f_8u_C3R() is deciphered as follows:

- nppi indicates an NPP image-processing algorithm.

- Filter is true to its name; it applies a filter (a.k.a. stencil).

- Border indicates that the algorithm handles cases where the stencil runs off the edge of the image. The last argument, NPP_BORDER_REPLICATE, says that the necessary "halo" values are equivalent to replicating the value of the nearest pixel.

- 32f indicates that the stencil contains 32-bit floats.

- 8u indicates that the input data consists of 8-bit unsigned chars.

- C3 says that the image data has three color channels.

- R indicates operation on a rectangular ROI.

The function ends by copying the filtered image data back to the host and freeing the memory allocated for the device arrays.

The rest of the `main.cpp` is almost the same as the `sharpen` app from Chapter 5, "Stencils and Shared Memory," with the exception of the data array being an array of `unsigned chars`, and the Npp8u being the NPP library's type name for `unsigned char`.

That completes the code description, and it is time to build and run the application. Listing 8.12 shows the Makefile needed for building this application in Linux. You should confirm that the `sharpen_npp` app reproduces the same output as the `sharpen` app for the sample image shown in Figure 5.4.

Navigating the NPP Documentation

Let's take a moment to get some perspective on where all the NPP code came from. How do you find an NPP algorithm that does what you want? How do you determine what to pass as arguments? NPP offers thousands of algorithms, so finding the right one can be challenging, but it is not impossible. All of the NPP algorithms are described in the comprehensive documentation [10]. This virtual tome (currently over 3,000 pages in length) can seem overwhelming at first, so let's break it down into manageable pieces.

Chapters 1–4 of the NPP Documentation ("NVIDIA Performance Primitives," "General API Conventions," "Signal-Processing Specific API Conventions," and "Image-Processing Specific API Conventions") total about 20 pages of material that is worth reading for general background if you plan to use NPP.

Once you've been through that material, you can focus on Chapter 5, "Module Index," which provides a full list of NPP's modules. (Image-processing capabilities include Arithmetic and Logical Operations, Color Sampling and Conversion, Compression, Labeling and Segmentation, Data Exchange, Filtering, Geometric and Linear Transformations, Morphological Operations, Statistical Operations, Memory Management, and Threshold/Compare Operations.) For each module, the functions are listed along with links to the detailed documentation.

For our example of image sharpening, we employed a 2D convolution with a custom filter, so only a few candidates had to be inspected to identify the Convolution module as useful and click on the link to the relevant page number (p. 1221 in Version 7.5). There one finds several pages of related functions of various "flavors," but, after reading the first four chapters of the NPP documentation, it is not too difficult to find one that has the right flavor and the appropriate specification of input and output datatypes. We chose `nppiFilterBorder32f_8u_C3R()` for the reasons listed above (i.e., a 32-bit `float` filter that handles 8-bit unsigned char images with three color channels, a border, and a rectangular ROI). Having identified a function of choice, clicking on the function name links to the parameter specifications (also listed above). Note that some of the more complicated parameters offer links to more detailed explanations.

MORE IMAGE PROCESSING WITH NPP

Let's embellish our app to not only sharpen an image, but to also produce an image that permutes (or swaps) the color channels or performs pixel-wise addition of shading values from a second image and computes a measure of how different the result is from the original image. You might take a look at the NPP documentation to see what functions you can find to produce images like those shown in Figure 8.4.

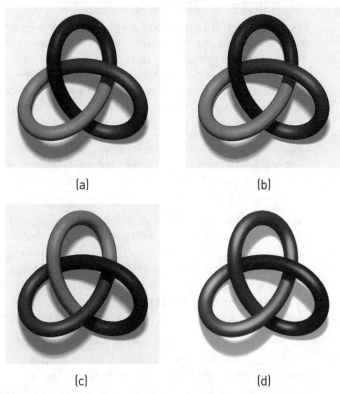

(a)

(b)

(c)

(d)

Figure 8.4 Rendering of the tricolor trefoil (a) original RGB, (b) sharpened, (c) colors swapped from RGB to BGR, (d) pixel-wise sum of original and color-swapped images. (Full-color versions of these images are available at www.cudaforengineers.com.) (Adapted from original image by Jim.belk on Wikimedia Commons, http://commons.wikimedia.org/wiki/File:Tricoloring.png)

For the specified operations, we identified the NPP function calls:

- **Permuting color channels.**

```
nppiSwapChannels_8u_C3R(d_in, kNumCh*w*sizeof(Npp8u), d_out,
kNumCh*w*sizeof(Npp8u), oSizeROI, aDstOrder);
```

The function name deciphers as NPP image-processing algorithm for swapping channels in an 8-bit, 3-channel rectangular image. The only new argument is the final one, which specifies the channel permutation. In our example, we permute RGB⟶GBR with the following specification:

```
const int aDstOrder[3] = {1, 2, 0};
```

(Note that aDstOrder[3] = {0, 1, 2} would leave the image unchanged.) These two lines of code (definition of aDstOrder and call of nppiSwapChannels_8u_C3R()) can be substituted for the nppiFilterBorder32f_8u_C3R() call on lines 28–30 of Listing 8.13 to perform color swapping instead of sharpening.

- **Pixel-wise addition.** nppiAdd_8u_C3RSfs() performs pixel-wise summation. The function call for adding the output data, d_out, to the input image data, d_in, and overwriting the results into d_out produces the following:

```
nppiAdd_8u_C3RSfs(d_in, kNumCh*w*sizeof(Npp8u), d_out,
kNumCh*w*sizeof(Npp8u), d_out, kNumCh*w*sizeof(Npp8u), oSizeROI, 1);
```

The suffix Sfs indicates that the function includes scaling to deal with output ranges that may exceed the input range of 8-bit unsigned integers. Since we can get sums of up to 255 + 255 (and all larger values would get clipped to 255, producing washout), we specify a scale factor exponent of 1 so the sum gets divided by $2^1 = 2$ to ensure results on [0,255] without clipping large values. Note that the resulting image was a bit dark, so we brightened it up by adding a constant to every pixel value as follows:

```
const Npp8u aConstants[3] = {32, 32, 32};
nppiAddC_8u_C3IRSfs (aConstants, d_out, kNumCh*w*sizeof(Npp8u),
oSizeROI, 0);
```

- **Computing image distance.** nppiNormDiff_L2_8u_C3R() computes the Euclidean distance between images (or the L^2-norm of the image difference). Note that the norm difference algorithm requires allocation of memory for intermediate results, so a few additional lines of code are needed. The code for setting up and calling nppiNormDiff_L2_8u_C3R() is shown in Listing 8.14. The distance measures are computed on lines 7–8 and printed to the command window on lines 11–13. This snippet can be inserted below the NPP call that modifies the image to compute the image distance between the input image and the modified output image.

Listing 8.14 Snippet for computing the "distance" between images using `nppiNormDiff_L2_8u_C3R()`

```
1    Npp64f *aNorm = 0;
2    cudaMalloc(&aNorm, 3 * sizeof(Npp64f));
3    Npp8u *pDeviceBuffer = 0;
4    int bufferSize;
5    nppiNormDiffL2GetBufferHostSize_8u_C3R(oSizeROI, &bufferSize);
6    cudaMalloc(&pDeviceBuffer, bufferSize);
7    nppiNormDiff_L2_8u_C3R(d_in, kNumCh*w*sizeof(Npp8u), d_out,
8      kNumCh*w*sizeof(Npp8u), oSizeROI, aNorm, pDeviceBuffer);
9    Npp64f res[3];
10   cudaMemcpy(res, aNorm, 3*sizeof(Npp64f), cudaMemcpyDeviceToHost);
11   for (int i = 0; i < 3; ++i) {
12     printf("%f\n", res[i]/(w*h));
13   }
```

Sample results are shown in Figure 8.4. The input image (a) is shown top-left; the sharpened image (b) is shown top-right; the color-swapped version (c) is shown lower-left; and the sum of the original and color-swapped images (d) is shown on lower-right. While it may not be easy to visually distinguish the original and sharpened images, we can distinguish them based on the normed image distances. Note that the image distance is computed component-wise; that is, with separate values for the red, green, and blue channels. If you want a single scalar distance, you can convert to grayscale first with the code shown in Listing 8.15.

Here is a summary of the results of computing distances from the input image:

- **Input image.** All three color channels produce a normed difference of 0.0 (The distance between anything and itself should be zero, so this is a good sign.)

- **Sharpened image.** The normed difference values for red, green, and blue channels are 0.01122, 0.01131, and 0.01129, respectively.

- **Color-swapped image.** The normed differences are 0.08716, 0.08813, and 0.08521 for red, green, and blue, respectively. Converting to grayscale produces a distance norm of 0.07697. Not surprisingly, the grayscale distance measure is less sensitive to color swapping than the color specific measures.

- **Sum of original and color-swapped images.** The RGB normed differences are 0.05028, 0.04999, and 0.04877. Grayscale conversion gives 0.04375. Note that the scaled sum averages the original and color-swapped images, producing an image distance that is much smaller than for the color-swapped image but still significantly larger than for the sharpened image.

Listing 8.15 Snippet for converting to grayscale then computing image distance

```
 1 // Allocate memory for a double.
 2 Npp64f *pNormDiff = NULL;
 3 cudaMalloc(&pNormDiff, sizeof(Npp64f));
 4
 5 // Allocate memory for scratch buffer.
 6 Npp8u *pDeviceBufferGray = NULL;
 7 int bufferSizeGray;
 8 nppiNormDiffL2GetBufferHostSize_8u_C1R(oSizeROI, &bufferSizeGray);
 9 cudaMalloc(&pDeviceBufferGray, bufferSizeGray);
10
11 // Convert to grayscale.
12 nppiRGBToGray_8u_C3C1R(d_in, kNumCh*w*sizeof(Npp8u), d_temp_gray1,
13   w*sizeof(Npp8u), oSizeROI);
14 nppiRGBToGray_8u_C3C1R(d_temp, kNumCh*w*sizeof(Npp8u), d_temp_gray2,
15   w*sizeof(Npp8u), oSizeROI);
16
17 // Grayscale norm diff.
18 nppiNormDiff_L2_8u_C1R(d_in, kNumCh*w*sizeof(Npp8u), d_temp,
19   kNumCh*w*sizeof(Npp8u), oSizeROI, pNormDiff, pDeviceBufferGray);
20
21 // Get and print result.
22 Npp64f res = 0;
23 cudaMemcpy(&res, pNormDiff, sizeof(Npp64f), cudaMemcpyDeviceToHost);
24 printf("%f\n", res/(w*h));
```

While some navigation skills are required to get through the documentation, NPP provides a large number of algorithms for image and signal processing that are developed, tested, and maintained by expert programmers for your convenience.

Linear Algebra Using cuSOLVER and cuBLAS

We now arrive at another area that is significant in terms of both library development and library usage: solving systems of linear algebraic equations. The focus on linear algebra libraries predates GPU computing, and the significant and widely used CPU-based linear algebra libraries include the Basic Linear Algebra Subprograms (**BLAS**) and the higher level Linear Algebra Package

(**LAPACK**) [11]. cuBLAS is NVIDIA's GPU-accelerated implementation of the BLAS library [12]. cuSOLVER, introduced into the CUDA Toolkit in Version 7.0, is a GPU-accelerated analog of LAPACK [13]. cuSOLVER contains three separate libraries:

- cuSolverDN provides factorization and solution methods for dense matrices.

- cuSolverSP solves sparse and least-squares problems based on sparse QR factorization.

- cuSolverRF accelerates refactorization methods used for multiple matrices that share a sparsity pattern.

While cuBLAS and cuSOLVER provide a large number of functions, here we will focus on just three of them that combine to serve a useful function: solving the multiple linear regression or least-squares problem.

Once again, we'll jump right into a concrete example that aims to compute a linear model of the hourly energy production rate (b) of a power plant based on four input variables: temperature (T), exhaust vacuum (V), ambient pressure (P), and relative humidity (H). The resulting model will express the output as a linear function of the inputs

$$c_0 + c_T * T_i + c_V * V_i + c_H * H_i + c_P * P_i = b_i$$

and if we had five sets of measurements to determine the five unknown coefficients c_0, c_T, c_V, c_H, and c_P, then this would be a nice, simple 5×5 matrix problem that could be done by hand. However, thanks to a generous data donation of Combined Cycle Power Plant data to the University of California-Irvine Machine Learning Repository [14,15], over 9,500 sets of measurements are available. (Note that we have changed the variable names slightly for ease of presentation.) So, instead of a small, well-determined problem (five equations with five variables), we have a large and highly-overdetermined problem (i.e., one with many more equations than variables). We'll leave it up to you to explore the full data set and construct an example based on the first nine sets of measurements. (Doing the larger computation is not the issue, but inputting the full data set and constructing the matrix involves reading in a .csv file, which is out of need-to-know territory for this book.)

Each measurement corresponds to an equation with values of the measured variables that get multiplied by the five unknown coefficients and summed to produce a measured value of **b**. We can then collect the equations into the single

$$res\ R^{-1}res^T$$
$$= res\ (QR)^{-1}res^T$$
$$= res\ R^{-1}Q^{-1}res^T = res\ R^{-1}Q^Tres = res R^{-1}(res Q)^T$$

matrix equation $Ac = b$ where A is the 9×5 matrix composed of columns that are the vector of measurements of each variable (e.g., the first column of A is the vector of measured temperatures), b is the vector (or 9×1 matrix) of measured power production rates, and we want to solve for the vector (or 5×1 matrix) of coefficients $c = [c_0, c_T, c_V, c_H, c_P]^T$. Such a system is not directly solvable, but it can be put into a tractable form using QR factorization [16,17]. The basic idea is that any matrix A can be expressed in terms of two matrices Q and R with the following special properties:

- $QR = A$

- Q is orthonormal (its inverse is the same as its transpose) so $Q^TQ = I$, the identity matrix.

- R is upper triangular.

Applying the factorization $A = QR$ and multiplying both sides of the matrix equation by Q^T, we get $Q^TQRc = Q^Tb$. The left side simplifies (because $Q^TQ = I$ and $IR = R$), and we end up with $Rc = Q^Tb$, which is tractable because R is upper triangular. The last equation only involves the last entry of c, so we can solve for that entry directly and back substitute to solve for the earlier entries in turn. The actual data for the problem is shown in Table 8.1.

With the problem description complete, we can focus on the library implementation of the three major steps:

1. The QR factorization of a dense matrix is provided by the function `cusolverDnSgeqrf()`. The name combines the name of the dense matrix library (`cusolverDn`), an indicator of float data type (`S`), and the abbreviated command to get the QR factorization (`geqrf`).

2. The modified right-hand side Q^Tb is computed with `cusolverDnSormqr()`. This name combines the dense matrix library, with the data type indicator, and an abbreviation for "overwrite matrix by multiplying with Q from QR decomposition" (`ormqr`).

3. Backsolve $Rc = Q^Tb$ for c using `cublasStrsm()`. Here the name consists of the relevant library (`cublas`), the data type indicator (`S` for float), and an abbreviation for "triangular solve matrix" (`trsm`).

The code for the library-based implementation of the multiple linear regression example is shown in Listing 8.16.

Table 8.1 Data from the Combined Cycle Power Plant Data Set

T	V	P	H	B
8.34	40.77	1010.84	90.01	480.48
23.64	58.49	1011.40	74.20	445.75
29.74	56.90	1007.15	41.91	438.76
19.07	49.69	1007.22	76.79	453.09
11.80	40.66	1017.13	97.20	464.43
13.97	39.16	1016.05	84.60	470.96
22.10	71.29	1008.20	75.38	442.35
14.47	41.76	1021.98	78.41	464.00
31.25	69.51	1010.25	36.83	428.77
6.77	38.18	1017.80	81.13	484.31

Listing 8.16 `linreg/main.cpp` for solving multiple linear regression example with cuSOLVER and cuBLAS

```
1 #include <stdio.h>
2 #include <cuda_runtime.h>
3 #include <cusolverDn.h>
4 #include <cublas_v2.h>
5
6 #define MIN(X, Y)  ((X) < (Y) ? (X) : (Y))
7
8 int main() {
9   // Create A (m by n) and b (m by 1) on host and device.
10   const int m = 9, n = 5;
11   const int lda = m, ldb = m;
12
13   float A[m*n] = {
14     1.0, 1.0, 1.0, 1.0, 1.0, 1.0, 1.0, 1.0, 1.0,
15     8.34, 23.64, 29.74, 19.07, 11.8, 13.97, 22.1, 14.47, 31.25,
16     40.77, 58.49,56.9,49.69,40.66,39.16,71.29,41.76, 69.51,
17     1010.84, 1011.4, 1007.15, 1007.22, 1017.13, 1016.05, 1008.2,
18     1021.98, 1010.25,
19     90.01,74.2,41.91,76.79,97.2,84.6,75.38,78.41, 36.83};
```

```
20    float b[m] = {
21      480.48, 445.75,438.76,453.09,464.43, 470.96,442.35,464, 428.77};
22
23    float *d_A = 0, *d_b = 0;
24    cudaMalloc(&d_A, m*n*sizeof(float));
25    cudaMemcpy(d_A, A, m*n*sizeof(float), cudaMemcpyHostToDevice);
26    cudaMalloc(&d_b, m*sizeof(float));
27    cudaMemcpy(d_b, b, m*sizeof(float), cudaMemcpyHostToDevice);
28
29    // Initialize the CUSOLVER and CUBLAS context.
30    cusolverDnHandle_t cusolverDnH = 0;
31    cublasHandle_t cublasH = 0;
32    cusolverDnCreate(&cusolverDnH);
33    cublasCreate(&cublasH);
34
35    // Initialize solver parameters.
36    float *tau = 0, *work = 0;
37    int *devInfo = 0, Lwork = 0;
38    cudaMalloc(&tau, MIN(m,n)*sizeof(float));
39    cudaMalloc(&devInfo, sizeof(int));
40    const float alpha = 1;
41
42    // Calculate the size of work buffer needed.
43    cusolverDnSgeqrf_bufferSize(cusolverDnH, m, n, d_A, lda, &Lwork);
44    cudaMalloc(&work, Lwork*sizeof(float));
45
46    // A = QR with CUSOLVER
47    cusolverDnSgeqrf(cusolverDnH, m, n, d_A, lda, tau, work, Lwork,
48                     devInfo);
49    cudaDeviceSynchronize();
50
51    // z = (Q^T)b with CUSOLVER, z is m x 1
52    cusolverDnSormqr(cusolverDnH, CUBLAS_SIDE_LEFT, CUBLAS_OP_T, m, 1,
53                     MIN(m, n), d_A, lda, tau, d_b, ldb, work, Lwork,
54                     devInfo);
55    cudaDeviceSynchronize();
56
57    // Solve Rx = z for x with CUBLAS, x is n x 1.
58    cublasStrsm(cublasH, CUBLAS_SIDE_LEFT, CUBLAS_FILL_MODE_UPPER,
59                CUBLAS_OP_N, CUBLAS_DIAG_NON_UNIT, n, 1, &alpha, d_A,
60                lda, d_b, ldb);
61    // Copy the result and print.
62    float x[n] = {0.0};
63    cudaMemcpy(x, d_b, n*sizeof(float), cudaMemcpyDeviceToHost);
64    for (int i = 0; i < n; ++i) printf("x[%d] = %f\n", i, x[i]);
65
66    cublasDestroy(cublasH);
67    cusolverDnDestroy(cusolverDnH);
68    cudaFree(d_A);
69    cudaFree(d_b);
70    cudaFree(tau);
71    cudaFree(devInfo);
72    cudaFree(work);
73    return 0;
74 }
```

The code starts with directives to include the necessary libraries and define a useful MIN utility macro. The main() function starts with declarations of relevant sizes including the number of rows m and columns n in the augmented matrix (i.e., **A** with 1's appended as its first column as the parameter that multiplies c_0) and the leading dimension of each side (both m in this case). Lines 13–21 hard-code the input data, and you would want to replace this with something that reads data from a file to handle a larger problem. Lines 23–27 allocate device memory and transfer the data for **A** and **b**. Lines 29–44 handle the prep work including calling a library function on line 43 to determine the size of the working buffer needed for the computation. Lines 47, 52, and 58 then call the three principal library functions discussed above to compute the QR factorization, construct the modified left-hand side, and backsolve for the vector of unknown coefficients that are copied back to the host and printed on lines 63–64. The remaining lines do the cleanup by destroying the contexts that were created and freeing the allocated memory.

The Makefile for running the code in Linux is shown in Listing 8.17. In Visual Studio under Windows, cublas.lib and cusolver.lib must be added to the list of additional linker input dependencies as described in the "Linking Library Files" sidebar earlier in this chapter. See Figure 8.3.

Listing 8.17 linreg/Makefile

```
1 NVCC = /usr/local/cuda/bin/nvcc
2 NVCC_FLAGS = -g -G -Xcompiler -Wall
3 LIBS += -lcublas_static -lcusolver_static -lculibos
4
5 all: main.exe
6
7 main.exe: main.cpp
8    $(NVCC) $(NVCC_FLAGS) $< -o $@ $(LIBS)
```

Running the code on the first nine samples in the data set produces the following values for the unknown coefficient vector:

$$c = \begin{bmatrix} 834.18, & -2.149, & -0.378, & -0.300, & -0.209 \end{bmatrix}^T$$

The linear regression relationship is

$$b = 843.18 - 2.149 * T - 0.378 * V - 0.300 * P - 0.209 * H$$

and we can test it by plugging in other samples from the data set (which is why we kept an extra sample that was not included in the computation). Substituting the values from the last row of Table 8.1 into the regression formula produces $b = 483.21$, which differs from the tabulated value by 0.2%.

One last note about error handling: Methods shown in Appendix D, "CUDA Practicalities: Timing, Profiling, Error Handling, and Debugging," for error handling are totally valid for use with the cuBLAS and cuSOLVER API, since the `helper_cuda.h` function `checkCudaErrors()` is capable of handling cuBLAS and cuSOLVER errors. While omitted for clarity here, we encourage you to wrap all your CUDA calls, including cuBLAS and cuSOLVER, in `checkCudaErrors()` for error handling when developing cuBLAS and cuSOLVER applications.

cuDNN

Machine learning has become one of the hottest topics in GPU computing, so you should know about cuDNN, the NVIDIA CUDA Deep Neural Network library, and NVIDIA DIGITS, the deep learning training system. cuDNN includes implementations of widely used deep learning frameworks, include Caffe, Theano, and Torch. For details, visit the cuDNN website at https://developer.nvidia.com/cudnn and the DIGITS website at https://developer.nvidia.com/digits.

ArrayFire

Finally, we touch briefly on ArrayFire, which is described as follows [18]:

> ArrayFire is a high performance software library for parallel computing with an easy-to-use API. Its array based function set makes parallel programming more accessible.

ArrayFire may be of interest to those of you who come from a Matlab background, because the programming style more closely resembles Matlab than C. ArrayFire is also open source and multiplatform, so it can take advantage of GPU-based SIMT parallelism but can also execute on other hardware (with appropriate adjustment of performance expectations). Apps built with ArrayFire can be very concise, and if you are interested, you should check out their examples to get a more concrete feel for its capabilities.

Summary

We have sampled just a few of the CUDA-powered libraries that are at your disposal. We hope the sample codes motivate you to further explore the libraries available to help you be both more effective and more efficient in your coding endeavors.

Suggested Projects

1. The Thrust example that estimated π generated the random coordinates on the interval [0,1] by generating vectors of random integers and then dividing by the largest value produced by the random integer generator, RAND_MAX, with both operations performed on the host. This particular random number generator is exclusively a host function, so that computation needs to be done on the host. However, there is no good reason not to do the division in parallel on the device. Modify the code to generate random numbers on the host, but to do the division in parallel on the GPU, use thrust::transform with a device vector.

2. Consider the following issues with the cuRAND version of the π estimator shown in Listing 8.10.

   a. If you run the app multiple times, do you keep getting the same answer? Is that a good thing or a bad thing for a Monte Carlo algorithm?

   b. Experiment with changing the seed value on line 11. Does that produce a new result? If you run the app again with the new seed value, do you reproduce the new result?

   c. Explore cuRAND to learn about states and offsets. Revise the code so that repeated runs of the app use different sets of random numbers and produce (appropriately) different outcomes.

3. Modify dist1D_fused to create dist2D_fused, an app that performs the same function as dist2D from Chapter 4, "2D Grids and Interactive Graphics," using Thrust. A suggested approach is to use a counting iterator to provide a virtual flat index and a functor that computes the row and col indices, converts them to x, y coordinates, and computes the distance from the reference point.

4. Use NPP to verify (quantitatively) that sharpen and sharpenNPP produce the same results for a given input image.

5. Create an interactive image-processing app to demonstrate some of the capabilities offered by NPP. (Build upon the OpenGL interop capability of the

$$Area = \frac{count\ in}{total} \cdot 1 = \frac{\pi r^2}{4} = \frac{\pi \cdot 1^2}{4} \Rightarrow \pi = \frac{count\ in}{total} \cdot 4$$

flashlight app or the image display capabilities of CImg or some other library of your choosing.)

6. Implement the π estimator using thrust::tuple and thrust::zip_iterator, as illustrated in Listing 8.9.

7. Incorporate code for reading a standard input file format such as comma-separated-value (CSV), and experiment with applying the linear regression app to larger data sets.

References

[1] Michael D. McCool, Arch D. Robison, and James Reinders, *Structured Parallel Programming: Patterns for Efficient Computation* (New York, NY: Elsevier, 2012).

[2] NVIDIA Corporation, "Thrust," NVIDIA Developer Zone, CUDA Toolkit Documentation, 2015, http://docs.nvidia.com/cuda/thrust.

[3] Jared Hoberock and Nathan Bell, Thrust Project website, 2015, http://thrust.github.io.

[4] "C++ Reference," 2015, http://en.cppreference.com.

[5] Mark Harris, "Expressive Algorithmic Programming with Thrust," *Parallel Forall* (blog), 2012, http://devblogs.nvidia.com/parallelforall/expressive-algorithmic-programming-thrust/.

[6] OpenMP Architecture Review Board, OpenMP, 2015, http://openmp.org.

[7] Intel, "Threading Building Blocks." (2015) https://www.threadingbuildingblocks.org.

[8] Jared Hoberock and Nathan Bell, Thrust wiki page, 2015, https://github.com/thrust/thrust/wiki.

[9] NVIDIA Corporation, "Thrust and cuRAND Example," NVIDIA Developer Zone, CUDA Toolkit Documentation, 2015, http://docs.nvidia.com/cuda/curand/device-api-overview.html#thrust-and-curand-example.

[10] NVIDIA Corporation. *NVIDIA Performance Primitives (NPP) Version 7.0* [NPP Library Documentation], 2015, http://docs.nvidia.com/cuda/pdf/NPP_Library.pdf.

[11] Edward Anderson et al., *LAPACK Users' Guide* (Philadelphia, PA: SIAM, 1999).

[12]   NVIDIA Corporation, "cuBLAS," NVIDIA Developer Zone, CUDA Toolkit Documentation, 2015, http://docs.nvidia.com/cuda/cublas.

[13]   NVIDIA Corporation, "cuSOLVER" NVIDIA Developer Zone, CUDA Toolkit Documentation, 2015, http://docs.nvidia.com/cuda/cusolver.

[14]   M. Lichman, "Welcome to the UC Irvine Machine Learning Repository!" UCI Machine Learning Repository, 2013, http://archive.ics.uci.edu/ml.

[15]   Pinar Tufekci, "Prediction of Full Load Electrical Power Output of a Base Load Operated Combined Cycle Power Plant Using Machine Learning Methods," *International Journal of Electrical Power & Energy Systems* 60 (2014): 126–40. http://dx.doi.org/10.1016/j.ijepes.2014.02.027.

[16]   Gene H. Golub and Charles F. Van Loan, *Matrix Computations, Fourth Edition* (Baltimore, MD: Johns Hopkins University Press, 2012).

[17]   William H. Press, Saul A. Teukolsky, William T. Vetterling, and Brian P. Flannery, *Numerical Recipes: The Art of Scientific Computing* (New York, NY: Cambridge University Press, 1992).

[18]   P. Yalamanchili et al., ArrayFire, 2015, http://www.arrayfire.com/docs/index.htm.

Chapter 9

Exploring the CUDA Ecosystem

The collection of resources (including books, websites, blogs, software, and documentation) related to CUDA is often referred to as the "CUDA ecosystem." This final chapter provides a collection of pointers to materials that may prove helpful in your further explorations of the CUDA ecosystem. Short descriptions are provided to help you identify materials that are more likely to be relevant to particular aspects or applications of CUDA.

The Go-To List of Primary Sources

We start off with the short list of resources you should definitely know about.

CUDA ZONE

The primary resource to take advantage of is NVIDIA's CUDA Zone website at https://developer.nvidia.com/cuda-zone, which you may have already visited to download the CUDA toolkit and/or to register as a CUDA developer. The page currently offers connections to six categories of links including the following:

- **About CUDA** provides a very general overview and links to case studies in a wide variety of application domains including bioinformatics, computational fluid and structural mechanics, design automation, and imaging.

- **Getting Started** offers links to programming languages (we have been using C/C++, but CUDA is also accessible from Fortran, Python, Matlab, Mathematica, and others), compiler directives (which ask the compiler to try to parallelize computations based on your existing code), and optimized libraries (so you can use parallel codes written, tested, and maintained by other people). Links are also provided to help identify CUDA-compatible hardware and to sign up for an online parallel programming class. (More on that below.)

- **Tools & Ecosystem** has links to applications, libraries, analysis tools, and tools for managing a GPU cluster.

- **Academic Collaboration** provides links to available education and training materials.

- **CUDA Downloads** is where you go to get new versions of CUDA along with Getting Started Guides and Release Notes.

- **Resources** offers a large collection of links grouped by category. A couple of them deserve special note:

  - **Docs and References** links to CUDA's Online Documentation, including Release Notes, Getting Started Guides, and Programming Guides. *Spending some time exploring the CUDA Toolkit documentation can be a very worthwhile investment. You should plan on visiting here regularly.*

  - **Education & Training** gives links to **GTC** presentations and GTC Express Webinars. GTC stands for **GPU Tech Conference**, an annual gathering of GPU professionals and enthusiasts held each Spring in San Jose, California. Each year hundreds of CUDA-related talks are presented, and the vast majority are recorded and made available online. GTC Express Webinars are the year-round online extension of GTC, providing talks on additional topics. There are some very good GTC talks, and you should check out the selection in your areas of interest.

OTHER PRIMARY WEB SOURCES

CUDA development is definitely an activity for which the internet is your friend. When you run into obscure errors, *copying an error message and pasting it into your favorite search engine is one of the best ways to get useful assistance.* However, there are a number of other particular web-based resources you should know about. Here are some favorites:

- The **Parallel Forall** (abbreviated "‖∀" by those who are more inclined toward mathematical notation) blog, http://devblogs.nvidia.com/parallelforall/. This blog regularly presents useful and enlightening posts by experts like Mark Harris, Chief Technologist for GPU Computing Software at NVIDIA.

- When you do a web search for help with a particular topic or error message, if you find a link to **StackOverflow** with a recent date, check it out. StackOverflow describes itself as follows: "Stack Overflow is a question and answer site for professional and enthusiast programmers. It's 100% free, no registration required." What makes it great for our purposes is that some very knowledgeable CUDA experts respond to questions posted there. Entering [cuda] in the search box at StackOverflow will produce CUDA-specific results: https://stackoverflow.com/questions/tagged/cuda.

- **Wikipedia's CUDA page**, https://en.wikipedia.org/wiki/CUDA. This is a handy location for details about compute capability of particular GPUs, along with supported features and technical specs that depend on compute capability.

ONLINE COURSES

There are three online courses to know about that contain significant CUDA content:

- **Udacity CS344: Intro to Parallel Programming** uses CUDA to introduce essential concepts in parallel computing. The course description goes as follows: "This class is for developers, scientists, engineers, researchers, and students who want to learn about GPU programming, algorithms, and optimization techniques." The presenters are Professor John Owens of UC Davis and Dr. David Luebke, Senior Director at NVIDIA Research. Students can start the class free of charge on their own schedule. The concise and well-crafted presentations are interspersed with quick quizzes and programming assignments. It is a computer science class, so significant C/C++ programming experience is expected, and even if you do not have the expected background, the explanations in the early presentations are quite worth your while (including the brilliant analogy of describing the contrast between CPU and GPU computing in terms of school buses and sports cars).

- **Heterogeneous Parallel Programming** is based on a course offered at the University of Illinois that aims at parallel systems involving CPUs and GPUs. The early part of the course is based on CUDA, while the later portion deals with other parallel platforms (OpenCL, OpenACC, and C++AMP). The lectures are presented by Professor Wen-mei Hwu (whose name will appear again in the list of books below), and the content has been updated since the initial offering in 2012. The course, which lasts nine weeks and has run January through April in recent years, has been offered free of charge through Coursera.

- **Programming Massively Parallel Processors with CUDA** presents recordings of the lectures from a course offered at Stanford in the spring of 2010. The lectures are given by Dr. Jared Hoberock and Dr. Nathan Bell (who were both involved in the creation of Thrust) and a handful of guest speakers. Significant programming background is expected, and some of the material is now a bit dated, but the explanations given in the early part of the course and the applications discussed later are of high quality. The videos are available for download free of charge from iTunes.

CUDA BOOKS

Since CUDA's debut in 2007, eight years have passed, and that is about how many CUDA books are presently available that you should be aware of. Here are brief descriptions of each:

1. *CUDA by Example: An Introduction to General-Purpose GPU Programming* by Jason Sanders and Edward Kandrot. Addison-Wesley: 2011. ISBN-13: 9780131387683.

   This is the book that got many people, including one of the authors (DS), started in the CUDA world. It is a well-written, attractive, compact book that is worth a look by every CUDA learner. The example-based approach is effective and inspires active engagement. Note, however, that *CUDA by Example* is aimed at experienced C programmers, not at a general technical audience. A significant portion of the content involves dealing with multiple computation streams, which becomes relevant when you want to take advantage of multiple GPUs or hide latency by having one stream transfer data while another stream is performing computations. (We consider multiple-stream programming a more advanced topic that is not need-to-know material for CUDA newcomers—which is why we have not broached the subject until now.) Note also that *CUDA by Example*, which has been out for about three-fourths of the entire period since CUDA's release, is understandably out of date in a few regards including handing of OpenGL interoperability and reliance on utility functions (in `cutil.h`) that were distributed with early versions of the CUDA Samples but never officially supported. (These utilities have now been supplanted by the `helper` files in more recent versions of CUDA.) All in all, a really good book. If a second edition comes out, we will be buying it!

2. *Programming Massively Parallel Processors: A Hands-On Approach* (Applications of GPU Computing Series) by David B. Kirk and Wen-mei Hwu. Morgan Kaufmann: 2010. ISBN-13: 9780123814722.

This is another of the early entries in the CUDA book market. It is aimed at a broader technical audience and assumes some (but not extensive) C programming background and shares the goal of efficiently preparing the reader to undertake their own CUDA projects. It provides background material introducing CUDA (as well as a chapter on OpenCL, an alternative platform for parallel computing on heterogeneous systems) and treats examples including matrix multiplication, MRI reconstruction, and molecular visualization.

3. *CUDA Application Design and Development* by Rob Farber. Morgan Kaufmann: 2011. ISBN-13: 9780123884268.

This book assumes significant programming background but introduces CUDA from scratch. The text is at a sufficiently advanced level to do serious treatments of examples including machine learning and real-time processing of streaming video. The author is responsible for a nice series of posts on CUDA programming at *Dr. Dobb's Journal* and is well-equipped to present nontrivial CUDA topics in an engaging and understandable manner. (Sadly, *Dr. Dobb's Journal* has ceased operations, so new posts are no longer appearing.)

4. *CUDA Programming: A Developer's Guide to Parallel Computing with GPUs* (Applications of GPU Computing Series) by Shane Cook. Morgan Kaufmann: 2012. ISBN-13: 9780124159334.

This is another book aimed at professional development of CUDA applications (in the author's words, use of "CUDA in real applications, by real practitioners"). It assumes an existing knowledge of C/C++, is recent enough to cover Kepler hardware (i.e., GPUs with compute capability 3.X), and has an emphasis on writing high-performance code.

5. *CUDA Handbook: A Comprehensive Guide to GPU Programming* by Nicholas Wilt. Addison-Wesley: 2013. ISBN-13: 9780321809469.

This book is true to its title. It is a comprehensive handbook of all things CUDA written by one of the originators of CUDA. It is not a book for beginners, but as you get into details of more significant CUDA projects, you will find that answers to many of your "what?" "how?" and "why?" questions reside in this book. With its 2013 publication date, the *CUDA Handbook* is more up to date and explicitly covers CUDA through Version 5.0 and hardware including the Kepler architecture.

6. *Professional CUDA C Programming* by John Cheng, Max Grossman, and Ty McKercher. Wiley: 2014. ISBN-13: 9781118739327.

As it says in the title, this book is aimed at professional CUDA code development. The organization is aimed at providing experienced coders with exposure to the various aspects of CUDA rather than presenting examples to engage CUDA newcomers. As the authors say in the preface, this is "a book written *by* programmers, *for* programmers, that focus[es] on what programmers need for production CUDA development." When you get to the point where you have created significant projects and you are ready to enhance their organization and/or performance, this book will be worth a look. If you are one of the lucky few who has the resources to hire staff to create your CUDA projects, your staff will likely want to have access to this book. With a 2014 release date, the content is reasonably up to date. Example codes are designed to run on a Linux system using CUDA 6.0 or higher and hardware architectures at or beyond Kepler (i.e., compute capability ≥ 3.0).

7. *GPU Computing Gems: Emerald Edition and Jade Edition* (Applications of GPU Computing Series) edited by Wen-mei Hwu. Morgan Kaufmann: 2011. ISBN-13: 9780123849885 (Emerald Edition), 9780123859631 (Jade Edition).

This two-volume set is in the spirit of the well-known *GPU Gems* series but focuses specifically on using the GPU for computing. The two volumes together offer dozens of examples (about 1,400 pages worth) detailing applications of GPU computing by leading practitioners in the field. When you need code for a specific purpose, if you can find it as a GPU Gem, you can rely on getting code that is efficient, well-tested, and reliable.

8. *CUDA Fortran for Scientists and Engineers: Best Practices for Efficient CUDA Fortran Programming* by Gregory Ruetsch and Massimiliano Fatica. Morgan Kaufmann: 2013. ISBN-13: 9780124169708.

If you are a Fortran user (or have existing Fortran codes that you want to parallelize), this book may be for you.

Further Sources

The sources listed previously are ones that, at the time of this writing, are known to exist and be of significant use. However, development of the CUDA ecosystem is accelerating, and the list of relevant sources continues to grow. Here are some links you might want to explore.

CUDA SAMPLES

It would be an oversight not to mention that the CUDA download includes a collection of example codes called the CUDA Samples (or the CUDA SDK Samples in some earlier versions). These sample codes can be useful when you need to see an implementation of a particular CUDA function or feature. When you want to get going on a new project, if you can find a related sample code, it might provide some suggestions (and/or questions) about how to get started in the right direction. Samples that employ special libraries or features can also provide a source of information about necessary build customizations such as inclusion of additional header files or linking of additional library files.

CUDA LANGUAGES AND LIBRARIES

From the CUDA Zone, select **Tools & Ecosystem**, then check out the growing variety of CUDA-compatible languages and APIs (application programming interfaces) as well as the collection of libraries (beyond Thrust, NPP, cuRAND, cuSOLVER, cuBLAS, and ArrayFire introduced in Chapter 8, "Using CUDA Libraries"). For a list of current items, see https://developer.nvidia.com/gpu-accelerated-libraries. There may be a nontrivial learning curve to get started with new languages or libraries, but you may well make up the time and effort by using code that is thoroughly tested, optimized, and maintained.

MORE CUDA BOOKS

The accelerating growth of CUDA is attested to by the suddenly increasing number of books on the subject. While the "go to" books were listed previously, this additional list includes some more specialized research-oriented books:

1. *Generation of Radiographs from 3D Anatomical Models Using the GPU: Parallel DRR Algorithms Using CUDA GPUs* by Andre Cardoso. Lambert Academic Publishing: 2012. ISBN-13: 9783838378756.

2. *CPU-Based Application Transformation to CUDA: Transformation of CPU-Based Applications to Leverage on Graphics Processors Using CUDA* by Anas Mohd Nazlee and Fawnizu Azmadi Hussin. Lambert Academic Publishing: 2012. ISBN-13: 9783659171215.

3. *Accelerating MATLAB with GPU Computing: A Primer with Examples* by Jung W. Suh and Youngmin Kim. Morgan Kaufmann: 2013. ISBN-13: 9780124080805.

4. *Designing Scientific Applications on GPUs* (Chapman & Hall/CRC Numerical Analysis and Scientific Computing Series) by Raphael Couturier. Chapman and Hall/CRC: 2013. ISBN-13: 9781466571624.

5. *GPU Power for Medical Imaging: A Practical Approach to General-Purpose Computing with CUDA Machine Learning* by Francisco Xavier. Lambert Academic Publishing: 2014. ISBN-13: 9783659251894.

6. *Parallel Computing for Data Science: With Examples in R, C++ and CUDA* (Chapman & Hall/CRC The R Series) by Norman Matloff. Chapman and Hall/CRC: 2015. ISBN-13: 9781466587014.

7. *Multicore and GPU Programming: An Integrated Approach* by Gerassimos Barlas. Morgan Kaufmann: 2015. ISBN-13: 9780124171374.

As with other aspects of CUDA, the list of available books is rapidly changing and keeping an eye on the "go to" sources to find out about new developments should be an ongoing activity.

Summary

Well, we've made it to the end of the book. Congratulations on your persistence, and we sincerely hope that the rewards will be commensurate with the investment of time and effort. If, in the process of working your way through the book, you have run into examples that prompt thoughts of interesting projects, then we have achieved our mission and you are on your way to accomplishing new and amazing things using the power of massively parallel computing made readily available with CUDA.

While many people are talking about how 3D printing (another cutting edge technology that is near and dear to our hearts) represents a major force to democratize manufacturing, you are now personally engaged in the democratization of parallel computing. We hope that you put the new resources at your disposal to good use to further your own interests and maybe even advance the knowledge of humanity. Thanks again for sharing the journey, and good luck as you continue your travels in the exciting world of CUDA.

Suggested Projects

At this point you should be maximally qualified to pursue some further CUDA challenges, so here they are.

1. Identify a CUDA library, language, or API with features/functions that look useful and apply them to a problem of personal interest.

2. Identify an interesting CUDA Sample, and figure out what it is supposed to do and how it accomplishes that goal. Write up your description and share it with your CUDA-savvy friends.

3. Find an interesting GTC talk to watch. (If you do not have well-identified personal interests, start with one of the keynote talks, which uniformly involve a quality presentation of significant and interesting content.) Write up a quick synopsis to share with interested friends.

4. Go to http://stackoverflow.com and enter [cuda] in the search box. Click on the votes tab and read the ten top-rated questions and answers.

5. Check out some of the content from an online CUDA class.

6. Locate a copy of another CUDA book and see if you can find some content relevant to your purposes.

7. Find a newly released CUDA book. Check out the content and presentation style. Write a review to share with your friends.

8. Come up with the latest, greatest application of CUDA's massively parallel computing power.

Appendix A

Hardware Setup

A CUDA-enabled parallel computing system includes both hardware and software components. Here we deal with the necessary hardware component: a CUDA-enabled GPU. We start by describing how to determine if your system has a CUDA-enabled GPU. That procedure depends on operating system, so read the section (Windows, OS X, or Linux) that applies to your system. (If the manufacturer of your system was nice enough to put a green NVIDIA sticker in a visible location, you can note the model and proceed directly to the section on "Determining Compute Capability.") We then discuss how to acquire and/or install a CUDA-enabled GPU, which depends on your hardware platform. Once again, read the section that applies to you.

Checking for an NVIDIA GPU: Windows

Right-click on the desktop. If the pop-up menu does not have an entry for the NVIDIA Control Panel, continue to the section on "Upgrading Compute Capability." If NVIDIA Control Panel is available, click to open it and then click the Home icon.

A sample Home window is shown in Figure A.1. The bottom line of the green NVIDIA CONTROL PANEL rectangle shows the model of the NVIDIA GPU installed on the system (here a GeForce 840M). Once you've identified your GPU, proceed to the section on "Determining Compute Capability."

Figure A.1 Home screen of the NVIDIA Control Panel showing the presence of an NVIDIA GPU

Checking for an NVIDIA GPU: OS X

From the Apple menu, select About This Mac where the Displays tab provides information about both the monitor and GPU on your system, as shown in Figure A.2. In the case shown, the system has a GeForce GT 650M. Note the

Figure A.2 The Displays tab in the About This Mac window showing the presence of an NVIDIA GPU

model of your graphics card (if you have one) and proceed to the section on "Determining Compute Capability." If no NVIDIA GPU is listed, proceed to the section on "Upgrading Compute Capability."

Checking for an NVIDIA GPU: Linux

From the command line (which can be accessed under Ubuntu via the keyboard shortcut Ctrl+Alt+t), enter the following command:

```
lspci | grep -i nvidia <Enter>
```

to produce a list of peripheral devices installed on your system. (ls is short for list and pci is the communications bus that connects between the CPU and peripheral devices such as your graphics card. The full list of installed PCI devices is piped to grep, the pattern-matching tool, to search the list for nvidia in a case-insensitive manner, as indicated by -i). On one of our Linux systems, lspci produces the following output: 01:00.0 VGA compatible controller: NVIDIA Corporation GF108 [GeForce GT 620] (rev a1), indicating the presence of a GeForce GT 620 graphics card.

If your system has no installed NVIDIA card, proceed to the section on "Upgrading Compute Capability." If you do have an installed NVIDIA card, note the model and proceed to the section on "Determining Compute Capability."

Determining Compute Capability

The NVIDIA CUDA website provides a full list of CUDA cards and the associated GPU compute capability. Go to https://developer.nvidia.com/cuda-gpus to find the compute capability of your GPU.

The major categories of CUDA-enabled GPUs currently include Tesla, Quadro, NVS, GeForce, and TEGRA/Jetson. All three systems discussed above have GeForce cards, so we click on the link to CUDA-Enabled GeForce Products and look in the appropriate column (Desktop Products or Notebook Products) to find the listing for our GPU. The sample Windows system is a notebook computer with a GeForce 840M whose compute capability is 5.0. The sample Mac has a GeForce GT 650M that has compute capability of 3.0. The sample Linux system has a GeForce GT 620 that has compute capability 2.1.

Go to the appropriate column to find your card and its compute capability. If you have an installed GPU with compute capability of at least 2.0 and you are satisfied with that, you can proceed to Appendix B, "Software Setup," to do your software installation.

Why Upgrade Compute Capability?

- If you do not have an installed card with compute capability of at least 2.0, then you need to upgrade your compute capability before you can run the codes discussed in this book.

- If you know you have a special interest in managed memory (which we use for one example in Chapter 3, "From Loops to Grids"), you need compute capability of at least 3.0.

- If you know you are interested in dynamic parallelism (which is not covered in this book), you need compute capability of at least 3.5. For further details about compute capability, see the documentation at the NVIDIA CUDA Zone or Wikipedia's CUDA page: https://en.wikipedia.org/wiki/CUDA.

- If you want to do large double-precision computations, you should seriously consider a Tesla card (which will require additional resources in terms of both price and power connectors).

Hardware Nomenclature

While we have been loosely talking about installing a GPU, names like GeForce 840M actually designate a graphics card, not the GPU itself. In this case, the graphics card includes a model GM108 GPU that has Maxwell class architecture. So when discussing CUDA hardware, there are four major designations: the model name/number of the card, the model name/number of the GPU, the compute capability, and the architecture class. For our purposes, the primary focus is on the graphics card name/number (because that is the most available identifier when inspecting your system or shopping for new hardware) and the compute capability (which is the info given for apps that have special requirements). However, you should also be aware of GPU architecture that refers to the general plan for the layout of the components of the GPU including processing units, memory, and so on. The nomenclature history of NVIDIA's CUDA architectures goes as follows:

- Tesla: The earliest CUDA cards (starting in 2007) with compute capabilities ranging from 1.0 to 1.3.

- Fermi: The second-generation of CUDA cards (starting in 2010) with compute capabilities 2.0 and 2.1. A Fermi class card will suffice for almost everything in this book.

- Kepler: The third-generation of CUDA cards (starting in 2012) with compute capabilities ranging from 3.0 to 3.7. A Kepler class card can do everything covered in the book.

- Maxwell: The fourth-generation of CUDA cards (starting in 2014) with compute capability 5.x.

- Pascal: The fifth-generation of CUDA cards is planned for release in 2016. Stay tuned to find out if the compute capability designation continues to be based on prime numbers (or perhaps the Fibonacci sequence)... .

Upgrading Compute Capability

The possibilities for upgrading compute capability depend on whether your hardware configuration is set by the manufacturer (typical of Macs and notebooks) or open for modification (typical of Windows and Linux desktop systems).

MAC OR NOTEBOOK COMPUTER WITH A CUDA-ENABLED GPU

If you use a laptop/notebook computer or a Mac, you probably have limited access for installing new hardware components. In such situations, a compute capability upgrade translates to the purchase of a system that includes a CUDA-enabled card.

Apple uses GPUs from different vendors in different models and years, so if you want to run CUDA under OS X, you need to shop around for a Mac with an NVIDIA graphics card.

For notebook computers, CUDA-ready systems make up a small portion of the market, but they are available at reasonable prices. Systems that have an "integrated" Intel GPU and a CUDA-enabled NVIDIA GPU (sometimes identified as **Optimus** systems) provide a good environment, because the integrated GPU can serve your display needs (i.e., send graphics to your monitor), while the NVIDIA GPU is dedicated to computing. Notebook computers with CUDA-enabled GPUs are often labeled as "gaming notebooks." You can also go to NVIDIA's Notebook web page (http://www.nvidia.com/object/notebooks.html) and follow the links there to vendors offering notebooks with your preferred GPU.

We should mention power consumption before we end the discussion of notebook computers. Some very powerful gaming systems are now available that contain the current high end of mobile GPUs; that is, cards in the GeForce GTX 900M series. These systems are powerful in terms of both computational performance and heat production; such high-end cards need to dissipate about 100W and require serious fans and heat-exhaust ducts. It is always worth shopping around to find what best suits your needs, but there is currently a nice "sweet spot" involving systems with the GeForce 840M that offer 384 computing cores, compute capability 5.0, and 2 GB of GPU memory, while consuming only about 30W of power. Passive heat dissipation is sufficient for such systems, so they can be both lightweight and quiet while still packing a lot of computing "punch."

DESKTOP COMPUTER

If you have a desktop PC, you should be able to install an add-on GPU, provided you have enough of a sense of adventure to open up your computer's case (after turning off the power, of course). Once the case is open, there are two key items to look for:

- PCIe-3.0 x16 slots on the motherboard

- Cables from the power supply with PCIe power connectors

Figure A.3(a) shows a desktop PC with the case opened to expose the motherboard and power supply. Figure A.3(b) shows a blow-up of the region on the motherboard with the peripheral connectors. The fine print at the left edge indicates the connector type. This system has two PCIe x16 slots: the blue connector at the top labeled PCIEX16_1 and the white slot below labeled PCIEX16_2. (Boxes have been drawn to indicate the location of the labels.)

If your system has a PCIe x16 slot, you can install a CUDA-enabled graphics card. The simple approach is to install a CUDA card that gets its power directly from the PCIe x16 slot and needs no additional power connectors. One such card is the GeForce GTX 750 Ti, which has 640 cores, compute capability 5.0, and peak power rating of 60W (so a 300W power supply will suffice). If you really have a small case, you may want to check out something like a GeForce GT 620 (with 96 cores and compute capability 2.1). The GeForce GT 620 is not exactly a computing powerhouse, but it is a single-height, half-width card that fits (with a little squeezing) into the smallest case we've encountered.

The desktop PC shown in the figures has two PCIe x16 slots and additional PCIe power connectors, so it can accommodate two CUDA graphics cards, including

(a) (b)

Figure A.3 (a) Desktop PC with case opened to show the hardware. The box indicates the region of peripheral connectors on motherboard. (b) Blow-up of peripheral connectors including two PCI Express x16 slots. Boxes highlight identifying labels: `PCIEX16_1` and `PCIEX16_2`.

one higher-end card that requires additional power. Figure A.4 shows the desktop PC with a low-power GeForce GT 610 card installed in the `PCIEX16_1` slot and a high-power GeForce GTX 980 installed in the `PCIEX16_2` slot. The box indicates where the additional power cables connect to the GeForce GTX 980, and the inset shows an enlargement of this region with the power disconnected to make the PCIe 6-pin and 6+2-pin connectors visible. If you have the luxury of two graphics cards, this configuration with a low-end card to drive the display and a higher-end card to do the computing is a good setup for CUDA purposes.

Once you have inspected your system for PCIe x16 slots and PCIe power connectors, you'll have an idea of what kind of graphics card is right for you. (If you can spot the wattage of your power supply, that is another useful piece of information.) You can then go to the CUDA GPUs page (https://developer.nvidia.com/cuda-gpus) and select the card of interest, then click on `Specifications` and look for details about power connectors and power supply capacity.

When you have identified a model of interest, paste the model number into a search engine to check details of price and availability. New GPUs hit the market

Figure A.4 Desktop computer with a GPU installed in each of the two PCI Express x16 slots: a GeForce GT 610 in the `PCIEX16_1` slot and a GeForce GTX 980 in the `PCIEX16_2` slot. The smaller rectangle shows the additional power connections to the GTX 980. The larger rectangle shows an enlargement with the power disconnected to make the connectors visible.

regularly and prices change over time, so expect to find new and improved opportunities. Engage in a bit of recreational GPU shopping, identify your GPU of choice, and place an order with your favorite vendor.

When your GPU arrives, installation should be pretty straightforward. Make sure your computer is turned off, then remove the cover (if the case is not already open from when you checked for PCIe slots, power connectors, etc.). Remove the GPU from its packaging and insert its "tabs" into a PCIe x16 slot. Note that it should only fit in one orientation (with the metal plate at the back of your case so that you can secure the card to the case with a screw). Fit it into the slot securely, connect additional power cables as necessary, and close up the case.

After powering up your system, connecting to the internet, and starting the computer, your system should recognize the new hardware and download driver software. To check that the system recognizes your new hardware, repeat the "Checking for an NVIDIA GPU" process to view the graphics cards installed on your system. Your hardware install is now complete, and you can proceed to Appendix B, "Software Setup."

Appendix B

Software Setup

Once you have a system with an appropriate GPU, all you need to enter the CUDA-powered world of massively parallel computing is some software. In this appendix, we'll cover the software you need and how to install it. Note that the install procedures are operating-system dependent, so we present separate sections for Windows, OS X, and Linux systems.

Windows Setup

Let's assume you have a recent vintage PC (anything that currently runs Windows 7 or above should suffice) and get right down to business. Key steps include the following:

- Create a system restore point.

- Install the Microsoft Visual Studio Integrated Development Environment (IDE).

- Install CUDA software, a single install that includes the CUDA Toolkit, CUDA Samples, Nsight Visual Studio Edition (IDE plug-in), and the CUDA driver for your GPU.

Note that this presentation describes the currently available versions of the software, namely, Microsoft Visual Studio 2013 Community Edition, Nsight Visual Studio Edition 4.7, and CUDA 7.5.

CREATING A RESTORE POINT

It is prudent to create a restore point before any software install so you have a known functional configuration to return to in case anything unexpected occurs. From the Windows Start menu, select `Control Panel` and type "Create a restore point" in the search box (near the upper right corner). Click on the search result to open the `System Protection` tab in the `System Properties` window. To create a restore point, click on the `Create...` button near the bottom of the window.

INSTALLING THE IDE

There are two major pieces of software to download, the CUDA Toolkit and the Microsoft Visual Studio IDE. Install Visual Studio first because the CUDA Toolkit includes specialized Nsight software for debugging and analyzing CUDA code that plugs into Visual Studio. All of this software is subject to ongoing development, so new versions are released regularly. Here, we go through the installation of a combination that is known to be compatible:

* Microsoft Visual Studio 2013 Community Edition

* CUDA 7.5 with Nsight 4.7

Go to www.visualstudio.com (or enter "Visual Studio 2013 Community Edition" into your favorite search engine) and follow the instructions given there to download and install Visual Studio. Note that the install of Visual Studio will likely take some time and provide an opportunity for a nice coffee break (or two).

INSTALLING THE CUDA TOOLKIT

With Visual Studio installed, you are now ready to enter the CUDA Zone. We mean this literally because "CUDA Zone" is NVIDIA's name for the portion of its website devoted to CUDA: https://developer.nvidia.com/cuda-zone. There you will find information about CUDA, related tools and resources, materials to help you get started, training and courseware, and (most relevant for our current purposes) downloads (as shown in Figure B.1).

The first time you visit the CUDA Zone, scroll all the way to the bottom of the page, then click on the link to the `Developer Program` (under the `GET INVOLVED` heading). Sign up as a registered CUDA developer to make sure you have access to the full set of available CUDA resources.

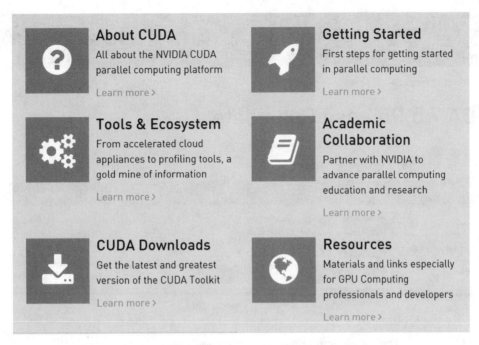

Figure B.1 Links available in the CUDA Zone

After you have registered as a CUDA developer, return to the CUDA Zone page. Clicking on the `CUDA Downloads` icon brings you to the current CUDA Downloads page, as illustrated in Figure B.2.

Note that Figure B.2 shows the CUDA 7 Downloads page because CUDA 7.5 is currently a release candidate and, as of this writing, has not yet been officially

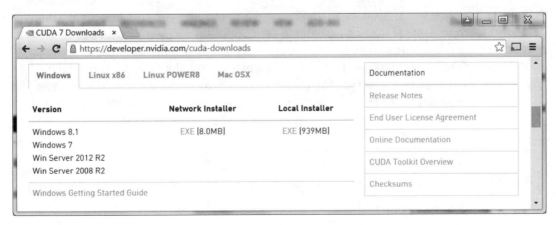

Figure B.2 The CUDA Zone page for downloading CUDA 7.0

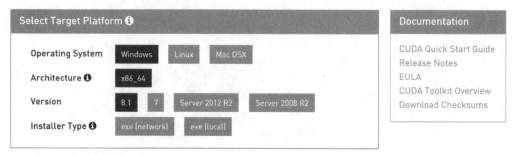

Figure B.3 CUDA 7.5 release candidate download page

released (which will have changed by the time you read this). If you search in the CUDA Zone, you can also find the download page for the release candidate if one is available. The download for the CUDA 7.5 release candidate is shown in Figure B.3. Note that the documentation links can be very useful. If the version you download has a Quick Start Guide, you should definitely give it a look.

Whether downloading an officially released version of CUDA or a release candidate, select the version that corresponds to your operating system and then choose one of the two executable (EXE) files: the Network Installer or the Local Installer. The Network Installer is much smaller, but you will need to be connected to the internet when you run the executable and do the actual software install. The Local Installer involves a much larger (and more time consuming) download, but the executable can run and perform the software install without an ongoing connection to the internet.

Click on your preferred installer. When the CUDA download is complete, open the executable file and click OK to verify the temporary folder where the extracted files will be stored. After extracting the files, the CUDA installer will open and go through the following steps, each of which require you to perform an action:

1. Perform a system compatibility check and present a license agreement that you accept by clicking on the AGREE AND CONTINUE button.

2. Present the option of Express or Custom installation. Unless you really have a specific reason to do something custom, select Express installation and click NEXT to start the installation process.

3. When the installer is ready to install the CUDA driver for your GPU, a Windows Security window pops up and asks, "Would you like to install this device software?" You will then need to click the Install button to enable installation of the "NVIDIA Display Adapters" driver software.

Flicker Alert!

Note that during the driver installation your screen may flicker or even go completely black for a few seconds. There is no need to panic because that is completely expected. (The system restore point we created before starting the install is another reason not to panic.)

While the installation will take several minutes, the installer conveniently takes care of four software components that formerly required separate installations:

- CUDA Toolkit: the basic software foundation of CUDA

- CUDA GPU Device Driver: the software that tells your specific CUDA-enabled GPU how to work in the CUDA environment

- NSight Visual Studio Edition: the software that integrates with the IDE for debugging and profiling CUDA code running on the GPU

- CUDA Samples: the official collection of sample CUDA applications

When the install is complete, you should see a window like the one in Figure B.4 indicating the components that were (or were not) actually installed.

Click NEXT to proceed, then click the boxes to Launch Documentation and Launch Samples and click CLOSE to exit the installer (see Figure B.5).

Figure B.4 Window displayed at the conclusion of a CUDA install

Figure B.5 CUDA installer ready to close and launch documentation and samples

INITIAL TEST RUN

After completing the install, it is time for a couple of test runs: one to verify that things are working properly and one to quantify the performance of your system. Both of these goals can be accomplished using the CUDA Samples, a collection of a few dozen example CUDA applications provided with the CUDA software distribution.

If you selected `Launch Samples` at the end of your CUDA install, you already have a File Explorer open to the CUDA Samples folder as shown in Figure B.6.

If you did not choose Launch Samples during install, you can access the CUDA Samples as follows. Under Windows 7, open the Windows Start menu and select `All Programs` ⇒ `NVIDIA Corporation` ⇒ `CUDA Samples` ⇒ `V7.5` ⇒ `Browse CUDA Samples`. Under Windows 8, click the arrow at the bottom of the `Start` page to get to the `Apps` page, scroll across to the `NVIDIA`

Figure B.6 CUDA `Samples/7.5` directory with the `Samples_vs2013` solution file highlighted

Corporation apps, and click on Browse CUDA Samples. Your file browser should then resemble Figure B.6. The folders hold collections of related code samples that need to be compiled and built into executables before we can run them. The necessary details of building executables with Visual Studio is covered in Appendix C, "Need-to-Know C Programming," but for now, let's build executable versions of the full set of CUDA Samples, which remarkably takes only two clicks of the mouse and one press of a function key. Hover the mouse over the Samples_vs2013 file and verify that the pop-up menu shows Type: Microsoft Visual Studio Solution to make sure you have the correct file, then double-click to open the file with Visual Studio.

When Samples_vs2013 opens, the Visual Studio window should resemble Figure B.7, and all you need to do is press the F7 function key to start the build process. (Building all the samples will take some time, so plan on an extended

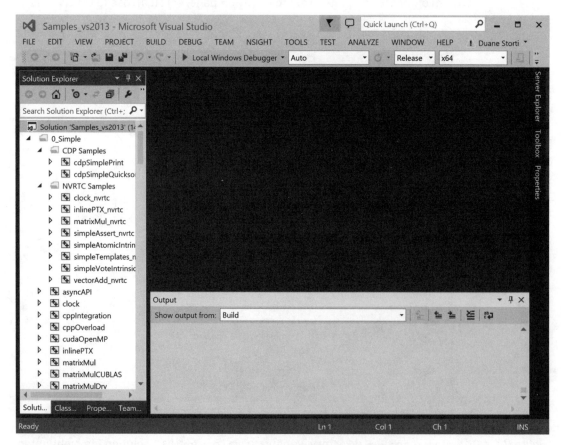

Figure B.7 The Samples_vs2013 Solution file open in Visual Studio

coffee break at this point.) Once you start the build process, a green progress bar will appear at the bottom of the Visual Studio window and then disappear when the build is complete.

Once the build process is complete, the executable files are all available in a subfolder of the bin folder shown in Figure B.6. Double-click on bin ⇒ win64 ⇒ Release to get to the directory containing the Samples executables. (You may find it convenient set the File Explorer View to sort by Type, so the executable files appear together in alphabetical order.) You can then double-click on an executable file to run a particular CUDA Sample. At this point, we really want to verify that things are working properly, so an appropriate choice is the deviceQuery sample, which prints the system's CUDA capabilities to the console. However, if you double-click on the icon for the deviceQuery executable file, the results are printed and the console window closes too quickly for most people to read the output. We'll get around this by running the sample in a different way:

1. In Visual Studio, select TOOLS ⇒ Visual Studio Command Prompt to open a console window.

2. In the File Explorer, right-click on the Release folder (under bin/win64), and select Copy address as text.

3. At the command prompt, type cd (for change directory), then right-click and choose Paste to insert the path where the CUDA Sample executables are located. Hit Enter to change to that folder.

4. At the command prompt, type deviceQuery <Enter> to execute the deviceQuery sample from the command line.

You should see results from deviceQuery similar to those shown in Figure B.8, where the utility correctly reports one CUDA Capable Device and identifies the make and model of the GPU (GeForce 840M), the version of CUDA it is running (7.5), the compute capability (5.0), the memory capacity (2048 MB, a.k.a. 2GB), the number of CUDA cores on the device (384), and numerous other properties that may become of interest later.

If you have managed to produce a similar result on your system, then congratulations are in order because you have just completed your first execution of a CUDA program on your system. Admittedly the deviceQuery application provides only a very limited impression of your CUDA capabilities, but more interesting examples lie ahead.

Figure B.8 Command prompt showing output from deviceQuery

At this point, we have accomplished the goal of verifying that your CUDA software is functioning (along with your CUDA-enabled graphics card). You can now return to Chapter 1, "First Steps," or proceed to Appendix C, "Need-to-Know C Programming," to learn the necessary aspects of C programming.

OS X Setup

While we refer to Macs running OS X as members of the class of Linux systems in other portions of the book (because the way programs are built is the same in both platforms), there are some significant differences in the CUDA setup procedure. This section aims to provide what you need to know about setting up your CUDA-enabled Mac to actually run CUDA.

DOWNLOADING AND INSTALLING THE CUDA TOOLKIT

Once you have verified that you have a CUDA-enabled GPU, you can move on to install the necessary software, including Xcode and the CUDA Toolkit.

Xcode is the official suite of software development tools for OS X, and it can be obtained free of charge through Apple's App Store application. Once you've obtained Xcode, install the command-line tools by entering the following command in a terminal window: `xcode-select --install`.

Once the Xcode command-line tools are installed, you are ready to download the CUDA Toolkit installer from the CUDA Downloads page. Go to https://developer .nvidia.com/cuda-downloads, select the Mac OSX option (as shown in Figure B.9), and then select the network or local installer. (Network installer requires an internet connection during the installation process.) After downloading, double-click on the downloaded file to start installation of the CUDA Toolkit, then follow the directions prompted by the CUDA Toolkit installer.

After the installation is over, open your shell's configuration file with TextEdit (for the bash shell, with `open -e ~/.bash_profile`) and add the following two lines:

```
export PATH=/usr/local/cuda/bin:$PATH
export DYLD_LIBRARY_PATH=/usr/local/cuda/lib:$DYLD_LIBRARY_PATH
```

The next time you open your command-line `nvcc`, the NVIDIA C Compiler (which you will use to compile your CUDA code) should be in the system path. You can use the command `nvcc --version` to check your installed version of `nvcc`.

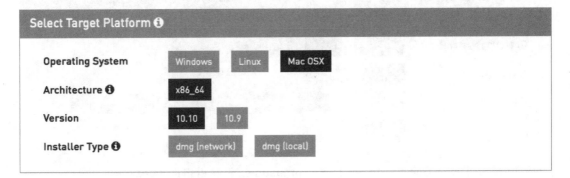

Figure B.9 CUDA 7.5 Downloads page for OS X

You have now completed the OS X–specific part of the setup, and you are ready to proceed to the "Installing Samples to the User Directory" and "Initial Test Run" subsections of the "Linux Setup" section that follows.

Linux Setup

There are a number of Linux distributions (distros) that the CUDA toolkit supports. The Linux distros that are compatible with CUDA 7.5 are listed under the Linux option at https://developer.nvidia.com/cuda-downloads, as shown in Figure B.10. Here we describe a sample installation based on Ubuntu 14.04, which is a long-term support (LTS) release. For other distros, the installation procedure should be very similar, and the extra steps that are required are described at https://docs.nvidia.com/cuda/pdf/CUDA_Getting_Started_Linux.pdf.

PREPARING THE SYSTEM SOFTWARE FOR CUDA INSTALLATION

Before doing the CUDA install, make sure that you have the GNU Compiler Collection (GCC) installed from the command line (which can be accessed under Ubuntu via the keyboard shortcut Ctrl+Alt+t) by typing gcc --version. If instead of a GCC version number, you get an output like command not found or currently not installed, then you should install gcc with the command sudo apt-get install gcc.

DOWNLOADING AND INSTALLING THE CUDA TOOLKIT

Go to the CUDA Downloads page https://developer.nvidia.com/cuda-downloads, select the Linux option (as shown in Figure B.10), then select the local or network

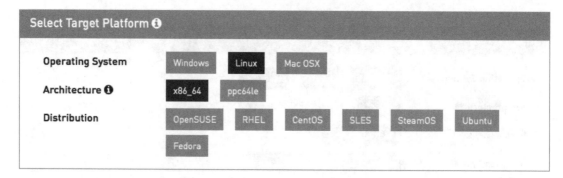

Figure B.10 CUDA 7.5 Downloads page with compatible Linux distributions

installer corresponding to your operating system. (Network installer requires an internet connection during the installation process.)

Clicking on the link will download a software repository package. Right-click on the repository package icon, select `Open with the Ubuntu Software Center`, then click on the `Install` button. When the repository installation is complete, open the command-line interface and execute the following steps:

- Update the repository information on your system with `sudo apt-get update`.

- Install the CUDA Toolkit with `sudo apt-get install cuda`.

After the CUDA install is complete, you may be prompted to restart your computer, but let's postpone the restart and take care of updating search paths so your system will be able to locate the CUDA Toolkit files. Here are the necessary steps:

- Open your profile configuration with a text editor (e.g., `gedit ~/.profile`).

- At the end of the file, add the line `export PATH=/usr/local/cuda/bin:$PATH`, and save the file.

- Open your UNIX shell start-up file with a text editor (e.g., `gedit ~/.bashrc`). At the end of the file, add the line `export LD_LIBRARY_PATH=/usr/local/cuda/lib64:$LD_LIBRARY_PATH` and save the file.

At this point, you should exit the text editor and restart your system (so that it will put the changes into effect). After the restart, check that the changes were successful with `printenv | grep cuda`. If your system successfully locates the CUDA files, you should get output resembling the following:

```
LD_LIBRARY_PATH=/usr/local/cuda/lib64:
PATH=/usr/local/cuda/bin:/usr/local/sbin:/usr/local/bin:...
```

You can also use the command `nvcc --version` to ensure that `nvcc` (the NVIDIA C Compiler, which you will use to compile your CUDA code) is currently installed and included in your path.

INSTALLING SAMPLES TO THE USER DIRECTORY

The CUDA Toolkit comes with sample applications that are copied to system directories. Since users do not have permission to write or edit files in the system directories (and you will want to be able to modify the sample applications), it is a good idea to copy the entire set of samples to a location where you have write access. The CUDA Toolkit includes a script for this purpose, and executing `cuda-install-samples-7.5.sh` ~ copies the samples to `~/NVIDIA_CUDA-7.5_Samples`. To view your copy of the samples, make the newly created samples directory your current directory with `cd ~/NVIDIA_CUDA-7.5_Samples` and view the sample directories with `ls`.

INITIAL TEST RUN

We encourage you to explore the full range of sample applications; to compile them all at once, go to your CUDA Samples directory and type `make` (note that this will take a while). Once all samples are compiled successfully, let's run the `deviceQuery` sample as a simple test of CUDA capability. The `deviceQuery` sample code is located in a subdirectory of `1_Utilities`, so change your working directory with `cd 1_Utilities/deviceQuery` and run the executable with `./deviceQuery`. The results of the `deviceQuery` application will be displayed in the terminal window. Sample results from one of our test systems are shown in Figure B.11, where we can see that the system has a GeForce GT 650M GPU with compute capability 3.0, 512 MB of memory, and 384 CUDA cores.

So you've now run a CUDA app to verify that your CUDA software is working properly (along with your CUDA-enabled graphics card). You can now return to Chapter 1, "First Steps," or you can continue on to Appendix C, "Need-to-Know C Programming," to cover the essentials of C programming.

```
● ● ●                              1. bash (bash)
bash-4.3$
bash-4.3$ ./deviceQuery
./deviceQuery Starting...

 CUDA Device Query (Runtime API) version (CUDART static linking)

Detected 1 CUDA Capable device(s)

Device 0: "GeForce GT 650M"
  CUDA Driver Version / Runtime Version          7.5 / 7.5
  CUDA Capability Major/Minor version number:    3.0
  Total amount of global memory:                 512 MBytes (536543232 bytes)
  ( 2) Multiprocessors, (192) CUDA Cores/MP:     384 CUDA Cores
  GPU Max Clock rate:                            900 MHz (0.90 GHz)
  Memory Clock rate:                             2508 Mhz
  Memory Bus Width:                              128-bit
  L2 Cache Size:                                 262144 bytes
  Maximum Texture Dimension Size (x,y,z)         1D=(65536), 2D=(65536, 65536), 3D=(4096, 4096, 4096)
  Maximum Layered 1D Texture Size, (num) layers  1D=(16384), 2048 layers
  Maximum Layered 2D Texture Size, (num) layers  2D=(16384, 16384), 2048 layers
  Total amount of constant memory:               65536 bytes
  Total amount of shared memory per block:       49152 bytes
  Total number of registers available per block: 65536
  Warp size:                                     32
  Maximum number of threads per multiprocessor:  2048
  Maximum number of threads per block:           1024
  Max dimension size of a thread block (x,y,z): (1024, 1024, 64)
  Max dimension size of a grid size    (x,y,z): (2147483647, 65535, 65535)
  Maximum memory pitch:                          2147483647 bytes
  Texture alignment:                             512 bytes
  Concurrent copy and kernel execution:          Yes with 1 copy engine(s)
  Run time limit on kernels:                     Yes
  Integrated GPU sharing Host Memory:            No
  Support host page-locked memory mapping:       Yes
  Alignment requirement for Surfaces:            Yes
  Device has ECC support:                        Disabled
  Device supports Unified Addressing (UVA):      Yes
  Device PCI Domain ID / Bus ID / location ID:   0 / 1 / 0
  Compute Mode:
     < Default (multiple host threads can use ::cudaSetDevice() with device simultaneously) >

deviceQuery, CUDA Driver = CUDART, CUDA Driver Version = 7.5, CUDA Runtime Version = 7.5, NumDevs = 1,
Device0 = GeForce GT 650M
Result = PASS
bash-4.3$ []
```

Figure B.11 Output from running the `deviceQuery` Sample utility

Appendix C

Need-to-Know
C Programming

This appendix covers the basics of C programming that provides our jumping off point for CUDA programming. We start from scratch with a general description of the C language and then cover the procedures for creating, compiling, and executing C language apps. By the end of the appendix, we will have fully discussed `dist_v1` and `dist_v2`, the two distance apps that will serve as our initial examples for parallelization with CUDA.

Characterization of C

Here is the very short version of the three basic characteristics of the C programming language you need to know about:

- C is a **compiled** language, so we will write code in a version of C that is recognizable to humans (i.e., the code consists of familiar-looking words and punctuation marks), and we will use a software tool called a compiler (which can be invoked from the command line or from the **Integrated Development Environment** or **IDE**) to convert the human-recognizable code to machine code that the computer's processing units can "understand" and execute.

The above description of compilation is a simplification of what actually happens, but the details of linkers, PTX code, and so forth, do not qualify as need-to-know from our current perspective. (If you decide you do need to know these details, *C Programming in Easy Steps*, by Mike McGrath, provides a nice, concise description [1], and CUDA-specific details are covered in the "CUDA C Programming Guide" [2].)

Compilation is one of those classic "good news/bad news" things. The good news is that compiled code can be quite efficient and allow you to create programs that make efficient use of your computer's processing capabilities. The bad news is that we have to pay the price of some extra effort during the code development process. Each time we edit code, we need to stop, recompile, and check for errors before running the new version of the program. We'll have a firsthand look at those steps soon. (The typical alternative to a compiled language is an **interpreted** language, where an explicit compilation step is avoided, usually by paying a price in terms of lack of syntax checking before the execution and lower performance at execution time.)

- C is a **typed** language, so each time we define a variable we need a declaration statement that tells the system what type of data the variable corresponds to. Since the system knows how much memory is needed to store each data type, type declarations are consistent with the theme of putting in a little extra effort so the computer can use its resources efficiently when running your program.

- C arguments are **passed by value** (as opposed to **passed by reference**). For our purposes, this becomes especially important when we discuss handling arrays of data. When you write a function that has an array as input or output, should the system make a copy of the array (which might turn out to be convenient but use up a lot of your limited memory) to operate on? The authors of the C language placed a premium on the efficient use of memory and chose not to make a copy. Instead they decided to use a **pointer**, a single piece of data that tells where the existing array can be found in the system memory. (Any standard C reference book [3,4,5] will include extensive discussion of pointers and pointer arithmetic. We will avoid getting bogged down in pointer arithmetic.) The presentation of pointers associated with the dist_v2 app near the end of this appendix aims to provide what you need to know about pointers for the purposes of getting started with CUDA.

With those few generalities covered, let's delve into the necessary details.

C Language Basics

A C program consists of a sequence of statements each having a standard syntax and generally ending with a semicolon. The kinds of statements we will use most frequently involve declaration of variables, assignment of values, function definitions, function calls, and execution control. The standard syntax for each statement includes one or more reserved keywords, punctuation, and possibly some bracketing that you need to get exactly right. (Remember that despite all of its processing power, your computer is a very literal device that only knows about your actual code and not your intent in writing it. The bad news is that sometimes you will have to pay considerable attention to the details of your code; the good news is that your development environment should include syntax checking tools that greatly reduce the burden on you as the programmer.)

Speaking of syntax details, let's get out in front of issues related to punctuation, brackets, and so forth, by stating a few general rules:

- Parentheses ( ) are used for a couple of purposes:

  - Grouping of arguments in functions and control statements.

  - Indicating the precedence order for operations in a mathematical formula, so (1+2)*3 evaluates to 9 while 1+(2*3) evaluates to 7. It turns out that 1+2*3 also evaluates to 7 since multiplication has precedence over addition, but it is generally safer to take charge of such issues explicitly rather than assuming that the system will correctly determine your intent.

- Braces { } are used to group sets of statements and for values in array initializations.

- Square brackets [ ] are used for indexing entries in arrays. In array declarations, an integer in square brackets indicates the number of elements in the array.

- The number or hash sign, #, indicates preprocessor instructions. These lines of code are not really part of the C language and do not end with a semicolon.

  - We use #include to include code from other files. For example, #include <stdio.h> includes the standard input-output header, and #include "aux_functions.h" includes the code from the aux_functions.h file located in the same directory.

  - We use #define to simplify the management of constants (and occasionally functions) that may appear in numerous places throughout the code.

- The basic arithmetic operations of addition, subtraction, multiplication, and division are indicated with the usual symbols (+, -, *, /), and two of those are also used for other purposes:

  - The asterisk, *, is also used in association with pointers (which we will introduce below).

  - The slash character, /, also shows up in file paths and, perhaps most importantly, in comments. The double slash, //, indicates that the remainder of the line is a comment (i.e., not part of the code that the compiler converts to machine language), and comments that extend across multiple lines can be created by starting with /* and terminating with */.

Data Types, Declarations, and Assignments

The C language includes several built-in or **primitive data** types including int, float, double, and char, which provide representations for integers, real numbers, and characters. Note that we are talking about digital computing, so each data type is stored in a fixed amount of memory and has a finite range of representation. The computer's memory is binary, and the fundamental storage unit, a single 0 or 1, is a **bit**. It is often convenient to lump bits together into a group of 8 called a **byte**. A char, which translates to a character code, typically uses 1 byte of storage, while an int or float typically uses 4 bytes (or 32 bits) of storage. These sizes can be system dependent (and modifiers like long, short, and unsigned can affect things), but C includes an operator called sizeof() that helps us to avoid getting hung up on such details.

Each time we introduce a new variable, we need to specify its data type so the system will know essential properties (notably how much memory must be allocated to store a value associated with the variable). Such a specification is done using a **declaration** statement with the following syntax:

```
typeName variableName;
```

where typeName is a known data type (such as int, float, or char) and variableName is whatever name you choose for your variable. There are a few guidelines to abide by when choosing variable names:

- Start names with a letter, not a number or special character.

- Avoid reserved keywords. (There are a few dozen keywords, and the full list is available online [6].)

- Do not include arithmetic operators, punctuation characters, or spaces.

- Underscores are allowed and are frequently used in CUDA. (We will be seeing a lot of names like h_out and d_out).

- Feel free to mix upper- and lowercase to make names readable. Names in C are case sensitive, so myname and myName are both valid and distinct. Appending words with an initial uppercase character is a useful naming convention that is called **camelCase** because of the apparent humps.

- my name—with a white space in the middle—is *not* a valid name.

- my_name is a valid and distinct alternative. Connecting words with underscores is often referred to as **snake_case** or **under_score**.

Once we have declared a variable, we can associate a value with the variable using an **assignment** statement which has the following syntax:

```
myName = myValue;
```

where myName is the variable we declared and myValue is a value of the appropriate type (so you can think of a single equals sign as the assignment operator). For example, we can declare an integer named myInt as follows:

```
int myInt;
```

and then assign to myInt the value 8 as follows:

```
myInt = 8;
```

We can also combine these operations of declaration and assignment into a single initialization statement with the following syntax:

```
typeName varName = varValue;
```

so our two lines of sample code above can be replaced by the single line

```
int myInt = 8;
```

The C language not only supports all of the usual arithmetic operations (addition, subtraction, multiplication, and division) but also provides the convenient alternative of combining arithmetic operations and assignment into a single statement known as **compound** or **augmented assignment**; for example, `i += j` is equivalent to `i = (i + j)`.

Defining Functions

C supports functions as a way of creating a single name as shorthand for a collection of statements. Functions provide an essential mechanism for organizing code into "chunks" that are testable (to enhance reliability and maintainability) and reusable (to prevent repetition). Functions also provide a context for **scoping**, so we can create variables that are only locally accessible within the function. We will see that being able to create variables whose scope is limited to a particular function allows for convenient reuse of variable names, which actually reduces confusion rather than creating it.

The following is the basic syntax for defining a function:

```
returnType functionName(type0 arg0, type1 arg1, …, typeLast argLast)
{
    statement0;
     …;
    statementLast;
}
```

We can define a function to `return` a value (that could, for example, be assigned to a variable), and `returnType` specifies the data type of the value to be returned. The function name is followed by parentheses containing a comma-separated list of zero or more entries, each of which is a **typed argument** consisting of the data type (`type0`, etc.) followed by a white space and then the argument name (`arg0`, etc.).

Note that the definition of the generic syntax is not exactly concise, so it is useful to create some abbreviations:

- *args* is shorthand for a comma-separated sequence of arguments (i.e., it replaces `arg0, arg1, … , argLast`.

- *typedArgs* is shorthand for a comma-separated sequence of typed arguments (i.e., it replaces `type0 arg0, type1 arg1, … ,typeLast argLast`).

- *statements* is shorthand for a semicolon-separated sequence of statements (i.e., it replaces `statement0; statement1; … ; statementLast`).

The syntax for defining a function then simplifies to something that should be both easier to read and easier to remember:

```
returnType functionName(typedArgs)
{
    statements
}
```

We will return to define and execute many other functions, but for the purposes of creating our first program, let's focus on creating a function named main() because all C programs have a main() function that specifies where to start and what to include in the execution of the program.

Building Apps: Create, Compile, Run, Debug

It is time for our first C program, and we will keep it very simple. The program consists of a main() function that contains code to declare variables and assign values to those variables. The code for the app is shown in Listing C.1.

Listing C.1 `declare_and_assign/main.cpp`

```
1 int main()
2 {
3    int i;
4    float x;
5    i = 2;
6    x = 1.3f;
7
8    return 0;
9 }
```

Note that our main() takes no arguments, so the parentheses that hold the argument list are empty. We declare two variables, an integer i and a float x, and then we assign them the values 2 and 1.3f, respectively. (Appending f to a number indicates a float value.) At the end of main(), we follow convention by returning the value 0 (consistent with the declaration that main() returns an integer) to indicate successful completion.

We now go through the full procedure of creating, compiling, executing, and debugging the program before we go on to more complicated (and more interesting) programs. The details of accomplishing these steps will depend on your platform and development software, so we provide separate descriptions for Windows and Linux systems.

BUILDING APPS IN WINDOWS

The time has come to put your development environment to work, so start Visual Studio, and create a new project (either from the `Visual Studio Start Page` or by selecting `File ⇒ New`). From the list of installed templates, select `NVIDIA ⇒ CUDA 7.5 Runtime` (if it is not already selected by default), and enter a name for your app. Figure C.1 shows the Visual Studio's pop-up window as it should look when you are ready to hit `OK` to create the a new project named `declare_and_assign`, which is what this simple app aims to do. (Note that this particular example contains only C code and nothing specific to CUDA, but we'll start now to get some practice for creating the CUDA projects that lie ahead.)

Figure C.2 shows the Visual Studio window as it appears upon opening the new project. The `Solution Explorer` pane on the left shows the files associated with the project, including a CUDA file named `kernel.cu`, which is open to show its code in the upper-right pane.

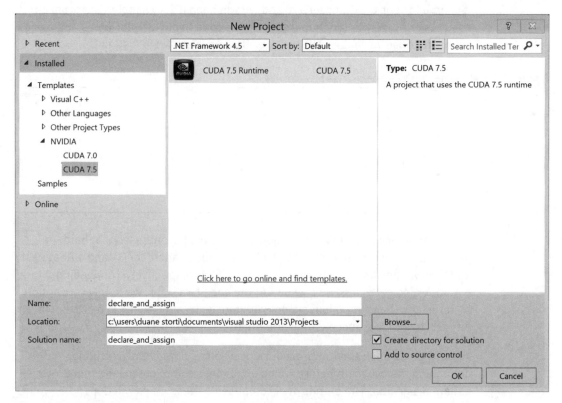

Figure C.1 Creating a new CUDA project in Visual Studio

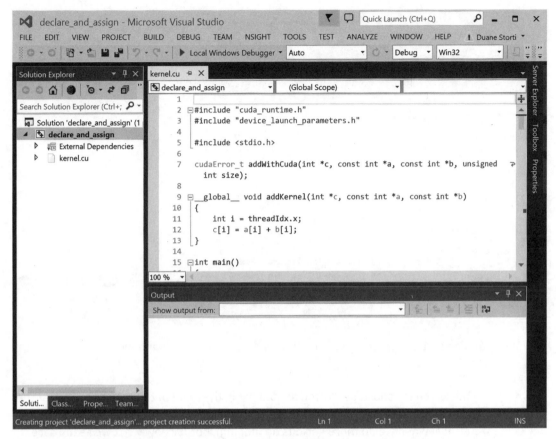

Figure C.2 The Visual Studio window upon creation of the new project

By default, a new project opens with code for a simple CUDA app that adds two arrays. Since this app involves only C code and not CUDA code, let's add `main.cpp` into the project and delete `kernel.cu` as follows:

1. Select PROJECT ⟹ Add New Item.

2. Select C++ file, and enter the name `main.cpp` as shown in Figure C.3.

3. Enter the code from Listing C.1 into `main.cpp`.

4. Remove `kernel.cu` from the project by right-clicking on its icon in the Solution Explorer pane and selecting Remove ⟹ Delete.

Having entered the code, the next steps involve compilation and execution. The code can be compiled/built by selecting BUILD ⟹ Build solution or using

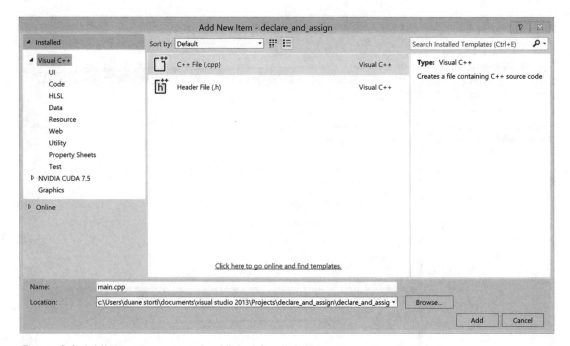

Figure C.3 Adding `main.cpp` using Visual Studio's `Add New Item` window

the keyboard shortcut `F7`. You should get in the habit of taking a good look at the messages that appear in the `Output` pane (since these messages will become critical when we do more serious debugging), but for now what we really care about is seeing something like

```
=== Build: 1 succeeded, 0 failed, 0 skipped ===
```

at the end of the output messages to tell us that the executable has been successfully created.

We can then run the executable by selecting `DEBUG` ⇒ `Start without debugging` or using the keyboard shortcut `Ctrl+F5`. Go ahead and execute the app. What happens? You should see a console window open with the message `Press any key to continue...` and pressing a key should close the console window.

While this is not very exciting, it should also not be very surprising since we did not include any code to provide output. Why did we avoid the obligatory statement to print "Hello World" to the console? First of all, it would require a tangential discussion of input/output formats that can wait until a bit later. Second, and perhaps more importantly, printing items of interest to the console is an ill-advised way to keep track of what is happening in your programs. Instead, let's start right away to become accustomed to using our development tools.

To be concrete, let's say we want to make sure that our variables actually get assigned values as intended. The preferred approach is to run the program in debug mode, which requires that the code has been compiled in debug mode. So reset your `Solution Configurations`, located below the `HELP` menu, from `Release` to `Debug` and `Solution Platforms` to `x64` (not `win32`), as shown in Figure C.4.

When executing in `Debug` mode, we can step through the execution line by line using the `DEBUG` ⇒ `Step Into` or the keyboard shortcut `F11`, but going through the whole program one step at a time becomes inconvenient for longer codes.

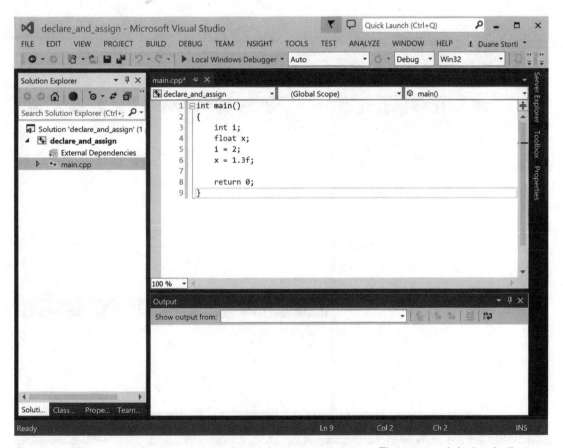

Figure C.4 The Visual Studio window after deleting `kernel.cu`. The upper-right box indicates the `Solution Configurations` and `Solution Platforms`.

The preferred alternative is to set specific **breakpoints** at which to do status checks. For example, let's set a break point at line 5, where i gets assigned a value. One way to do this is to just click in the code pane at the start of line 5 and then select DEBUG ⇒ Toggle break point or use keyboard shortcut F9. A large red dot appears at the left edge of the pane indicating the location of the break, and you can click in that location to toggle the break point on and off. Now if we start debugging with F5 (and the breakpoint toggled on), execution proceeds to the break point, and you can observe the current values of the variables in the Locals pane, as shown in Figure C.5. At this point you should see values for i and x that have no specific significance because no assignments have been executed yet.

After taking an execution step (by pressing F11) so the arrow moves to line 6, the Locals pane should resemble that shown in Figure C.6, where i now has a recognizable value that is displayed in red in the Locals pane.

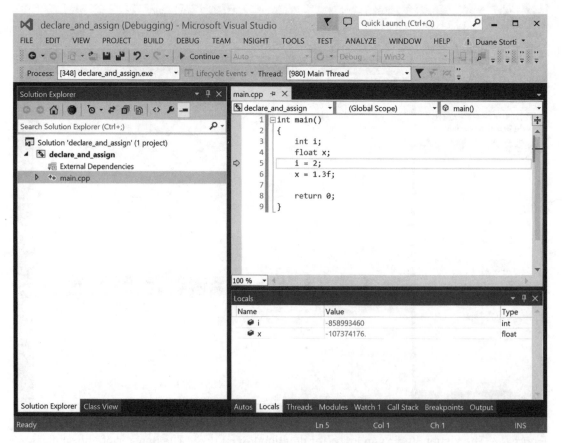

Figure C.5 Executing declare_and_assign in Debug mode at line 5

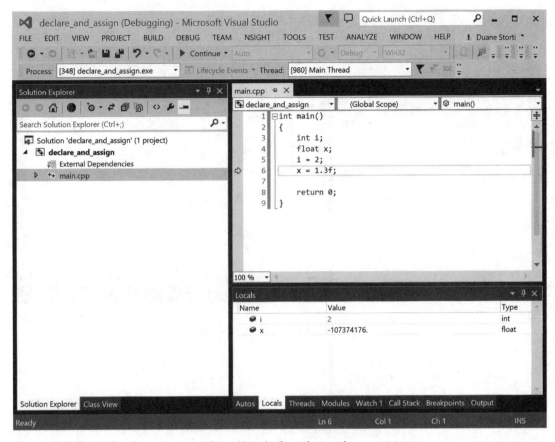

Figure C.6 Execution in `Debug` mode at line 6 after the assignment `i=2`

After one more execution step (via F11), the information presented in the Locals windows has changed, as shown in Figure C.7. The value shown for i is now displayed in black (only the assignment from the most recent statement is displayed in red) and a recognizable value is displayed in red for the variable x. Note that the value is not exactly 1.3, but it is the best possible approximation in a binary system with the given level of precision.

At this point, you can step through the last line or select DEBUG ⇒ Stop Debugging to terminate execution. We have now completed running our first C app, and if you only use Windows and not Linux/OS X, you can skip ahead to the section on "Arrays, Memory Allocation, and Pointers."

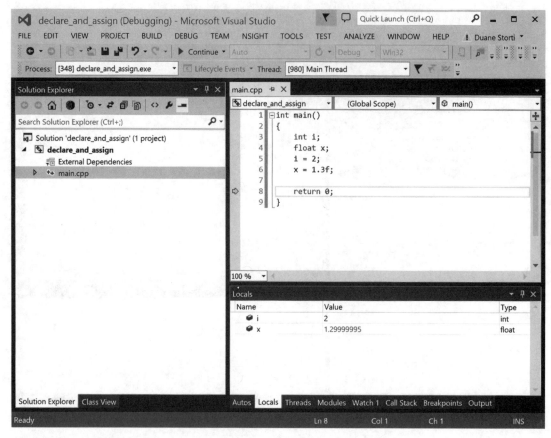

Figure C.7 Executing in `Debug` mode at line 8 after both assignments

BUILDING APPS IN LINUX

Here, we go through the process of creating an app under Linux/OS X using the following software:

- Use a text editor: For purposes of simplicity, our presentations in this book use the default editors `gedit` on Ubuntu and `TextEdit` on OS X. However, we recommend that you check out our text editor of choice, Sublime Text 3 with CUDA C++ language package, which is available on all platforms.

- `gmake` (GNU Make) automates the compilation/linking process.

- `nvcc` (NVIDIA CUDA Compiler) compiles the source code.

- `cuda-gdb` (NVIDIA CUDA debugger) debugs the executable.

Throughout the book, Makefiles for automating the compile/link process are provided when necessary. Complete documentation on GNU Make is available on GNU's website [7].

To create the `declare_and_assign` app under Linux/OS X, we need to compile the source code presented in Listing C.1 and link with the necessary libraries. In this simple case with a single file, `main.cpp`, containing the source code, we can generate the executable from the terminal with the command:

```
nvcc -g -G -Xcompiler -Wall main.cpp -o main.exe
```

which parses as follows:

- `nvcc` invokes the NVIDIA CUDA compiler.

- `-g` (shorthand for `--debug`) tells the compiler to generate debug information for the host code.

- `-G` (shorthand for `--device-debug`) tells the compiler to generate debug information for the device code.

- `-Xcompiler` (shorthand for `--compiler-options`) combined with `-Wall` tells the compiler to generate warning messages during compilation.

- `main.cpp -o main.exe` tells `nvcc` to get `main.cpp` as input and store the output as `main.exe`.

Alternatively, we can create a Makefile that controls the generation of executables from the source. Makefiles offer numerous advantages that become especially important when the project involves multiple source files. We introduce Makefiles here, and we will provide Makefiles for our apps. The `Makefile` for `declare_and_assign` is given in Listing C.2.

Listing C.2 `declare_and_assign/Makefile`

```
main.exe: main.cpp
    nvcc -g -G -Xcompiler -Wall main.cpp -o main.exe
```

Makefile Syntax

Makefiles include variable assignments and rules. A variable assignment such as `NVCC = /usr/local/cuda/bin/nvcc` looks much like a C assignment (without the semicolon terminator) and allows you to just write `NVCC` as shorthand for the full path in the remainder of the Makefile. A rule consists of three parts: targets, dependencies, and commands. The first line of a rule consists of the target (followed by a colon) and the dependencies. The remaining lines of a rule are a sequence of commands, each of which is indented with a TAB character. (To avoid problems, be sure to indent with TAB and not spaces.)

An equivalent shorthand version of the Makefile is given in Listing C.3.

Listing C.3 Shorthand version of `declare_and_assign /Makefile`

```
NVCC = /usr/local/cuda/bin/nvcc
NVCC_FLAGS = -g -G -Xcompiler -Wall

main.exe: main.cpp
    $(NVCC) $(NVCC_FLAGS) $< -o $@
```

Files in the Build Process

A detailed discussion of the steps in the process of building an executable app from source code is not on our critical path to CUDA, but here is a brief summary for those who are interested. We will write high-level code into source files with the extension .cpp for C/C++ code, .cu for source that includes CUDA code, and .h or .cuh for header files. The preprocessor produces another version of the C/C++/CUDA code with directives handled. The compiler then produces assembly code, and the assembler processes the assembly code into machine code stored in object files with the .o extension. The linker puts the object files together to produce the executable file.

With the code and the Makefile at our disposal, we are ready to create the executable app. Perform the following steps to create the `declare_and_assign` app:

1. Create a `projects` directory to store your projects. Using the cd command in the terminal, change to the `projects` directory.

2. Create a directory for this project with `mkdir declare_and_assign`, and change to that directory with `cd declare_and_assign`.

3. Create the file `main.cpp` with `gedit main.cpp` (for OS X, first `touch main.cpp` and then `open -e main.cpp`).

4. Enter the contents of the Listing C.1 into `main.cpp`.

5. Create the `Makefile` with `gedit Makefile` (first, `touch Makefile` and then `open -e Makefile` on OS X).

6. Enter the contents of the Listing C.2 into `Makefile`.

7. Compile the source file by typing `make`.

Now that the executable is ready, run the application and inspect the results as shown in Figure C.8 by using the debugger as follows:

1. Load the executable into the debugger with `cuda-gdb main.exe`.

2. Start debugging with `start` and display local variables with `info locals`. The first step goes to line 5 (the first execution statement), and the first `info locals` shows values of i and x that have not yet been initialized to their intended values.

3. Go to the next instruction with `next`, and check local variable values again. We are now at line 6, and `info locals` tells us that i has now been set to 2, but x will still be undefined.

4. Repeat the previous step to get to line 8, and observe that `info locals` now shows the assigned values for both i and x. Note that the value of x is not exactly `1.3`, but it is the best possible approximation in a binary system with the given level of precision.

5. Finish running the application with `continue` and leave the debugger with `quit`.

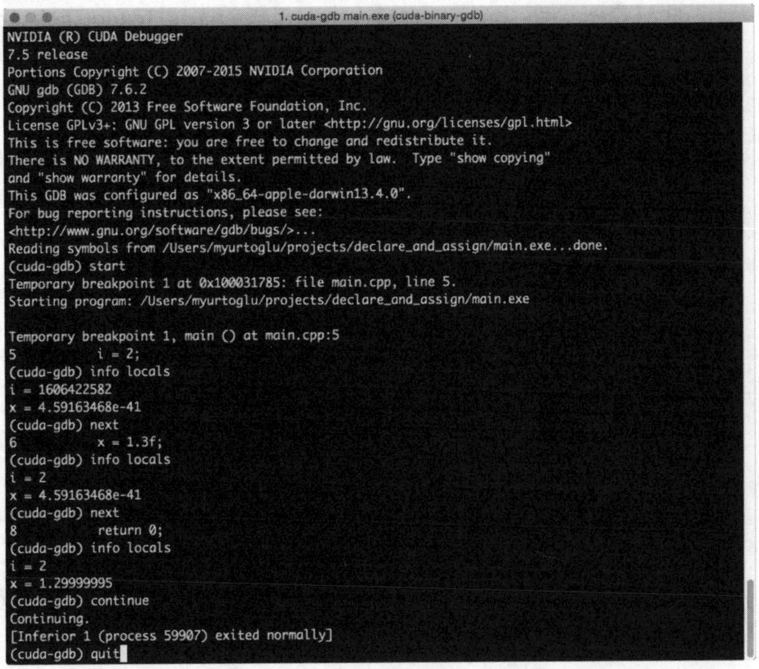

Figure C.8 `cuda-gdb` commands and results during debugging
`declare_and_assign`

We have now completed running our first C app, and we'll move on to the other aspects of the C language that are essential for our purposes.

Arrays, Memory Allocation, and Pointers

We have now created, compiled, executed, and debugged a simple C program, so it is time to gradually add in the elements of C that we will need, starting with arrays and control statements including the for loop.

To store more than one item of a particular type, you can use an **array** that is an indexed sequence of variables of a given type. The apps dist_v1 and dist_v2 at the end of this appendix provide examples of where we store the input values and/or the output values in arrays.

Let's get concrete and think about integer input values and floating point output values. As with regular variables, the name of an array is established by a declaration statement that looks very much like the declaration of a variable except that there are square brackets after the name to indicate that it is an array. In the declaration, a constant inside the square brackets indicates the length of the array. In other statements, the integer in the square brackets indicates the index of an element in the array.

Here let's create an input array of integers named in. We can declare an array in to hold 3 integer values and an array out to hold 3 float values as follows:

```
int in[3];
float out[3];
```

There are a few important things to note regarding array declarations:

- Memory is allocated for a fixed number of entries, so the entry in the square brackets must be a constant value specified at compile time. Dynamic resizing of the array is not supported in C. A common way to handle this employs the #define directive, as in the sample code below (which also includes examples of single-line and multiline comments):

```
#define  N 3 //Compiler directive has no semicolon.
/* The lines below declare 2 arrays.
   Each array has length N. */
int     in[N];
float   out[N];
```

- Recall that the indexing scheme in C starts counting at 0, so the elements of the array are `in[0]`, `in[1]`, and `in[2]`.

- As with simple variables, you can combine the declaration with assignment of initial values. For example, `int in[] = {1,2,3};` declares the array of 3 elements (here the square brackets can be left empty, as the length of the array is inferred from the list of initial values) and assigns initial values equivalent to `in[0] = 1; in[1] = 2; in[2] = 3;`.

- We are being a bit cavalier in the presentation of arrays up to this point. We have not yet said anything to indicate that the declaration `int in[] = {1,2,3};` does anything different from creating 3 integer variables and assigning each of them sequentially a value from the list in the braces. What is really happening is that the name we declare serves as a pointer to the first element in a contiguous block of memory of the appropriate size (equal to the number of elements times the number of bytes per element; here `N*sizeof(int)`). The element number (contained in the square brackets) tells the system how many steps of the appropriate size (i.e., the number of bytes needed to store each element of the given type) to take in the memory space to find the value of the specified element in the array. We are, in fact, being intentionally cavalier at this point, because this distinction is not yet important. We will return to look at the necessary details of explicitly handling pointers in the sample codes below that include functions with arrays as inputs or outputs, and we will cover explicit memory allocations when we discuss creating arrays on the device (GPU) side in Chapter 2, "CUDA Essentials," and beyond.

- Resist the urge to try to assign entire arrays in one fell swoop. Yes, you can create another array of 3 integers by `int inCopy[3];` but `inCopy = in` will not assign all of the elements of the new array `inCopy` to have values matching the corresponding elements in `in`. Instead, it just generates an error message because C just does not work that way. Such assignments need to be accomplished one element at a time—which provides a perfect segue into a brief discussion of control statements.

Control Statements: `for`, `if`

Control statements allow you to specify the circumstances under which certain portions of your code will (or will not) execute. In C, there are a handful of control statements that you need to know how to use, but for now we will focus on `for` and `if`.

THE for LOOP

The for statement is the quintessential embodiment of sequential programming in that it involves explicit specification of an iteration or loop index variable. The code within the loop is repeatedly executed for one value of the loop index after another until an exit criterion is met. Note that the for loop is an essential location on our path to parallel computing with CUDA, because our initial parallelizations will involve conversion of sequential for loops.

The syntax of a for loop has the following form:

```
for (start; test; increment)
{
    statements
}
```

where start is ordinarily a statement that declares the loop index variable and assigns it an initial value, test is a statement that specifies the exit condition, and increment is usually a statement that specifies how to change the value of the loop index after each trip through the loop. The braces contain the sequence of statements to be executed during each trip through the loop.

To be concrete, let's tackle the problem mentioned previously of copying the entries from one array (named in) into another (named inCopy). Here is the sample code:

```
#define N 3
int main()
{
    int in[] = {1,2,3};
    int inCopy[N];

    for (int i=0; i < N; ++i)
    {
        inCopy[i] = in[i];
    }

    return 0;
}
```

We start with a #define compiler directive to replace the symbol N with the number 3 (which serves as the constant needed for the array length), and then continue with the obligatory main() function. As before, we declare in and assign its entries the values 1 through 3. Declaration of inCopy as an array of 3 integers is followed by the for loop using a specific instance of the syntax described above. The loop index is an int named i with initial value 0. (Note that the scope of i is limited to this loop. The same symbol appearing outside of the loop refers to a distinct variable, so there is no need to come up with a novel loop index name for each loop.) The iterations continue until i no longer has a value less than N (which was replaced by 3), and ++i increases the value of i by 1 after each trip through the loop. Since each trip through the loop copies the ith entry in in into the corresponding position in inCopy, and i is initialized with value 0, during the first trip through the loop, inCopy[0] is assigned the value stored in in[0], which is 1. The value of i is increased from 0 to 1, and execution returns to the top of the loop. Since i has value 1 (and N has been replaced by 3), the continuation condition i < N is satisfied, and a second trip is made through the code in the loop, during which inCopy[1] is assigned the value stored in in[1]; that is, 2. The process continues (assigning values for entries up to and including inCopy[2]) until i is incremented to have value 3, at which point the continuation test fails and we exit from the loop. Execution proceeds to the final line in main(), and the integer value 0 is returned to indicate completed execution.

Recall that entries in an array in C are indexed starting at 0; this is a common coding pattern. To execute some code with each entry in an array (as either input or output), use a for loop with an iterator initialized to zero and incremented at each iteration with an execution test that the iterator value is less than the number of elements (because an array of length N has elements with indices 0, 1, ..., N − 1). Note that some other languages use other indexing schemes, but for writing C code, we want to get used to counting from 0.

A final note should be made here. Our descriptions of arrays have been a bit figurative to this point and have not involved any real mention of pointers. We will rectify this in the sample programs that follow, where we construct functions whose inputs and/or outputs are stored in arrays.

THE if STATEMENT

The keyword if allows you to specify that a section of code will execute only when a test condition is satisfied. The selection of test conditions includes equality (==), inequality (!=), and ordering—greater than (>), less than (<), greater than or equal to (>=), less than or equal to (<=). The composition of multiple conditions can be specified using the logical operations "and" written as &&, "or" written as ||, and complement or "not" written as !. C represents FALSE as 0, so (a > b) is really shorthand for ((a > b) != 0), which asks whether the truth of a > b is not FALSE.

The standard syntax is the following:

```
if (condition)
{
    statements
}
```

You can also include `else` clauses to specify alternative statements to execute when the condition is not satisfied. The standard syntax is the following:

```
if (condition)
{
    statements
}
else if (condition)
{
    statements
}
else
{
    statements
}
```

This provides fundamental support for computations that involve doing different things in different situations. As a concrete example, assume that we have declared an integer n and assigned n a value, and we want to assign y the rectified version of x (i.e., y = x if x > 0; y = 0 if x <= 0). The following code using `if-else` syntax will do the job:

```
if (x > 0)
{
    y = x;
}
else
{
    y = 0;
}
```

Relevant items to know about `if` statements:

- Semicolons terminate the statements inside the braces, but no semicolon is needed after the braces.

- There's more than one way to get things done, and you will see alternatives to this structure that can be convenient (and still readable), especially when the braces contain only one or two statements. The code for assigning to y the rectified value of x can be written more compactly as

  ```
  if (x > 0) y = x; else y = 0;
  ```

  or using the ternary operator `? :` as

  ```
  y = (x > 0) ? x : 0;
  ```

  but we find that use of braces and indentation helps make code more readable. (We'll see later that initial format shown with full braces and indentation is most compatible with debugging tools.) Figure out the style that works for you, and stick with it.

OTHER CONTROL STATEMENTS

Control statements that combine a condition test with repeated (or looping) evaluation are accomplished with the keywords while and do. You can have the execution skip an index value with continue or escape from a loop entirely using break or goto. Multiple, distinct execution paths that are determined by the value of an expression can be specified using a switch statement with multiple case values and can optionally include a default path. Please refer to standard C language sources for complete details [5].

Sample C Programs

We are now ready to construct the first apps on our direct path to CUDA. The apps compute the distance from a reference point to each of *N* equally spaced points on the interval from 0 to 1. Here, we construct two versions, dist_v1 and dist_v2, which also appear in Chapter 1, "First Steps," as our initial examples to be converted to parallel CUDA apps.

The two distance apps are designed to produce the same output, but they are structured in different ways:

1. dist_v1 uses a for loop to call a function that evaluates the distance for a single input value. This version offers the simplest candidate for initial parallelization.

2. dist_v2 has a bit more structure. The input values are stored in an array, and the for loop is moved into a function named distanceArray(), which is called once to compute and store all of the output distance values. Parallelization of dist_v2 will take a bit more work, but it provides a structure that is well-suited for parallelization with CUDA.

dist_v1

The code for dist_v1 is shown in Listing C.4.

Listing C.4 dist_v1/main.cpp

```
1 #include <math.h>  //Include standard math library containing sqrt.
2 #define N 64    // Specify a constant value for array length.
3
4 // A scaling function to convert integers 0,1,...,N-1
```

```
 5 // to evenly spaced floats ranging from 0 to 1.
 6 float scale(int i, int n)
 7 {
 8   return ((float)i) / (n - 1);
 9 }
10
11 // Compute the distance between 2 points on a line.
12 float distance(float x1, float x2)
13 {
14   return sqrt((x2 - x1)*(x2 - x1));
15 }
16
17 int main()
18 {
19   // Create an array of N floats (initialized to 0.0).
20   // We will overwrite these values to store our results.
21   float out[N] = {0.0f};
22
23   // Choose a reference value from which distances are measured.
24   const float ref = 0.5f;
25
26   /* for loop to scale the index to obtain coordinate value,
27    * compute the distance from the reference point,
28    * and store the result in the corresponding entry in out. */
29   for (int i = 0; i < N; ++i)
30   {
31     float x = scale(i, N);
32     out[i] = distance(x, ref);
33   }
34
35   // It is conventional for main() to return zero
36   // to indicate that the code ran to completion.
37   return 0;
38 }
```

This code is designed to compute an output array (named out with length N=64) of distance values from a reference point ref to a grid of regularly spaced points on the interval 0.0 to 1.0 computed by scaling the loop index i. We start by including the header file for the standard math library (so we have access to the square root function sqrt()) and by specifying a constant value N (chosen to be 64) for the number of points and the length of the output array. The first function, scale(), defined on lines 6–9 converts an integer in the range 0, ..., $N - 1$ to a floating point coordinate value on the interval 0.0 to 1.0, while distance(), defined on lines 12–15, computes the distance between two points on a line.

The main() function begins by creating an array of N floats initialized to 0.0 (which will be overwritten to store our output) on line 21 and setting the reference point from which distances are measured, ref = 0.5f on line 24. The for loop then begins on line 29 and, for each value of the loop index (from 0 to N-1), the corresponding scaled location is computed and stored in x on line 31, and the distance from the reference point is computed and stored in out[i] on line 32. When i increments to N, the computation exits the for loop and main() returns the value 0 to indicate that the code has completed execution.

Convert the code in Listing C.4 to an executable app as follows:

- Under Windows

    1. Open Visual Studio and create a new project named dist_v1.

    2. Add a main.cpp file to the project: Select PROJECT ⇒ Add New Item, then select C++ file, enter the name main.cpp, and click Add. The extension .cpp stands for C++ and indicates that the contents should be compiled as C/C++ code. Contrast to .cu files, which contain CUDA code to be compiled with nvcc.

    3. Enter the code from Listing C.4 into main.cpp.

    4. Remove kernel.cu from the project by right-clicking on its icon in the Solution Explorer pane and selecting Remove.

    5. Set the compilation configuration to Debug and x64, and then select BUILD ⇒ Build solution or F7.

    6. Set a break point at line 37, and debug to inspect the results.

- Under Linux

    1. Create a dist_v1 directory.

    2. Create a new file main.cpp. Enter the code from Listing C.4 into main.cpp and save the file.

    3. Create the Makefile and enter the contents of Listing C.2 into Makefile.

    4. Compile the source file by typing make.

    5. Load the executable into the debugger with cuda-gdb main.exe.

    6. Set a breakpoint at line 37 with break main.cpp:37.

    7. Start debugging with run, and inspect the results.

Using the debugging tools to inspect the results, the procedure should be just like what you did with declare_and_assign above, but now you need to inspect the values stored in an array out. This requires no adjustment under Linux; info locals or print out will send the list of entries in the array out to the terminal. In Visual Studio's Locals pane, there will be a small triangle at the left side of the line where out appears, as shown in Figure C.9. Click on the triangle to open a scrollable list of the entries stored in out.

However you view your results, you should see values starting at 0.5 (the distance from a scaled value of 0 to the reference point at 0.5), decreasing toward zero near the middle of the array, and increasing back to 0.5 (corresponding to the distance from 0.5 to a scaled value of 1.0).

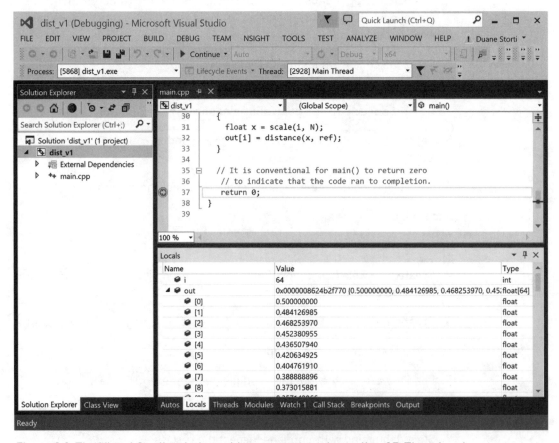

Figure C.9 The Visual Studio window with Debug execution at line 37. The triangle next to out in the Locals pane has been clicked to display a list of the entries in the array.

dist_v2

In the second version of the distance app, we create an array of all the input coordinate values and a function that computes distance values for the entire input array. The first version, dist_v1, is atypical in that there is no real input data (other than the reference location). Here we do something more typical and process an array of input data to produce an array of output data. (Here the input data is created with an initial for loop, but the same basic workflow would apply for input data read from a file or an input device.) We add a bit of structure by putting the functions (other than main()) in a separate file, aux_functions.cpp, and creating a corresponding header file, aux_functions.h, for inclusion. That said, let's get right to the code for dist_v2. The codes for main.cpp, aux_functions.h, and aux_functions.cpp are shown in Listings C.5, C.6, and C.7.

Listing C.5 dist_v2/main.cpp

```
 1 #include "aux_functions.h"
 2 #define N 64      // Specify a constant value for array length.
 3
 4 int main()
 5 {
 6    // Create 2 arrays of N floats (initialized to 0.0).
 7    // We will overwrite these values to store inputs and outputs.
 8    float in[N] = {0.0f};
 9    float out[N] = {0.0f};
10
11    // Choose a reference value from which distances are measured.
12    const float ref = 0.5f;
13
14    // Iteration loop computes array of scaled input values.
15    for (int i = 0; i < N; ++i)
16    {
17      in[i] = scale(i, N);
18    }
19
20    // Single function call to compute entire distance array.
21    distanceArray(out, in, ref, N);
22
23    return 0;
24 }
```

The code in main() has only minor changes from dist_v1/main.cpp shown in Listing C.4. There is an in array for the scaled input values in addition to the out array to store the output distances, and the work of the for loop (which previously computed the scaled input and then computed/stored the distance value) is split into two pieces. The for loop in main() now just computes and stores the scaled input values. The work of computing and storing the distance values is now relegated to distanceArray().

Note that main() includes calls to scale() and distanceArray(), whose definitions do not appear. We have already discussed that the compiler needs to know at least the function declaration or prototype in advance of the function call, and this need is met using the header files. In this case, we choose to define the auxiliary functions scale() and distanceArray() in a separate file named aux_functions.cpp. We then put a copy of the prototype for each of the auxiliary functions that should be callable from main() in the file aux_functions.h and include aux_functions.h at the top of main.cpp, and the compiler has access to all the necessary information.

The complete header file is shown in Listing C.6. The gist of the header file consists of the function prototypes and descriptive comments. In addition to the prototypes, there are three compiler directives that constitute the **include guard** (or **header guard**), which prevents compilation errors associated with attempts at redundant inclusion of prototypes.

Listing C.6 dist_v2/aux_functions.h

```
 1 #ifndef AUX_FUNCTIONS_H
 2 #define AUX_FUNCTIONS_H
 3
 4 // Function to scale input on interval [0,1]
 5 float scale(int i, int n);
 6 // Compute the distance between 2 points on a line.
 7 float distance(float x1, float x2);
 8 // Compute scaled distance for an array of input values.
 9 void distanceArray(float *out, float *in, float ref, int n);
10
11 #endif
```

The code for aux_functions.cpp is shown in Listing C.7. The scale() and distance() definitions are unchanged from dist_v1. The interesting addition is distanceArray(), a function that is supposed to take an array of input values (along with a reference location and array length) and produce an array of output values. This is our first encounter with a function whose arguments include arrays and a good opportunity for a reminder of the statement from the "Characterization of C" section about how C deals with functions of arrays: Instead of passing a whole array, C passes the value of a pointer that specifies the memory location where the array storage begins. C uses the asterisk to indicate pointer variable types in declarations, so distanceArray's first two arguments, float *out and float *in indicate pointers to an array of floats.

Listing C.7 `dist_v2/aux_functions.cpp`

```
 1 #include "aux_functions.h"
 2 #include <math.h>
 3
 4 float scale(int i, int n)
 5 {
 6   return ((float)i) / (n - 1);
 7 }
 8
 9 float distance(float x1, float x2)
10 {
11   return sqrt((x2 - x1)*(x2 - x1));
12 }
13
14 void distanceArray(float *out, float *in, float ref, int n)
15 {
16   for (int i = 0; i < n; ++i)
17   {
18     out[i] = distance(in[i], ref);
19   }
20 }
```

The body of `distanceArray()` consists of a `for` loop that reads `in[i]`, the `ith` element of the input array, computes the distance to `ref`, and stores the result at `out[i]`, the corresponding position in the output array. Note that the function prototype tells the compiler that `in` and `out` are pointers to `float`s, and neither the type nor the asterisk that appear in the prototype appear with the array name in the body of the function.

Pointer Arithmetic

Outside of declarations, the asterisk functions as the **dereference** operator that returns the value in the memory location stored by the pointer variable. While there are situations where explicit dereferencing is appropriate, it is not needed for our array operations. If the name of array is a pointer to the start of the array—for example, `in` points to the start of the input array—why don't we need an asterisk to access a value in the array? The answer is that we don't just use `in`. We think of `in` as an array so our code contains not `in`, but `in[i]`. The compiler decomposes `in[i]` to `*(in + i)`, which translates into English as "increment the pointer `in` by `i` and return the value stored at that location." Since `in` points to the start of the input array, and the compiler knows to increment the pointer by the amount of memory used to store a `float`, `in[i]` returns the value of the `ith` element. If you do include an asterisk, undesirable and unexpected things will occur because bits stored in the array will get unintended treatment as memory addresses.

Note that `distanceArray()` has return type `void`, which may seem a bit strange at first but is actually common in C. Since C passes arguments by value, a function cannot directly modify any of its arguments. If you want a C function to modify an entity (a variable or array element), the argument needs to be a pointer to the entity and not the entity itself. The pointer (the memory location of the entity) remains unchanged, but the function can store a new value at the entity's location; and all of this can occur without the function returning anything. (In Chapter 3, "From Loops to Grids," we will see that there are important classes of functions that must have type `void` and are not allowed to return a value.)

It is time to build and test the app. If you are running Linux, the procedure will be only slightly different from for `dist_v1`. In addition to creating a `dist_v2` directory with files `main.cpp`, `aux_functions.h`, and `aux_functions.cpp` containing the code from Listings C.5, C.6, and C.7, respectively, you will need to create a new Makefile in the `dist_v2` directory. The code for `dist_v2/Makefile` is given in Listing C.8. Build the app using `cuda-gdb`, set a breakpoint at the return statement at the end of `main()`, and verify that the results agree those from `dist_v1`.

Listing C.8 `dist_v2/Makefile`

```
NVCC = /usr/local/cuda/bin/nvcc
NVCC_FLAGS = -g -G -Xcompiler -Wall

all: main.exe

main.exe: main.o aux_functions.o
    $(NVCC) $^ -o $@

main.o: main.cpp aux_functions.h
    $(NVCC) $(NVCC_FLAGS) -c $< -o $@

aux_functions.o: aux_functions.cpp aux_functions.h
    $(NVCC) $(NVCC_FLAGS) -c $< -o $@
```

In Visual Studio, create a new `dist_v2` project, add `main.cpp` to the project, and delete `kernel.cu` just as you did for `dist_v1`. Then add new files `aux_functions.cpp` and `aux_functions.h` to the project. (Note that when you select `Project` ⇒ `Add New Item` ⇒ `C++`, you can choose to add a `.h` file or a `.cpp` file.) Enter the code from Listings C.5, C.6, and C.7 into the appropriate files, and compile in `Debug` mode. Set a breakpoint at the `return` statement at the bottom of `main()`, start debugging, and inspect the results in the `Locals` pane. Verify that the `in` entries increase from 0 to 1 in uniform increments and that the distance values in `out` agree with those computed using `dist_v1`.

Reading Messages and Warnings

If you follow the directions above, your compilation should succeed. However, sometimes things do not go exactly as planned, and we want to be prepared for such situations, so let's create one. Comment out #include <math.h> in aux_functions.cpp and rebuild the app. The compiler will generate an error message, and the point of this detour is to get you to pay attention to the errors and warnings generated at compile time. Figure C.10 shows the error message as it appears in the Visual Studio Output pane. The "bottom line" that indicates overall success or failure is important, but get used to looking beyond that. Two lines above, we learn that the specific error (error C3861) occurred at line 11 of aux_functions.cpp. There are now several useful tools at your disposal for resolving the problem. You can enter error C3861 and/or identifier not found in a search engine and find additional information: for example, "The compiler was not able to resolve a reference to an identifier, even using argument-dependent lookup." You can even click on the error in the Output pane to make the cursor go to the corresponding line in the code pane.

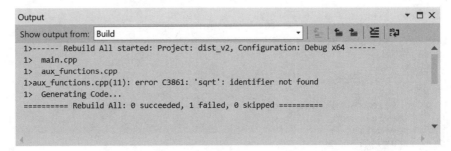

Figure C.10 Visual Studio Output pane showing error message generated from attempt at code compilation

These tools may be overkill for resolving the current issue, that sqrt is not recognized because we forgot to include the math library header, but we strongly advise you to get into the habit of actually looking carefully at the details—and not just the bottom line—when you compile.

dist_v2 WITH DYNAMIC MEMORY

We have now discussed most of the critical aspects of the C language for our needs, but there is one more topic that requires attention. The arrays we've created so far have had small constant lengths, so the arrays were small enough to fit in the stack memory. However, stack memory is limited, and you will produce segmentation fault errors if you just replace #define N 64 with #define N 20000000 in dist_v2/main.cpp. We need to take a different approach for array sizes that are larger (and large arrays are very relevant in the CUDA world) or not known at compile time. A modified version of dist_v2 that handles large arrays using **dynamic memory management** is shown in Listing C.9.

Listing C.9 dist_v2/main.cpp with dynamic memory management

```
 1 #include "aux_functions.h"
 2 #include <stdlib.h> // supports dynamic memory management
 3
 4 #define N 20000000 // A large array size
 5
 6 int main()
 7 {
 8   float *in = (float*)calloc(N, sizeof(float));
 9   float *out = (float*)calloc(N, sizeof(float));
10   const float ref = 0.5f;
11
12   for (int i = 0; i < N; ++i)
13   {
14     in[i] = scale(i, N);
15   }
16
17   distanceArray(out, in, ref, N);
18
19   // Release the heap memory after we are done using it.
20   free(in);
21   free(out);
22   return 0;
23 }
```

The revised code requires only a few changes:

- The stdlib.h header is included to support calling dynamic memory management functions.

- We create the arrays in and out on lines 8 and 9 by explicitly declaring pointers *in and *out to which we assign the values returned by calls to (float*)calloc(N, sizeof(float)), which allocates (and initializes to zero) enough contiguous memory to hold N floats. The calloc call returns the starting location of the allocated memory, and (float*) casts the value to be of type "pointer to float." The net result is that the name of the array is again a pointer to the array's starting location in memory; but now it is heap memory instead of stack memory, so the array size can be both large and determined at runtime.

- On lines 20 and 21, we free the memory that was allocated to store the arrays.

Replace the code in dist_v2/main.cpp with the revised version in Listing C.9, compile in debug mode, set a breakpoint at line 20 (after the computations but before the memory is freed), and start debugging.

Note that a different procedure is required for viewing array values in the heap. Using cuda-gdb under Linux, out [5000]@100 prints the values of 100 array elements starting at the 5,000th element. In Visual Studio, the array entries can no longer be inspected in the Locals pane (which only has access to stack memory), and a Watch window is used instead. (Select DEBUG ⇒ Windows ⇒ Watch ⇒ Watch1 if a Watch window is not already open.) Typing out+5000,100 in the Name column of the Watch window accesses 100 elments, starting with the 5,000th element in the array. (We are employing a bit of pointer arithmetic here, but do not get hung up on that detail.) Again, you may need to click on the triangle next to the name to view the entries on separate lines.

Having completed this appendix, you should know the essentials of C programming, including declaring and defining variables and functions, simple control structures, and basic array operations. You should also have a basic understanding of the example apps dist_v1 and dist_v2 that also appear in Chapter 1, "First Steps," and provide our initial case studies for parallelization with CUDA in Chapter 3, "From Loops to Grids."

References

[1] Mike McGrath, *C Programming in Easy Steps, Fourth Edition* (Southam, Warwickshire, UK: In Easy Steps Limited, 2012).

[2] NVIDIA Corporation, "CUDA C Programming Guide," NVIDIA Developer Zone, CUDA Toolkit Documentation, 2015, http://docs.nvidia.com/cuda/cuda-c-programming-guide/index.html#abstract.

[3] David Griffiths and Dawn Griffiths, *Head First C* (Sebastopol, CA: O'Reilly Media, 2012).

[4] Zed A. Shaw, *Learn C the Hard Way* (New York, NY: Addison-Wesley, 2016).

[5] Brian Kernighan and Dennis M. Ritchie, *The C Programming Language, Second Edition* (Englewood Cliffs, NJ: Prentice Hall, 1988).

[6] "C++ Keywords," cppreference.com, 2015, http://en.cppreference.com/w/cpp/keyword.

[7] Free Software Foundation, *GNU Make*, 2013, http://www.gnu.org/software/make/manual/make.html.

Appendix D

CUDA Practicalities: Timing, Profiling, Error Handling, and Debugging

This appendix aims to introduce some practical matters you will want to include in your skill set before getting too far along with your own development projects. In particular, we introduce the following:

- Execution timing and profiling

- Error handling

- CUDA debugging tools

Execution Timing and Profiling

When you start creating CUDA programs, you will want to be able to quantify the performance of your code. (If you did not care about performance, it is highly unlikely that you would have gotten started with CUDA.) While you can use the

standard C language timing methods, there are some issues with synchronization between the CPU and the GPU, so we will also look at the CUDA-specific
timing methods provided by CUDA C and Nsight.

STANDARD C TIMING METHODS

Modern versions of the C language include a library <time.h> that provides a
type definition clock_t for timing variables, a clock() function for getting the
current processor time used by the program so far, and the constant CLOCKS_
PER_SEC for converting the result of clock() to seconds. The simplest way
to present this approach is with an example, so let's use the standard C timing
approach to get a measurement of the kernel execution time and the time it
takes to copy the input data from the host to the device in our sample application
dist_v2_cuda from Chapter 3, "From Loops to Grids."

Listing D.1 shows dist_v2_cuda/kernel.cu with timing code added. In addition to the changes made in kernel.cu, increase the size of the array by editing
the line that sets the length of the array (N) in main.cpp as #define N 256000.

Listing D.1 dist_v2_cuda/kernel.cu with code inserted for CPU timing of memory transfer
of input data from host to device

```
1 #include "kernel.h"
2 #include <stdio.h>
3 #include <time.h>
4 #define TPB 32
5 #define M 100 // Number of times to do the data transfer
6
7 __device__
8 float distance(float x1, float x2)
9 {
10   return sqrt((x2 - x1)*(x2 - x1));
11 }
12
13 __global__
14 void distanceKernel(float *d_out, float *d_in, float ref)
15 {
16   const int i = blockIdx.x*blockDim.x + threadIdx.x;
17   const float x = d_in[i];
18   d_out[i] = distance(x, ref);
19 }
20
21 void distanceArray(float *out, float *in, float ref, int len)
22 {
23   float *d_in = 0;
24   float *d_out = 0;
25   cudaMalloc(&d_in, len*sizeof(float));
26   cudaMalloc(&d_out, len*sizeof(float));
27
```

```
28    // Record the clock cycle count before data transfer.
29    clock_t memcpyBegin = clock();
30    // Copy input data from host to device M times.
31    for (int i = 0; i < M; ++i)
32    {
33      cudaMemcpy(d_in, in, len*sizeof(float),
34               cudaMemcpyHostToDevice);
35    }
36    // Record the clock cycle count after memory transfer.
37    clock_t memcpyEnd = clock();
38
39    clock_t kernelBegin = clock();
40    distanceKernel<<<len/TPB, TPB>>>(d_out, d_in, ref);
41    clock_t kernelEnd = clock();
42
43    cudaMemcpy(out, d_out, len*sizeof(float), cudaMemcpyDeviceToHost);
44
45    // Compute time in seconds between clock count readings.
46    double memcpyTime =
47      ((double)(memcpyEnd - memcpyBegin))/CLOCKS_PER_SEC;
48    double kernelTime =
49      ((double)(kernelEnd - kernelBegin))/CLOCKS_PER_SEC;
50
51    printf("Kernel time (ms): %f\n", kernelTime*1000);
52    printf("Data transfer time (ms): %f\n", memcpyTime*1000);
53
54    cudaFree(d_in);
55    cudaFree(d_out);
56 }
```

Here is a summary of the highlights:

- The standard timing library is included via #include <time.h>.

- M constant is defined to repeat the data transfer M times.

- The changes in distanceArray() include

  - Storing initial and final CPU times for the memory transfer via memcpyBegin = clock(); and memcpyEnd = clock(); on lines 29 and 37

  - Looping the copy operation M times with a for loop

  - Storing initial and final CPU times for the kernel via kernelBegin = clock(); and kernelEnd = clock(); on lines 39 and 41

  - Converting the difference in recorded CPU time to seconds

Running this example on our OS X system with NVIDIA GeForce GT 650M produces the following results:

```
Kernel time (ms): 0.032000
Data transfer time (ms): 41.790000
```

The data transfer time turns out to be correct, but the kernel time is not.

Why is it that this approach seems to work for timing a memory transfer but not a kernel execution? This question brings up the important point that there are two very different classes of operations which occur in CUDA applications:

- **Synchronous operations** block the computation stream and prevent other operations from proceeding.

- **Asynchronous operations** allow other operations to proceed while the asynchronous operation is executed concurrently.

By default, data transfers are synchronous, so `cudaMemcpy()` finishes execution before the CPU can move on to other operations like reading the clock and recording the end time. Kernel launches, on the other hand, are asynchronous. As soon as the kernel is launched, the CPU moves on to its next task, and the clock value is read and assigned to `kernelEnd` before the kernel execution is complete. Now we are going to look at a CUDA-specific timing method based on CUDA events that is capable of timing both synchronous and asynchronous operations.

CUDA EVENTS

To avoid some of the issues associated with CPU/GPU synchronization and to provide finer resolution, CUDA includes its own timing mechanisms. The CUDA API includes a special data type, `cudaEvent_t`, along with several key functions used to work with CUDA events including the following:

- `cudaEventCreate()` and `cudaEventDestroy()` for creating and destroying events (just as their names suggest)

- `cudaEventRecord()` for recording the time

- `cudaEventSynchronize()` for ensuring completion of asynchronous functions

- `cudaEventElapsedTime()` for converting a pair of event records to an elapsed time (in milliseconds)

Once again, the most efficient way to present these functions is to show them in action, so we will jump right into the CUDA event approach to timing operations in distanceArray(). Listing D.2 shows an updated version of kernel.cu that uses the CUDA event API to time both the initial transfer of data from host to device and the kernel execution.

Listing D.2 dist_v2_cuda/kernel.cu modified to time memory transfer from host to device and kernel execution using CUDA events

```
 1  #include "kernel.h"
 2  #include <stdio.h>
 3  #define TPB 32
 4  #define M 100 // Number of times to do the data transfer
 5
 6  __device__
 7  float distance(float x1, float x2)
 8  {
 9    return sqrt((x2 - x1)*(x2 - x1));
10  }
11
12  __global__
13  void distanceKernel(float *d_out, float *d_in, float ref)
14  {
15    const int i = blockIdx.x*blockDim.x + threadIdx.x;
16    const float x = d_in[i];
17    d_out[i] = distance(x, ref);
18  }
19
20  void distanceArray(float *out, float *in, float ref, int len)
21  {
22    // Create event variables for timing.
23    cudaEvent_t startMemcpy, stopMemcpy;
24    cudaEvent_t startKernel, stopKernel;
25    cudaEventCreate(&startMemcpy);
26    cudaEventCreate(&stopMemcpy);
27    cudaEventCreate(&startKernel);
28    cudaEventCreate(&stopKernel);
29
30    float *d_in = 0;
31    float *d_out = 0;
32    cudaMalloc(&d_in, len*sizeof(float));
33    cudaMalloc(&d_out, len*sizeof(float));
34
35    // Record the event that "starts the clock" on data transfer.
36    cudaEventRecord(startMemcpy);
37    // Copy input data from host to device M times.
38    for (int i = 0; i < M; ++i)
39    {
40      cudaMemcpy(d_in, in, len*sizeof(float),
41                 cudaMemcpyHostToDevice);
42    }
43    // Record the event that "stops the clock" on data transfer.
44    cudaEventRecord(stopMemcpy);
45
```

```
46    // Record the event that "starts the clock" on kernel execution.
47    cudaEventRecord(startKernel);
48    distanceKernel<<<len/TPB, TPB>>>(d_out, d_in, ref);
49    // Record the event that "stops the clock" on kernel execution.
50    cudaEventRecord(stopKernel);
51
52    // Copy results from device to host.
53    cudaMemcpy(out, d_out, len*sizeof(float), cudaMemcpyDeviceToHost);
54
55    // Ensure timed events have stopped.
56    cudaEventSynchronize(stopMemcpy);
57    cudaEventSynchronize(stopKernel);
58
59    // Convert event records to time and output.
60    float memcpyTimeInMs = 0;
61    cudaEventElapsedTime(&memcpyTimeInMs, startMemcpy, stopMemcpy);
62    float kernelTimeInMs = 0;
63    cudaEventElapsedTime(&kernelTimeInMs, startKernel, stopKernel);
64    printf("Kernel time (ms): %f\n", kernelTimeInMs);
65    printf("Data transfer time (ms): %f\n", memcpyTimeInMs);
66
67    cudaFree(d_in);
68    cudaFree(d_out);
69  }
```

Note that we declared and created four events: startMemcpy and stopMemcpy for timing the data transfer and startKernel and stopKernel for timing the kernel execution. The cudaEventRecord() statements appear immediately before and after each operation (or segment of code) that we want to time, even for the asynchronous kernel launch. We insert the synchronization statements, cudaEventSynchronize(), just before the event records are converted to time using cudaEventElapsedTime(). Running the CUDA event timing on our OS X system with NVIDIA GeForce GT 650M produces the following results:

```
Kernel time (ms): 1.066176
Data transfer time (ms): 42.495968
```

Note that the data transfer time corroborates the standard C timing result, but this more accurate result for the kernel execution time shows that the C timing, which was 30 times smaller, missed a significant portion of the kernel execution.

PROFILING WITH NVIDIA VISUAL PROFILER

The CUDA Toolkit comes with **NVIDIA Visual Profiler (NVVP)**, a cross-platform visual profiling tool. We present a quick tour of NVVP, but you should see the full documentation for details at https://docs.nvidia.com/cuda/profiler-users-guide/index.html.

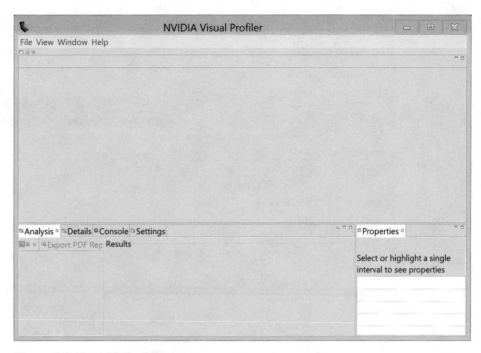

Figure D.1 The NVVP window

Launching NVVP (by typing nvvp in the Linux/OS X command line or by double-clicking the NVVP icon in Windows) opens the visual profiler window shown in Figure D.1.

Once the GUI application is running, click New Session from the File menu, and it will pop a Create New Session dialog as shown in Figure D.2.

Enter the path of the executable file for the CUDA app you would like to profile and select Next. (For applications requiring command line arguments, they can also be given in this dialog.) The Executable Properties window will open where you should be able to use the default settings and just click Finish.

Unless the Run guided analysis option was unchecked, NVVP will automatically run the application and generate a timeline of both host and device activity. Following the row labeled Compute, you should see something near the right edge of the timeline. Use the zoom tool and the sliders to see that it is actually a bar representing the kernel execution. Click on the bar to select distanceKernel() (and cause other items to fade), and look at the properties tab to see various kernel stats including Duration, which gives a timing of the execution in microseconds.

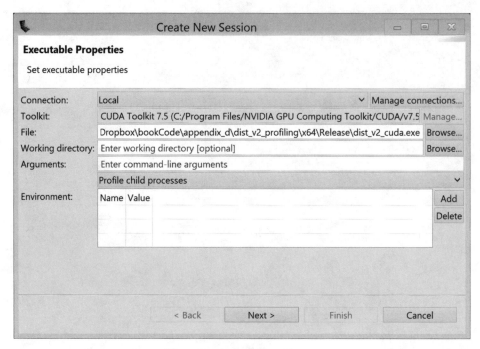

Figure D.2 Creating a new session dialog with `dist_v2_cuda.exe` (`dist_v2_cuda/main.exe` if you use the Makefile under Linux) chosen as executable

In addition to the timeline, the lower portion of the NVVP window provides a variety of tabs including `Analysis`, `Details`, `Console`, and `Settings`. Focusing on the `Analysis` tab, there are two icons suggestive of numbered and bulleted lists that correspond to **guided analysis** and **unguided analysis**. Guided mode takes the user step by step through different profiling metrics, whereas users select their own analysis path in unguided mode. With the `Default` row selected in the timeline, the `Details` tab contains a table with a row of data including timing for each memory copy and kernel launch in the profiled application. In Figure D.3, the details tab is shown for the `dist_v2_cuda` application.

To see how the kernel performed, let's select the guided analysis icon under the `Analysis` tab. The first step is to `Examine Individual Kernels`. In this case, there is only one kernel, which uses 100% of the GPU computation time and appears at the top of the `Performance Critical Kernel` list. Having identified a kernel, the next step is to `Perform Kernel Analysis`. NVVP indicates that `distanceKernel()` is using only a small fraction of both the compute capacity and the overall execution time. Most of the execution time is

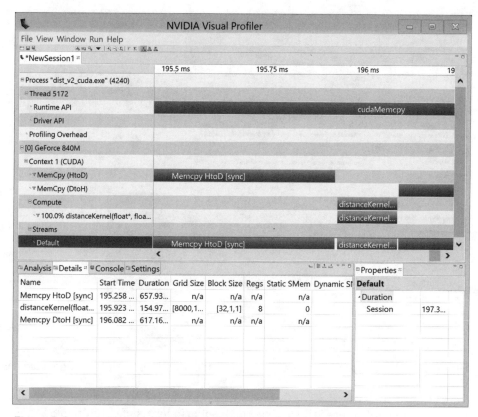

Figure D.3 `Details` tab showing a row for each memory copy and kernel launch in the `dist_v2_cuda` application

spent on memory transfers, and the app `Performance is Bound by Memory Bandwidth`. NVVP then prompts to `Perform Memory Bandwidth Analysis`, `Perform Compute Analysis`, and `Perform Latency Analysis`. Memory bandwidth analysis provides relevant stats on memory transfers and suggestions for enhancing performance. Compute analysis provides stats and suggestions on utilization of the capacity of the SMs, and latency analysis provides stats and suggestions relating to availability of requested data.

The bottom line here is that the `dist_v2_cuda` app needs to transfer a reasonable quantity of data (typically several hundred thousand `float` variables from host to device and back), and each thread has the nearly trivial job of computing a single distance value. The memory bandwidth analysis indicates that the execution time is limited by the maximum rate at which data can be transferred to and from device memory, and there is not much to be done here to improve the situation.

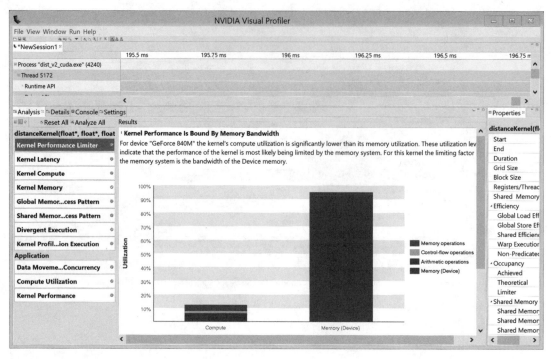

Figure D.4 Information on the `dist_v2_cuda` app produced by NVVP in unguided analysis mode

While there is not much worth doing in terms of optimizing `dist_v2_cuda`, the apps in Chapter 5, "Stencils and Shared Memory," provide examples of identifying memory transfer as a critical issue and enhancing efficiency using tiling and shared memory.

For completeness, let's also look at the unguided analysis mode which produces the information shown in Figure D.4. Again, memory bandwidth is identified as the limiting factor despite achieving device memory bandwidth equal to about 95% of the maximum capacity.

PROFILING IN NSIGHT VISUAL STUDIO

Timing and performance information can also be generated using Nsight Visual Studio. (If you are developing on one computer and running your CUDA code on another, see the Nsight documentation for details [1].) Start Visual Studio and select NSIGHT ⇒ Start Performance Analysis… to bring up an Activity page (possibly after responding to some dialogs requesting authorization to run Nsight Monitor) that includes several windows, as shown in Figure D.5:

- At the top of the activity page, there is an `Application Settings` window, in which you should not need to modify the default entries.

- Likewise, the entries in the `Triggers and Actions` window should not need changing.

- The important choices occur in the `Activity Type` window, which presents four options to choose from:

  - `Trace Application`
  - `Trace Process Tree`
  - `Profile CUDA Application`
  - `Profile CUDA Process Tree`

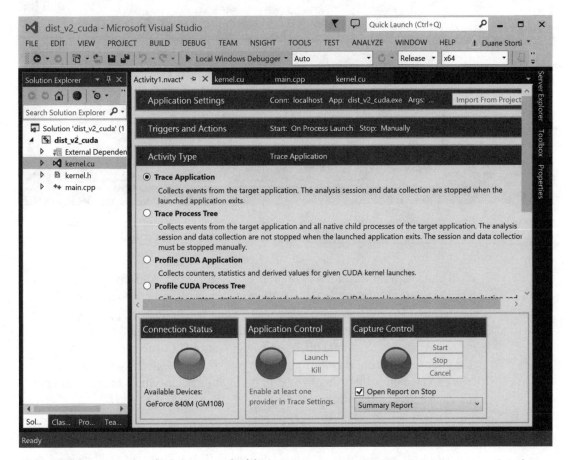

Figure D.5 `Activity` window opened with `NSIGHT ⇒ Start performance analysis...`

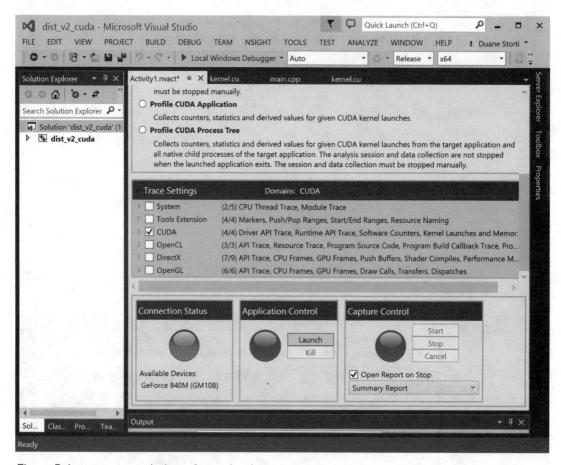

Figure D.6 Activity window after selecting `Trace Application` and scrolling down to open `Trace Settings` and selecting CUDA

We'll start with the default Activity Type, `Trace Application`, which causes Nsight to gather information while the program runs and produce a report when execution ends. When `Trace Application` or `Trace Process Tree` is selected, the next pane down is titled `Trace Settings` and allows you to choose what to collect data on, as shown in Figure D.6. Our immediate goal is to gather CUDA profiling information, so you should check the box next to CUDA. (You can also click the triangle next to CUDA and specify which of the CUDA subtopics to collect information on.)

Below `Trace Settings` there will be three small windows:

* On the left, `Connection Status` shows your GPU in the list of available devices below a big green disk (assuming Nsight has succeeded in connecting to your GPU).

- In the middle, `Application Control` provides the `Launch` button that is of immediate use.

- On the right, `Capture Control` becomes relevant when you want to start and stop the profiling manually.

When you click `Launch` in the `Application Control` window, your application will run, and an activity report window will open showing a `Summary Report` of the performance data gathered. The `Session Overview` reports the total running time over which data was collected, and the `CUDA Overview` shows the percentage use of both the CPU and GPU during the collection period. The pull-down menu that displays `Summary Report` also provides other options that you can explore. The option of most immediate interest is `Timeline`, which gives a visual history of the various CUDA-related operations that occurred during execution, as shown in Figure D.7. You can scroll through

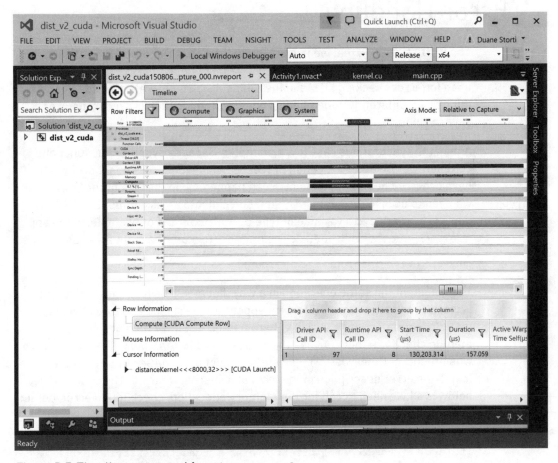

Figure D.7 Timeline generated for `dist_v2_cuda`

the captured data and `Ctrl+Drag` to expand or contract the timeline about your chosen moment of interest.

When you create a timeline for the `dist_v2_cuda` app, you are likely to be able to see the `cudaMemcpy()` calls, and you should practice zooming in on the timeline to find the kernel execution. If you click on the corresponding bar in the timeline (e.g., the bar labeled `distanceKernel` in the `Compute` row), you can go to the lower pane and click on `Row Information` and `Compute` to see detailed data on the kernel including the execution time (which agrees with the timing from NVVP to within a few microseconds).

For now, we've achieved the immediate goal of being able to get kernel execution timings, so let's move on to our next practical topic.

Error Handling

The CUDA functions that we use belong to the CUDA Runtime API [2]. CUDA Runtime API functions produce a return value of type `cudaError_t` that can be used for error checking [3]. As in the timing discussion, we will need to handle things a bit differently depending on whether the function is synchronous or asynchronous.

Again, the synchronous case is a bit simpler. Because synchronous functions complete before other execution proceeds, whatever errors might occur will have occurred before anything else can happen. So in the synchronous case, all we need to do is to turn our CUDA function call into an assignment of the function's return value to a variable of type `cudaError_t`. For example, in the app `dist_v2_cuda` we allocated device memory to store the input array as follows:

```
cudaMalloc(&d_in, len*sizeof(float));
```

To implement the same operation in a way that alerts us to errors that might arise, we make this same statement appear on the right-hand side of an assignment to a `cudaError_t` variable (here named err). We then use an `if` statement to check whether err has the value `cudaSuccess` indicating that no error was produced. Otherwise, we use the API function `cudaGetErrorString()` to get the error description in the form of a character string. The code snippet below is all we need to call for the memory allocation, check for an error, obtain an error description (if one exists), and print it to the screen:

```
cudaError_t err = cudaMalloc(&d_in, len * sizeof(float));
if (err != cudaSuccess) printf("%s\n", cudaGetErrorString(err));
```

If you want to avoid being left completely in the dark when things go wrong, you should get in the habit of adding this small amount of code every time you call a CUDA function.

Note that if you reuse a variable for your error checking, the type should appear in the statement where it is first used—and needs to be declared—but subsequent uses involve only assignment and not type declaration. Following the code snippet above to allocate memory for d_in with error checking, the allocation of memory of d_out with error checking is simply

```
err = cudaMalloc(&d_out, len * sizeof(float));
if (err != cudaSuccess) printf("%s\n", cudaGetErrorString(err));
```

If you want to keep things a bit cleaner, you can include a header from CUDA Samples, helper_cuda.h, which is found in the common/inc directory of the samples, and use the checkCudaErrors() function as a "wrapper" around your CUDA functions to print error messages to standard output. Add the line #include <helper_cuda.h> at the top of your code and invoke the allocation of GPU memory with error checking with

```
checkCudaErrors(cudaMalloc(&d_in, len * sizeof(float)));
```

The situation is a bit different for handling errors produced by kernel functions. The first difference to note is that the kernel itself has type void; that is, it does not return anything and that includes error values, so we will have to obtain errors from other function calls. There are also two separate classes of errors to handle: synchronous errors that arise during the kernel launch (e.g., if the kernel launch requests amounts of memory or grid sizes that are not available) and asynchronous errors that arise later during the kernel execution. We can catch the synchronous errors by calling the built-in function cudaGetLastError() or cudaPeekAtLastError() immediately after the kernel launch. To catch the asynchronous errors, we need to make sure that the kernel execution has completed, which we can ensure by calling cudaDeviceSynchronize(). The following code snippet illustrates a kernel launch with both synchronous and asynchronous error handling:

```
distanceKernel<<<len/TPB, TPB>>>(d_out, d_in, ref);
cudaError_t errSync = cudaGetLastError();
cudaError_t errAsync = cudaDeviceSynchronize();
if (errSync != cudaSuccess)
  printf("Sync kernel error: %sn", cudaGetErrorString(errSync);
if (errAsync != cudaSuccess)
  printf("Async kernel error: %sn", cudaGetErrorString(errAsync);
```

The cleaner version using the `helper_cuda.h` functions is as follows:

```
distanceKernel<<<len/TPB, TPB>>>(d_out, d_in, ref);
checkCudaErrors(cudaPeekAtLastError());
checkCudaErrors(cudaDeviceSynchronize());
```

where the first line is the kernel call, the second line provides information about kernel launch errors, and the third line provides information about kernel execution errors. It is worth noting that error checking is a huge help during development but also incurs some performance penalty, especially the `cudaDeviceSynchronize()` call, which can prevent other progress until the kernel finishes running. The desire for both efficient development and computational performance leads many developers to employ error checking during development but not to include it in released applications. `dist_v2_cuda`'s `kernel.cu` with error checking is provided in Listing D.3.

Listing D.3 `dist_v2_cuda/kernel.cu` modified to handle errors

```
 1 #include "kernel.h"
 2 #include <helper_cuda.h>
 3 #define TPB 3200
 4
 5 __device__
 6 float distance(float x1, float x2)
 7 {
 8   return sqrt((x2 - x1)*(x2 - x1));
 9 }
10
11 __global__
12 void distanceKernel(float *d_out, float *d_in, float ref)
13 {
14   const int i = blockIdx.x*blockDim.x + threadIdx.x;
15   const float x = d_in[i];
16   d_out[i] = distance(x, ref);
17 }
18
19 void distanceArray(float *out, float *in, float ref, int len)
20 {
21   float *d_in = 0;
22   float *d_out = 0;
23   checkCudaErrors(cudaMalloc(&d_in, len*sizeof(float)));
24   checkCudaErrors(cudaMalloc(&d_out, len*sizeof(float)));
25
26   checkCudaErrors(cudaMemcpy(d_in, in, len*sizeof(float),
27                             cudaMemcpyHostToDevice));
28
29   distanceKernel<<<len/TPB, TPB>>>(d_out, d_in, ref);
30   checkCudaErrors(cudaPeekAtLastError());
31   checkCudaErrors(cudaDeviceSynchronize());
32
33   checkCudaErrors(cudaMemcpy(out, d_out, len*sizeof(float),
34                             cudaMemcpyDeviceToHost));
```

```
35    checkCudaErrors(cudaFree(d_in));
36    checkCudaErrors(cudaFree(d_out));
37 }
```

Note that since we are including `helper_cuda.h`, build settings must be modified in order to find the header. Listing D.4 shows the Makefile modification that needs to be made to build the app with error handling. Visual Studio users can refer to the section "Using Visual Studio Property Pages" at the end of this appendix for details of how to specify the location of additional include directories.

Listing D.4 `dist_v2_cuda/Makefile` for building the app with error handling

```
 1 NVCC = /usr/local/cuda/bin/nvcc
 2 NVCC_FLAGS = -g -G -Xcompiler -Wall
 3 INC = -I/usr/local/cuda/samples/common/inc
 4
 5 all: main.exe
 6
 7 main.exe: main.o kernel.o
 8     $(NVCC) $^ -o $@
 9
10 main.o: main.cpp kernel.h
11     $(NVCC) $(NVCC_FLAGS) -c $< -o $@
12
13 kernel.o: kernel.cu kernel.h
14     $(NVCC) $(NVCC_FLAGS) $(INC) -c $< -o $@
```

Now, let's see an example of error handling by changing `#define TPB 32` on line 3 to `#define TPB 3200` and rebuilding the project. Running it gives the error message as follows:

`CUDA error at kernel.cu:30 code=9(cudaErrorInvalidConfiguration)`

Checking "CUDA Error Types" in the CUDA Runtime API Documentation's "Data types used by CUDA Runtime" section, we see that code 9 has the following definition: "This indicates that a kernel launch is requesting resources that can never be satisfied by the current device. Requesting more shared memory per block than the device supports will trigger this error, as will requesting too many threads or blocks." Thus, we indeed caught the error due to requesting too many threads per block (TPB) thanks to our error handling approach.

Finally, let's get to the error avoidance part. Many errors (some that will produce messages and some that will just produce incorrect calculation) can be avoided if we take a bit of care that our computational grids are compatible with both the problem size and the device capabilities. Typically, we need to deal with a problem with a given size (think array length for now), and we need to accomplish the dual goals of determining the number of blocks needed to cover the array length and making sure that we do not read or write beyond the end of the array. The usual trick to get this done simply and reliably employs some integer division and an `if` statement.

Suppose we want to compute the elements in an array of length N using blocks with block size TPB. If N happens to be an integer multiple of TPB, then N/TPB produces the requisite number of blocks. However, if N is something other than an exact integer multiple of TPB, then one additional block is required to cover the end of the array.

It turns out that no conditional test is required at this stage because there is a simple integer division that reliably produces the correct number of blocks:

```
GRIDSIZE = (N + TPB - 1)/TPB
```

Note, however, that if we use our standard formula to compute the index associated with a thread, the last block will contain entries associated with index values greater than N-1 (which should be the largest index value in an array of length N). This is where the `if` statement comes into play.

The conditional test `if (i < N) { }` should be wrapped around the code contained within the kernel definition to make sure that only the desired (and valid) entries are computed. An equivalent approach that many people find easier to read is to return from the kernel immediately when the test fails:

```
if(i >= N) return;
```

Again, we present an example for concreteness. The adjusted definition and launch of `distanceKernel()` become the following:

```
__global__
void distanceKernel(float *d_out, float *d_in, float ref, int len)
{
  int i = blockIdx.x * blockDim.x + threadIdx.x;
  if(i >= len) return;
  d_out[i] = distance(d_in[i], ref);
}
distanceKernel<<<((len + TPB - 1)/TPB, TPB>>>(d_out, d_in, ref, len);
```

The issue of ensuring that the launch parameters are valid is a bit more complicated because the limitations (including maximum number of threads in a block) are device specific. The viability of the kernel code itself is also device dependent because features like double-precision arithmetic and dynamic parallelism depend on the compute capability of the device on which the code is executed. As you develop applications, you get to choose which CUDA features to employ, but you are unlikely to get to choose which GPU is installed in the systems belonging to other people who may use your code. To deal with this reality, CUDA provides the following functions that inspect the installed devices so you can see if they meet the needs of your application:

- cudaGetDeviceCount() takes as input the address of an int variable and returns the number of installed CUDA-capable devices in the given int variable.

- cudaGetDeviceProperties() takes as input the address of a cudaDeviceProp struct and an integer device number and populates the cudaDeviceProp struct with the properties of the device with the given number.

Listing D.5 below gives a code snippet that illustrates counting CUDA devices and querying their properties.

Listing D.5 Snippet for querying select CUDA device properties

```
 1 #include <stdio.h>
 2
 3 int main() {
 4     int numDevices;
 5     cudaGetDeviceCount(&numDevices);
 6     printf("Number of devices: %d\n", numDevices);
 7     for (int i = 0; i < numDevices; ++i) {
 8         printf("--------------------------\n");
 9         cudaDeviceProp cdp;
10         cudaGetDeviceProperties(&cdp, i);
11         printf("Device Number: %d\n", i);
12         printf("Device name: %s\n", cdp.name);
13         printf("Compute capability: %d.%d\n", cdp.major, cdp.minor);
14         printf("Maximum threads/block: %d\n", cdp.maxThreadsPerBlock);
15         printf("Shared memory/block: %lu bytes\n",
16                 cdp.sharedMemPerBlock);
17         printf("Total global memory: %lu bytes\n",
18                 cdp.totalGlobalMem);
19     }
20 }
```

You now have the tools necessary to check the hardware limits of the device your code will run on so you can make adjustments or issue warnings as desired. See the documentation on the CUDA Runtime API for more details on the other members of cudaDeviceProp, and look at the code for the deviceQuery CUDA Sample for details of how to access the detailed information you may need. (If you are on a Windows system, you can also find property information in Visual Studio via NSIGHT ⇒ SystemInfo ⇒ CUDA Devices.)

Debugging in Windows

Here we take a look at the special tools Nsight provides for debugging CUDA code. To be concrete, let's return again to `dist_v2_cuda` with the immediate goal of being able to inspect the values computed within the kernel.

The first thing to note is that Nsight is specifically for CUDA code, so to benefit from Nsight's debugging tools, we need to set a breakpoint in a portion of the app involving CUDA code. A kernel function is definitely CUDA code, so let's start by putting a breakpoint (just as we did for regular debugging in Visual Studio) at the first line in `distanceKernel()`. Instead of using the DEBUG menu (or F5), go to the NSIGHT menu and select `Start CUDA Debugging`.

Execution should proceed to the breakpoint at the start of the kernel, and the content of the `Locals` window should resemble that shown in Figure D.8.

We are immediately confronted with the fact that the massive parallelism that gives CUDA its computational power also forces us to rethink our approach to debugging. Since there are many computational threads all executing together, there is a separate set of "local" values for each of the many computational threads that are executing in parallel, and it is neither practical nor desirable to try to display such a plethora of information for human consumption. What we

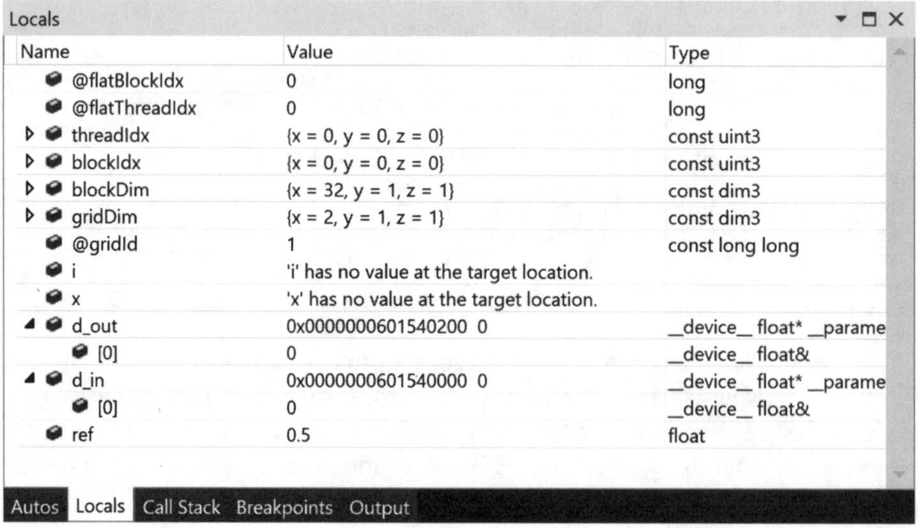

Name	Value	Type
@flatBlockIdx	0	long
@flatThreadIdx	0	long
▷ threadIdx	{x = 0, y = 0, z = 0}	const uint3
▷ blockIdx	{x = 0, y = 0, z = 0}	const uint3
▷ blockDim	{x = 32, y = 1, z = 1}	const dim3
▷ gridDim	{x = 2, y = 1, z = 1}	const dim3
@gridId	1	const long long
i	'i' has no value at the target location.	
x	'x' has no value at the target location.	
▲ d_out	0x0000000601540200 0	__device__ float* __parame
[0]	0	__device__ float&
▲ d_in	0x0000000601540000 0	__device__ float* __parame
[0]	0	__device__ float&
ref	0.5	float

Autos **Locals** Call Stack Breakpoints Output

Figure D.8 `Locals` window when execution hits the breakpoint at the first line of `distanceKernel()`

see from the `Locals` window displayed in Figure D.8 is that Nsight displays the variables and their values for a single representative thread. In this case, the information displayed involves `blockIdx` 0 and `threadIdx` 0. Reading down the list of variables, we can see the input value, `d_in[0]`, is 0 and that values have not yet been computed for the local variable `i` and the output `d_out[0]`.

Now we can start to step through the execution via menu selection (DEBUG ⇒ Step Into) or keyboard shortcut (F11). The updated `Locals` window, shown in Figure D.9, indicates that `i` (which combines `blockIdx`, `blockDim`, and `threadIdx` in the standard way) has been computed and assigned the value 0, so we are inspecting values for the first of 64 threads numbered 0 through 63. (Note that `@flatThreadIdx`, which appears near the top of the `Locals` window, is an alternative shorthand for this quantity.)

Taking another step forward in the execution with F11, you should see the cursor jump up to the definition of the device function `distance()`, which gets called in the next line of code. Another F11 step brings us into `distance()` where `sqrt()` is called, and the step after that should take you to the function prototype for `sqrt()` in `math.h`. Since debugging the standard math library functions is not on our agenda and we want to get back to our own code, we now step out of a function rather than stepping into one. This is accomplished via menu (DEBUG ⇒ Step Out) or keyboard shortcut (Shift+F11). Your first

Locals			▾ □ ×
Name	Value	Type	
● @flatBlockIdx	0	long	
● @flatThreadIdx	0	long	
▷ ● threadIdx	{x = 0, y = 0, z = 0}	const uint3	
▷ ● blockIdx	{x = 0, y = 0, z = 0}	const uint3	
▷ ● blockDim	{x = 32, y = 1, z = 1}	const dim3	
▷ ● gridDim	{x = 2, y = 1, z = 1}	const dim3	
● @gridId	1	const long long	
● i	0	int	
● x	'x' has no value at the target location.		
◢ ● d_out	0x0000000601540200 0	__device__ float* __parame	
● [0]	0	__device__ float&	
◢ ● d_in	0x0000000601540000 0	__device__ float* __parame	
● [0]	0	__device__ float&	
● ref	0.5	float	

| Autos | Locals | Call Stack Breakpoints Output |

Figure D.9 `Locals` window after stepping forward to the second line of `distanceKernel()`

Locals			▾ ☐ ✕
Name	Value		Type
🔵 @flatBlockIdx	0		long
🔵 @flatThreadIdx	0		long
▷ 🔵 threadIdx	{x = 0, y = 0, z = 0}		const uint3
▷ 🔵 blockIdx	{x = 0, y = 0, z = 0}		const uint3
▷ 🔵 blockDim	{x = 32, y = 1, z = 1}		const dim3
▷ 🔵 gridDim	{x = 2, y = 1, z = 1}		const dim3
🔵 @gridId	1		const long long
🔵 i	0		int
🔵 x	0		float
▲ 🔵 d_out	0x0000000601540200 0.5		_device_ float* _parame
🔵 [0]	0.5		_device_ float&
▷ 🔵 d_in	0x0000000601540000 0		_device_ float* _parame
🔵 ref	0.5		float

Figure D.10 `Locals` window at the last line of `distanceKernel()`

`Shift+F11` should get you back into `distance()`, and a second `Shift+F11` should put the cursor at the last line of `distanceKernel()` and produce a `Locals` window resembling that shown in Figure D.10.

Now we see that the desired value of 0.5 has been computed and stored in `d_out[0]`, but how do we see the information associated with other threads? Answers to this question can be found by exploring Nsight's debugging windows (accessible via `NSIGHT ⇒ Windows` in the menu structure).

- The `System Info` window (which is the only entry appearing before you `Start CUDA Debugging`) does not help with our current task, but is worth exploring when you want to know details about your system and the devices installed on it.

- The `CUDA Debug Focus` window allows us to choose the thread for which local information is displayed. For example, if you restart CUDA debugging (`DEBUG ⇒ Stop Debugging` followed by `NSIGHT ⇒ Start CUDA Debugging`), then select `NSIGHT ⇒ Windows ⇒ CUDA Debug Focus`, a window will pop-up allowing you to input the block and thread indices for the thread you wish to inspect. As a concrete example, let's leave the block index entry as 0,0,0 and change the thread index entry from 0,0,0 to 1,0,0. (Recall that our computational grid is one-dimensional, so only the first of the three numbers in each entry is currently relevant; multidimensional grids are covered in Chapter 4, "2D Grids and Interactive Graphics," and Chapter 7, "Interacting with 3D Data.") Stepping through the computation, we see that `i` gets assigned the value 1 (so we have shifted focus to the second of the 64 threads), but when we expand `d_in` and `d_out`, the values displayed are still those associated with index 0 instead of those associated with index 1. The problem is that the Locals window displays values of local variables and d_in and d_out are not local variables for any specific thread. (A thread only has access to the pointers that get passed as arguments to the kernel, and they provide direct access only to the initial element in each array (i.e., d_in[0] and d_out[0]).

A simple approach to overcoming this limitation is to create local variables so that each thread has a local copy of relevant data for display. For example, we might consider the following revised version of distanceKernel() where local variables y and d have been created for the input location and the output distance:

```
__global__
void distanceKernel(float *d_in, float *d_out, float ref, int len)
{
  int i = blockIdx.x * blockDim.x + threadIdx.x;
  float y = d_in[i];
  float d = distance(y, ref);
  d_out[i] = d;
  printf("distance = %f\n", d_out[i]);
}
```

After compiling with the new version of the kernel and starting CUDA debugging, we can change the CUDA focus to any allowable combination of thread and block indices and view the input and output values associated with z and d in the Locals window. (Note that local variable values may only be visible temporarily until the compiler optimizes them into oblivion.) At this point, however, we are still taking it on faith that the value computed for d gets stored properly in the d_out array. Following the general rule that it is dangerous and counterproductive programming practice to have faith in your computer (an extremely literal "creature") understanding what you mean to accomplish, we really need to have a way to directly inspect and verify the results stored in d_out, so let's continue down the list of windows provided by Nsight in search of such a tool:

- Start a new CUDA debugging session (DEBUG ⇒ Stop Debugging followed by NSIGHT ⇒ Start CUDA Debugging), then select NSIGHT ⇒ Windows ⇒ CUDA Info to open a window that can provide information about numerous aspects of your computation. For now, let's just take a quick look at two of the most relevant options. Select Warps from the drop-down menu, and you should see two lines corresponding to the thread warps for the blocks with index 0,0,0 and 1,0,0 as shown in Figure D.11.

At the far right, you should see an array of boxes indicating the computational lanes (one for each processing unit within a multiprocessor) where the threads in each warp get executed. Here the boxes are red to indicate that the

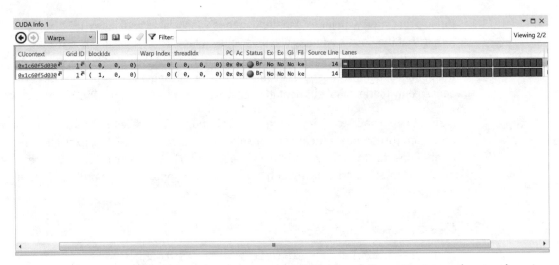

Figure D.11 CUDA Info window showing warps with focus on `threadIdx` = {0,0,0} and `blockIdx` = {0,0,0}

threads are at a breakpoint. You should also see a yellow arrow in one of the boxes indicating the current CUDA debug focus at `threadIdx` = {0,0,0} and `blockIdx` = {0,0,0}. You can shift the focus, just as we did using the CUDA Debug Focus window, by double-clicking on a box. Figure D.12 shows the CUDA Info window after shifting focus to `threadIdx` = {3,0,0} and

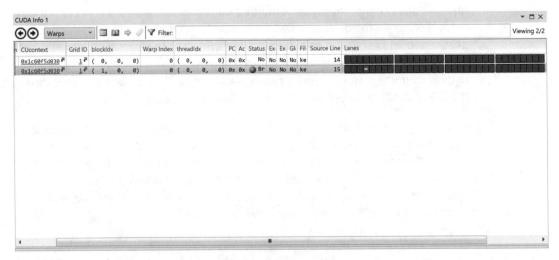

Figure D.12 CUDA Info window showing warps with focus on `threadIdx` = {3,0,0} and `blockIdx` = {1,0,0} after stepping beyond the breakpoint

blockIdx = {1,0,0} and stepping forward past the breakpoint. You can see that the focus arrow has moved, and you can verify in the Locals pane that the value of i has the corresponding value:

```
blockIdx.x * blockDim.x + threadIdx.x = 1*32 + 3 = 35
```

If you return to the drop-down menu and select Lanes, you should see a listing of the 32 threads in the focus warp along with their thread indices and activity status. While this will provide useful information for future purposes, it does not allow us to inspect the values stored in the d_out array, so let's move on to the next (and last) window offered.

- Select NSIGHT ⇒ Window ⇒ CUDA Warp Watch ⇒ CUDA Warp Watch 1 to open a window with a column that contains Name and Type followed by the numbers 0 to 31. If Name and Type strike you as suggestive of how variables are described in C, then your instincts are good, and if you enter a variable name in a column to the right of Name, you will be rewarded by seeing the column fill with the value of that variable for each thread in the focus warp. If you enter i, d_in[i], and d_out[i], and step to the last line of distanceKernel(), the CUDA WarpWatch1 window should fill with the index number, the input value, and the output distance computed for each thread in the focus warp as shown in Figure D.13.

  To view the values for another warp, shift the focus using the CUDA Debug Focus or CUDA Info window as discussed above. (When you shift to a new warp, execution will likely have proceeded only to the breakpoint, so you may need to step through the kernel code again to get to where the output values have been computed and stored.)

So far we have progressed from viewing local values one thread at a time to viewing them one warp at a time. To view an entire array of values in one fell swoop, we will directly inspect the memory where the array is stored. Set a breakpoint at the last line of the kernel, and start a new CUDA debugging session. Select DEBUG ⇒ Windows ⇒ Memory ⇒ Memory 1 (or use the keyboard shortcut Alt+6) to open a memory window. In the address box, enter d_out, 64 and select four columns. The first column gives a hex display of memory addresses and should not necessarily convey a lot of meaning. If the other columns do not contain recognizable values, right-click on the table and select a different display mode, for example, 32-bit Floating Point, and you should be able to view the computed distance values ranging from 0.5 down to about 0.008 and back up to 0.5, as shown in Figure D.14.

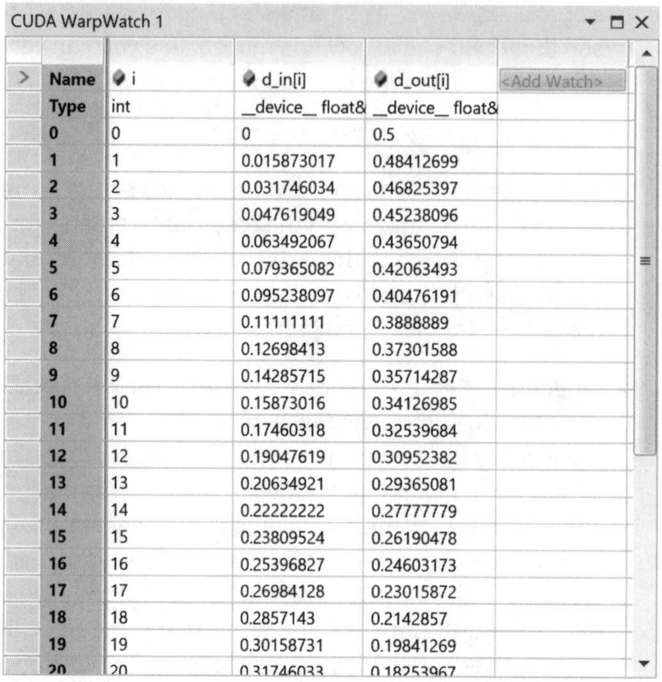

CUDA WarpWatch 1   ▼ □ ✕

>	Name	⬤ i	⬤ d_in[i]	⬤ d_out[i]	<Add Watch>
	Type	int	__device__ float&	__device__ float&	
	0	0	0	0.5	
	1	1	0.015873017	0.48412699	
	2	2	0.031746034	0.46825397	
	3	3	0.047619049	0.45238096	
	4	4	0.063492067	0.43650794	
	5	5	0.079365082	0.42063493	
	6	6	0.095238097	0.40476191	
	7	7	0.11111111	0.3888889	
	8	8	0.12698413	0.37301588	
	9	9	0.14285715	0.35714287	
	10	10	0.15873016	0.34126985	
	11	11	0.17460318	0.32539684	
	12	12	0.19047619	0.30952382	
	13	13	0.20634921	0.29365081	
	14	14	0.22222222	0.27777779	
	15	15	0.23809524	0.26190478	
	16	16	0.25396827	0.24603173	
	17	17	0.26984128	0.23015872	
	18	18	0.2857143	0.2142857	
	19	19	0.30158731	0.19841269	
	20	20	0.31746033	0.18253967	

Figure D.13 `Warp Watch 1` window at the last line of `distanceKernel()` showing first warp values for `d_in[i]` and `d_out[i]`

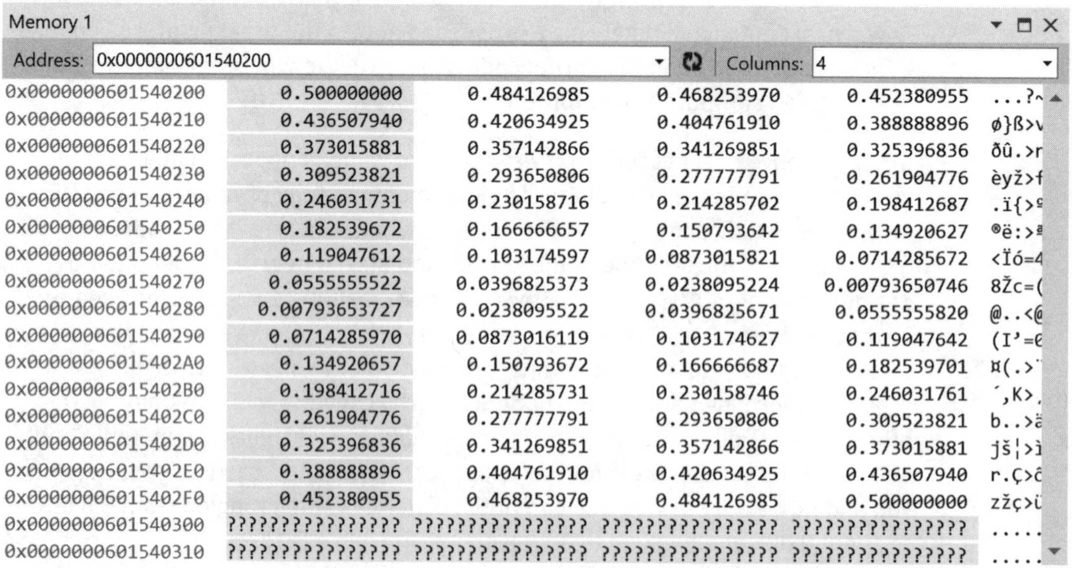

Memory 1   ▼ □ ✕

Address: `0x0000000601540200`   ▼ 🔁 Columns: `4`   ▼

```
0x0000000601540200    0.500000000    0.484126985    0.468253970    0.452380955   ...?^
0x0000000601540210    0.436507940    0.420634925    0.404761910    0.388888896   ø}ß>v
0x0000000601540220    0.373015881    0.357142866    0.341269851    0.325396836   ðû.>r
0x0000000601540230    0.309523821    0.293650806    0.277777791    0.261904776   èyž>f
0x0000000601540240    0.246031731    0.230158716    0.214285702    0.198412687   .ï{>º
0x0000000601540250    0.182539672    0.166666657    0.150793642    0.134920627   ®ë:>▪
0x0000000601540260    0.119047612    0.103174597    0.0873015821   0.0714285672  <Ïó=4
0x0000000601540270    0.0555555522   0.0396825373   0.0238095224   0.00793650746 8Žc=(
0x0000000601540280    0.00793653727  0.0238095522   0.0396825671   0.0555555820  @..<@
0x0000000601540290    0.0714285970   0.0873016119   0.103174627    0.119047642   (I'=€
0x00000006015402A0    0.134920657    0.150793672    0.166666687    0.182539701   ¤(.>`
0x00000006015402B0    0.198412716    0.214285731    0.230158746    0.246031761   ´,K>,
0x00000006015402C0    0.261904776    0.277777791    0.293650806    0.309523821   b..>ä
0x00000006015402D0    0.325396836    0.341269851    0.357142866    0.373015881   jš¦>ì
0x00000006015402E0    0.388888896    0.404761910    0.420634925    0.436507940   r.ç>ĉ
0x00000006015402F0    0.452380955    0.468253970    0.484126985    0.500000000   zžç>ù
0x0000000601540300    ?????????????? ?????????????? ?????????????? ??????????????  .....
0x0000000601540310    ?????????????? ?????????????? ?????????????? ??????????????  .....
```

Figure D.14 `Memory 1` window showing all 64 entries in `d_out` computed by `distanceKernel()` (arranged in 4 columns)

At this point, we have achieved our goal of being able to inspect values of variables, whether local to a thread or stored in an array, at various points during the execution of CUDA code. For further information and alternative examples, refer to "Using the CUDA Debugger" in the "Nsight Visual Studio Edition" [4].

Debugging in Linux

For Linux, NVIDIA Nsight Eclipse Edition provides a GUI front-end experience. However, in this section, we will use the non-GUI option, cuda-gdb, which is also the underlying debugger in Nsight Eclipse Edition. cuda-gdb is an extended version of gdb (GNU Debugger) and has all the gdb functionality plus the ability to debug the CUDA code on the device.

CUDA-GDB on OS X

As of CUDA 7.0, CUDA-GDB is deprecated on OS X. Thus, for Mac users, remote debugging on Linux may be a viable option.

In contrast to profiling, when debugging is the goal, the program must be compiled with debug information generated. To achieve this, the flags -g and -G must both be passed to the compiler in the compilation command. Also, as of today, single-GPU CUDA debugging is still a little bit problematic for Linux. On Linux, if your NVIDIA GPU has CUDA compatibility 3.5 or above, there is a beta feature available for debugging without any additional steps. If your GPU has CUDA compute capability less than 3.5, you can still do single-GPU debugging, but you need to turn off desktop manager and debug in console mode.

Now, go ahead and build the dist_v2_cuda app with printf() removed from the kernel (note that it must be built with the flags -g and -G). Once the app is built, load the executable to cuda-gdb with cuda-gdb main.exe. If you are debugging with desktop manager running (with a card of CUDA compute capability of at least 3.5), enter set cuda software_preemption on to make sure that the debugging on single GPU with GUI feature is turned on. Figure D.15 shows this step.

Put a breakpoint at the first line of distanceKernel() in kernel.cu with break kernel.cu:14 and another breakpoint at the end of main.cpp with break main.cpp:26, and run the program with the run command as shown in Figure D.16.

```
cuda-gdb main.exe
→ dist_v2_cuda  cuda-gdb main.exe
NVIDIA (R) CUDA Debugger
7.5 release
Portions Copyright (C) 2007-2015 NVIDIA Corporation
GNU gdb (GDB) 7.6.2
Copyright (C) 2013 Free Software Foundation, Inc.
License GPLv3+: GNU GPL version 3 or later <http://gnu.org/licenses/gpl.html>
This is free software: you are free to change and redistribute it.
There is NO WARRANTY, to the extent permitted by law.  Type "show copying"
and "show warranty" for details.
This GDB was configured as "x86_64-unknown-linux-gnu".
For bug reporting instructions, please see:
<http://www.gnu.org/software/gdb/bugs/>...
Reading symbols from /home/duane/Desktop/dist_v2/dist_v2_cuda/main.exe...done.
(cuda-gdb) set cuda software_preemption on
(cuda-gdb) show cuda software_preemption
Software preemption debugging is on.
(cuda-gdb)
```

Figure D.15 cuda-gdb's `software_preemption` option must be turned on before debugging.

```
cuda-gdb main.exe
(cuda-gdb) break kernel.cu:14
Breakpoint 1 at 0x4028ab: file kernel.cu, line 14.
(cuda-gdb) break main.cpp:26
Breakpoint 2 at 0x4025fa: file main.cpp, line 26.
(cuda-gdb) run
Starting program: /home/duane/Desktop/dist_v2/dist_v2_cuda/main.exe
[Thread debugging using libthread_db enabled]
Using host libthread_db library "/lib/x86_64-linux-gnu/libthread_db.so.1".
[New Thread 0x7ffff6131700 (LWP 3545)]
[Switching focus to CUDA kernel 0, grid 1, block (0,0,0), thread (0,0,0), device 0, sm 0, wa
rp 0, lane 0]

Breakpoint 1, distanceKernel<<<(2,1,1),(32,1,1)>>> (d_out=0x508a80200, d_in=0x508a80000,
    ref=0.5) at kernel.cu:14
14          const int i = blockIdx.x*blockDim.x + threadIdx.x;
(cuda-gdb) next
[Switching focus to CUDA kernel 0, grid 1, block (0,0,0), thread (0,0,0), device 0, sm 1, wa
rp 1, lane 0]
15          const float x = d_in[i];
(cuda-gdb) print i
$1 = 0
(cuda-gdb) cuda kernel block thread
kernel 0, block (0,0,0), thread (0,0,0)
(cuda-gdb) cuda block 1,0,0 thread 5,0,0
[Switching focus to CUDA kernel 0, grid 1, block (1,0,0), thread (5,0,0), device 0, sm 0, wa
rp 1, lane 5]
14          const int i = blockIdx.x*blockDim.x + threadIdx.x;
(cuda-gdb) next
[Switching focus to CUDA kernel 0, grid 1, block (1,0,0), thread (5,0,0), device 0, sm 1, wa
rp 2, lane 5]
15          const float x = d_in[i];
(cuda-gdb) print i
$2 = 37
(cuda-gdb)
```

Figure D.16 Setting breakpoints and debugging the app

Once the program pauses at line 14 of `kernel.cu`, the current focus and thread are shown along with the kernel launch parameters. Currently our index variable is not set. When you execute the current line with `next`, `print i` outputs 0, since we are in the first thread. You can see the information about current focus with the command `cuda kernel block thread`, or you can check the CUDA variables with `print threadIdx` and `print blockIdx`. Let's focus on another thread in the same block with `cuda thread 5,0,0`. Now, if you `print i`, it will show 5, which is the correct value for the sixth thread. Let's switch focus again to another thread in another block with `cuda block 1,0,0 thread 30,0,0`. Now, since the focus is on another block, we will see line number 14 again after the switching focus prompt. Execute it with `next`, and check the index value with `print i`. The result is 62, since we are on block 1 and thread 30 (32 × 1 + 30). Figure D.17 shows focusing on different threads.

Now, let's move to the next breakpoint, which is outside the kernel with `continue`. We are now in the `main()`. Type `info locals` to see the variables in this context. We have pointers to two host arrays, `in` and `out`. Let's see the contents of `out` by typing `print out[0]@64`. Values starting from 0.5 and ending at 0.5 should verify that the kernel did its job correctly. Now that the interesting part of the program is completed, let the program finish and exit successfully with `continue`. Figure D.18 shows these final steps.

```
cuda-gdb main.exe
(cuda-gdb) cuda thread 5,0,0
[Switching focus to CUDA kernel 0, grid 1, block (0,0,0), thread (5,0,0), device 0, sm 0, wa
rp 1, lane 5]
15          const float x = d_in[i];
(cuda-gdb) print i
$4 = 5
(cuda-gdb)
(cuda-gdb) cuda block 1,0,0 thread 30,0,0
[Switching focus to CUDA kernel 0, grid 1, block (1,0,0), thread (30,0,0), device 0, sm 1, w
arp 1, lane 30]
14          const int i = blockIdx.x*blockDim.x + threadIdx.x;
(cuda-gdb) next
[Switching focus to CUDA kernel 0, grid 1, block (1,0,0), thread (30,0,0), device 0, sm 1, w
arp 2, lane 30]
15          const float x = d_in[i];
(cuda-gdb) print i
$5 = 62
(cuda-gdb)
```

Figure D.17 Focusing on different threads and stepping

```
● ● ●    cuda-gdb main.exe
(cuda-gdb) continue
Continuing.

Breakpoint 2, main () at main.cpp:26
26          free(in);
(cuda-gdb) info locals
ref = 0.5
in = 0x664220
out = 0x664330
(cuda-gdb) print out[0]@64
$1 = {0.5, 0.484126985, 0.46825397, 0.452380955, 0.43650794, 0.420634925, 0.40476191,
  0.388888896, 0.373015881, 0.357142866, 0.341269851, 0.325396836, 0.309523821,
  0.293650806, 0.277777791, 0.261904776, 0.246031731, 0.230158716, 0.214285702,
  0.198412687, 0.182539672, 0.166666657, 0.150793642, 0.134920627, 0.119047612,
  0.103174597, 0.0873015821, 0.0714285672, 0.0555555522, 0.0396825373, 0.0238095224,
  0.00793650746, 0.00793653727, 0.0238095522, 0.0396825671, 0.055555582, 0.071428597,
  0.0873016119, 0.103174627, 0.119047642, 0.134920657, 0.150793672, 0.166666687,
  0.182539701, 0.198412716, 0.214285731, 0.230158746, 0.246031761, 0.261904776,
  0.277777791, 0.293650806, 0.309523821, 0.325396836, 0.341269851, 0.357142866,
  0.373015881, 0.388888896, 0.40476191, 0.420634925, 0.43650794, 0.452380955, 0.46825397,
  0.484126985, 0.5}
(cuda-gdb) continue
Continuing.
[Thread 0x7ffff7fd3740 (LWP 3929) exited]
[Inferior 1 (process 3929) exited normally]
(cuda-gdb)
```

Figure D.18 Continuing to the breakpoint in `main.cpp` and checking the final values. Note how the dynamic array values can be printed using the operators `[]` and `@` on the pointer.

Note that running the program successfully does not erase breakpoints automatically. Check the breakpoints set currently with `info breakpoints`, and delete the ones that are no longer necessary with `delete breakpoint n`, where n is the breakpoint number to be deleted, or delete all breakpoints at once with `delete breakpoints`.

In addition to the `gdb`/`cuda-gdb` commands/functionality demonstrated above, information is available about other features of `gdb`/`cuda-gdb` [5,6].

CUDA-MEMCHECK

The final CUDA tool we want to talk about is CUDA-MEMCHECK. CUDA-MEMCHECK is a very lightweight runtime error detector tool available on all platforms. It is used mainly to detect memory leaks, memory access errors, and hardware errors. Simply open a command prompt, change to the directory where the executable is stored, and enter `cuda-memcheck` followed by the name of the executable file (e.g., `cuda-memcheck main.exe` under Linux or `cuda-memcheck` `dist_v2_cuda.exe` in Visual Studio). The app will then run and report on the presence of memory access errors. If no errors are detected, your output will conclude with `ERROR SUMMARY: 0 errors`. For more information about CUDA-MEMCHECK, see the online documentation [7].

Using Visual Studio Property Pages

Visual Studio projects have associated Property Pages that provide a mechanism for specifying a wide variety of options for compiling and building apps. We will avoid getting into all the possible details and focus on two issues that are directly relevant for our CUDA development purposes. For apps that employ code libraries (e.g., the `flashlight` app from Chapter 4, "2D Grids and Interactive Graphics," which uses OpenGL libraries), it may be necessary to tell the system where to find the necessary header files (to be included during compilation) and object files (to be linked in as part of the executable). These two operations are accomplished by similar methods:

1. Right-click on the project name in the `Solution Explorer` pane and click on `Properties` at the bottom of the pop-up menu (or select `Alt+F7`).

2. Select `Configuration Properties` ⇒ `C/C++` ⇒ `Additional Include Directories` so that the properties page resembles Figure D.19.

3. Click on the ∨ icon that appears at the right side.

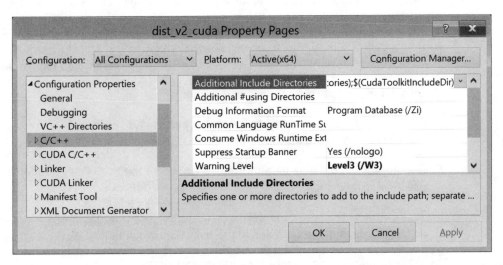

Figure D.19 `Property Pages` showing location of `Additional Include Directories`

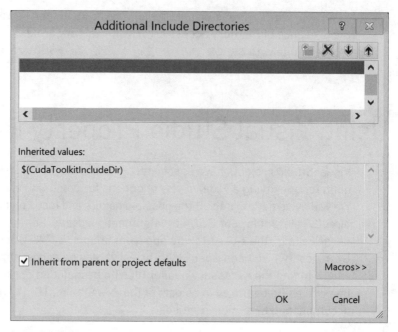

Figure D.20 `Additional Include Directories` dialog ready for entry of new directory path

4. Click on <Edit...> that appears below to open the `Additional Include Directories` dialog, as shown in Figure D.20.

5. Double-click in the blue bar, enter the path where the necessary header files are located, and click `OK`.

6. Select `Configuration Properties` ⇒ `Linker` ⇒ `Additional Library Directories` so that the properties page resembles Figure D.21.

7. Click on the ∨ icon that appears at the right side.

8. Click on <Edit...> that appears below to open the `Additional Library Directories` dialog as shown in Figure D.22.

9. Double-click in the blue bar, enter the path where the necessary header files are located, and click `OK`.

10. To link library files, select `Linker` ⇒ `Input` ⇒ `Additional Dependencies` ⇒ `Edit`, and add the libraries to the list as shown in Figure 8.3.

11. In the property page, `Apply` the change and hit `OK`.

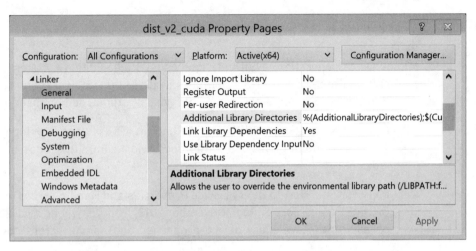

Figure D.21 `Property Pages` showing location of `Additional Library Directories`

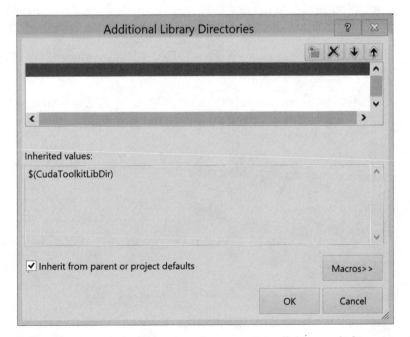

Figure D.22 `Additional Library Directories` dialog ready for entry of new directory path

References

[1] NVIDIA Corporation, "NVIDIA Nsight Visual Studio Edition 4.7 User Guide," NVIDIA Gameworks, 2015, http://docs.nvidia.com/gameworks/index .html#developertools/desktop/nsight_visual_studio_edition_user_guide.htm.

[2] NVIDIA Corporation, "NVIDIA CUDA Runtime API," NVIDIA Developer Zone, Cuda Toolkit Documentation, 2015, http://docs.nvidia.com/cuda/cuda-runtime-api/ index.html.

[3] Mark Harris, "How to Query Device Properties and Handle Errors in CUDA C/C++," *Parallel Forall* (blog), November 2012, http://devblogs.nvidia.com/ parallelforall/how-query-device-properties-and-handle-errors-cuda-cc/.

[4] NVIDIA Corporation, "NVIDIA Nsight Visual Studio Edition," NVIDIA Gameworks, 2015, https://docs.nvidia.com/gameworks/index.html#developertools/desktop/ nvidia_nsight.htm.

[5] Norman S. Matloff and Peter Jay Salzman, *The Art of Debugging with GDB, DDD, and Eclipse* (San Francisco, CA: No Starch Press, 2008).

[6] NVIDIA Corporation, "CUDA-GDB," NVIDIA Developer Zone, Cuda Toolkit Documentation, 2015, http://docs.nvidia.com/cuda/cuda-gdb/index.html.

[7] NVIDIA Corporation, "CUDA-MEMCHECK," NVIDIA Developer Zone, Cuda Toolkit Documentation, 2015, http://docs.nvidia.com/cuda/cuda-memcheck/index.html.

Index